THE PITCH
BRYCE COURTENAY

EDITED BY LESLEY DOW

MARGARET
Gee

Published by
Margaret Gee Publishing
an imprint of
Margaret Gee Holdings
Suite 2a, 61 Victoria Street, McMahons Point 2060
A.C.N. 005 604 464

First published in 1992

Distributed by Gary Allen Pty Ltd
9 Cooper Street, Smithfield NSW 2164

Copyright © 1992 Bryce Courtenay

All rights reserved. No part of this publication may be reproduced, stored in a retrieval system, or transmitted in any form or by any means electronic, mechanical, photocopying, recording or otherwise without the prior permission of the Publisher.

National Library of Australia
Cataloguing-in-Publication entry

Courtenay, Bryce, 1933-
  The pitch: selections from the Australian 1986-1991.

  ISBN 1 875574 14 X.

  1. Australia—Social conditions. 2. Australia—Social life and customs. I. Dow, Lesley. II. Title. III. Title: Australian (Sydney, N.S.W.: 1964).

994

Cover designed by Reno Visual Communications
Typeset by Midland Typesetters, Victoria
Printed by Australian Print Group, Victoria
Production by Vantage Graphics, Sydney

Bryce Courtenay

Born in South Africa in 1933, Bryce Courtenay has spent most of his adult life in Australia and has been a naturalized Australian since 1958. After completing his early schooling in South Africa, he worked for a year in the copper mines of Central Africa, after which he completed his education in England.

Arriving in Australia in 1958, he took a job as a junior copywriter with the advertising company McCann Erickson. Four years later he was appointed Creative Director and a board member. He stayed with McCann Erickson for ten years and then moved to J. Walter Thompson as Creative Director there. During Courtenay's term as Creative Director of McCann and subsequently of J. Walter Thompson, both became Australia's most awarded advertising agencies. In turn, each moved from fifth largest to third largest and fifth to second largest under his direction. He stayed a further four years at JWT before starting his own advertising agency. Harvie HRC was sold to the Clemenger Group in 1987 when Courtenay was offered a high profile position with George Patterson Advertising.

Bryce Courtenay is seen as having the rare ability to be both an award winning advertising man and an astute business builder. He has personally won most of the international and local awards available for advertising. In 1984 he won a gold medal at the New York Film Festival for best documentary. Perhaps his best known contribution to advertising is as the originator of 'Louie de Fly', the world's longest-running commercial.

Courtenay is considered an expert in his field and in November 1985 he was invited by the Chinese government to present a series of introductory lectures to the Chinese people on the subject of advertising and free enterprise. This three week lecture tour was the first on business communication to take place in China since the advent of the Communist state.

Courtenay is a keenly sought after speaker on the subject of free enterprise, marketing, advertising, business motivation, stress management and the spoken and written word for people in business.

As a writer and essayist Courtenay has been published in journals, magazines and newspapers in Australia, New Zealand, USA and the UK, most recently as a weekly columnist in *The Australian*. He has also run seventeen marathons, a clear indication of insanity.

Courtenay's first novel, THE POWER OF ONE, was published in hardcover in 1989 by Heinemann Australia and William Heinemann, UK and subsequently by Random House in USA and Little, Brown & Company in Canada. THE POWER OF ONE has also been sold to overseas publishers for translation into French, German, Danish, Swedish, Norwegian, Spanish, Portuguese, Italian, Dutch, Finnish and Japanese.

About his novel, THE POWER OF ONE, Courtenay says he wrote it because:

> ". . . he hungered for a book where the hero is larger than life and the plot satisfied the need all readers have, to become hopelessly involved in narrative action which contains, among other things, a belly full of laughs and a bucket full of tears."

Described as "a spellbinding story of cruelty, sadness, love and faith, filled with unforgettable characters, and told with great compassion and humour by a gifted new writer", Courtenay's novel was an immediate best-seller. It surpassed the publisher's expectations in terms of its commercial success, and was widely praised by readers as diverse as a class of young school boys to an Oxford Don. Heinemann Australia reprinted the book in 1989, 1990 (three times), and 1991 and it has sold well over one million copies worldwide.

Film rights to THE POWER OF ONE were sold to Village Roadshow Pictures and a Warner Bros movie has just been released in the USA and Australia.

Courtenay's sequel novel to THE POWER OF ONE, entitled TANDIA, was published in hardcover by Heinemann Australia and Willian Heinemann UK in June 1991. A paperback edition of the novel was published in Australia in March 1992 and, once again, Courtenay produced a best-seller.

Courtenay is currently writing his third book, entitled APRIL FOOL'S DAY, which describes his young son, Damon, a haemophiliac, who died of medically acquired AIDS on 1 April 1991. He is also planning to write a new series of novels, this time set in Australia.

Bryce Courtenay lives in Sydney with his wife, Benita, and two sons. He is still a Creative Director of Australia's largest advertising agency, George Patterson.

Contents

OF GENERAL INTEREST

1986 — 1
- Cashing in on Caxton's success by matching the medium with the message — 3
- Everyone needs the great Chinese clockwork fly-trap — 5
- Time to slot more women into the top positions — 11
- The real spirit of Christmas Day — 15

1987 — 19
- The trendy's sandwich proves hard to swallow — 21
- America's Cup is no excuse for a handout — 24
- Stimulating talk worth all the hot air — 27
- When hamburgers were made with love — 30
- Feminist talk more thunder than enlightening — 33
- Food for thought on a dog day mourning — 36
- Did you know that? Facts of absolutely no consequence — 39

1988 — 43
- Even big companies need pleasant party manners — 45
- Modify us if you like, but don't change us without our consent — 48
- The art of selling . . . from every perspective — 51
- The fountain of youth runs dry — 54
- The new, improved Constitution — 57
- Book sales business needs a really good dose of salts — 60
- Stuff the panda—how about a cute koala? — 63
- Mediocrity rules in the race to be president — 66
- How to beat the tradesmen rip-offs — 69

1989 — 73
- Kermit takes a back seat to the call of the wild frog — 75
- Glowing result from the potting shed — 79
- How to turn a case of Delhi belly into a ball in Lahore — 83
- Fear—a classy way to fleece fools perfected for centuries in Europe — 87
- A bird on the ground is worth more as PM — 91
- Fire of enthusiasm can revive that flickering candle — 94
- Forget the kid gloves when educating hoons — 98
- When a pregnant thought leads to a womb with a view — 101
- Only trifles can fulfil a certain need — 104

1990 107
  –Electrify visitors with a smile ...... 109 –
  The only person who can save the environment is you ...... 112 ✓
  –Good taste is for those who can't have fun ...... 115 –
  Sustaining development without a mess ...... 118 –
  A mayday call from Mr April 121
  How a little love could help remove our iron bars 124
  The politicians talk but we're not listening 128

1991 131
  Why do wars make our leaders popular? ...... 133 –
  –Dare your genius to walk the wildest way ...... 136 –
  Dobbing in the profiteers 140

1992 143
  –Why we get carried away by our flag ...... 145 –

ADVERTISING AND RELATED SUBJECTS

The Advertising Industry — 151
  Advertising: the words that seduce consumers 151
  Production values *aren't* everything 154
  Pep up your sales with spontaneity 157
  Louie de Fly, a fluke idea that became a legend 160
  The answer lies in asking questions 163
  With advertising, you'll never be alone 166
  Why VIPS are very important parts of the advertising system 170
  Telling you what's already on your mind 174

Advertising Agency–Client Relations — 177
  Even God and Aunt Dolly couldn't save Gossamer 177
  Thinking of a change? Call me first 183
  Spend your way out of the recession 187
  Trials of training clients 190
  Lovely little earners for the papers 193
  Emotion: bottle it up, add fizz, then sell it 196
  Small can truly be beautiful in advertising 200

Corporate Communications — 203
  Good manners are money in the bank 203
  Words are all we've got to communicate 206
  The writers who really earn their money 209
  How to make audiences sit up and listen 213
  Beware vulgar language of the quick buck 216
  Stimulation always beats information 219

The Australian Business Environment — 223
- FBT just a symptom of the disease — 223
- Why are we paying top price for a banana? — 226
- It's scrape, bump and thump from here, son — 229
- Our cult of failure is the biggest obstacle to success — 232
- Entrepreneurs prove power corrupts — 235
- Rugby success shows worth of team spirit — 238
- A dumb way to become a clever country — 242
- Give jobs to the young—our future depends on it — 246

Sales and Marketing — 249
- In the service of tomorrow's sales — 249
- Greener pastures across the Tasman — 253
- Instinct beats expertise on success scale — 256
- Home repairs—plumbing the depths — 259
- Here's how we become leading manufacturers — 263
- Cattlemen stake their export claim — 266
- Pride in products and services comes before a rise in business — 269
- Why you keep buying that same warm, friendly brand of soap — 272

The International Scene — 276
- Why Japan catches world with industrial pants down — 276
- Home-made excellence could make its mark — 280
- Brain strain a national gain — 283
- How to sell to those dreadful foreigners — 286
- We've got it, and they want it, but... — 289
- A little serious dreaming may do a world of good — 292
- A perfect opportunity to cash in on Japanese buyers — 295
- Let's ditch our desire for failure — 298
- How Japan and Germany beat the rest — 301

Dedication

To all those lovely people who, every Friday, rain or shine,
turn to the Business Section of *The Australian*
to find me. Thank you.

OF GENERAL INTEREST

1986

Cashing in on Caxton's success by matching the medium with the message

The year was 1746 and the place was a modest inn in the City of Westminster.

A group of friars, scribes from the local abbey, mingled with what passed for the literati of the day.

They had come to attend the launch of a new book, lured to the occasion less by the advent of the book than by the promise of free pork pies.

In truth, the occasion was unusual for two reasons.

The book was a secular title written not in Latin but in English and transcribed by an unknown layman, not by a calligrapher from the abbey.

A close examination of the invitations had shown that the text on each invitation was identical, not even the tiniest slip of the quill, not even the smallest detail was different.

This amazing consistency had led the abbey scribes to suspect that Master William Caxton, the author of the invitations, had a very superior talent.

The abbey's sneakiest choir boy had been despatched to Master Caxton's workshop to snoop around. He reported that there had been a strong smell of carbon black and linseed oil.

He had been told an incredible story of how Master Caxton could transcribe, in a matter of days, something that would take the scribes of the abbey several months to complete.

So here they were, munching pork pies and downing pots of honeyed ale, determined to ridicule this lay upstart for his ridiculous attempt to undermine the authority of the Church by emulating an idea of a fat German called Gutenberg.

The book, Canterbury Tales, impressed them not at all. Printed on common stock without illumination, it was a poor excuse for a manuscript.

POTENTIAL

But the potential of Master Caxton's movable type was not lost on them and clerical union solidarity was so effective that 59 years were to pass before the Bible was printed in English.

By this time the Church, which throughout the Dark Ages had held most printed knowledge in its cold, ecclesiastical grasp, had lost its grip.

The common man was coming to terms with the printed word and the world would never be the same again.

How soon after William Caxton's historical book launch the first newspaper appeared on the streets is a matter of historical conjecture.

But it did and the daily paper became a daily habit that cleansed the unwashed and did much to free the world from tyranny.

In Australia, three million newspapers are purchased every day. The reason is that a newspaper is an active medium. Conversely, television is a passive one.

If you are an advertiser this information is important. Used properly it will both make and save you a fortune.

If you are like most people you use a newspaper actively. You search through it to find things, like a clucky hen working through the fowl yard for a worm.

By the time you get to work you're armed to the teeth. You can talk on 10 different subjects for a minimum of 15 seconds each.

Which, by Australian standards, makes you an intellectual. A newspaper is active because it involves itself intimately with people and situations which readers have personally experienced or know and feel about.

Television, on the other hand, is passive.

With a sigh you plop yourself down in front of it and immediately there is an unspoken injunction: entertain me.

The fact that it seldom does in no way diminishes your expectations, because usually you fall asleep.

Scientists, while doing spectrum analysis at the Melbourne Institute of Technology, discovered the patterns set up in the brain when watching television were similar, in all respects, to those that take place during deep sleep.

Add to this the effect the average television commercial has on you, and you are forced to conclude that television is a very passive medium.

Yet advertisers still look upon television as the Everest of commercial achievement, despite the fact it is often unjustified on a cost per thousand or demographic basis.

Often it's not even the right emotional climate for the message.

If you are trying to sell any of the brainless commodities, such as fags, beer, soft drinks, candy, fast or snack foods, or some of the more frivolous shampoos or cosmetics then television is ideal.

But, if the product or service needs thinking about, needs explaining, persuasion, logic or intelligent comparison then it belongs in the print medium.

Products that need a little verbal massage, a little chewing on the fat of the proposition, need the magic of print.

In the end, print climbs the highest intellectual mountains.

The cost of making a major television commercial would buy 10 full pages in just about any metropolitan newspaper, where the readers are more or less prepared to think about a product actively.

People become addicted to caffeine, cigarettes, heroin and televison, but they become firm friends with a newspaper.

The point I am trying to make is that a newspaper is family.

A newspaper knows precisely who it is, not what it is. This "who" of a newspaper is very important.

People make an active decision to become involved with a particular newspaper—a commitment and a friendship that may last for a lifetime.

Every newspaper has a personality that is different from the others, and there are enough of them around to match a product with readers' aspirations.

An unknown journalist understood this perfectly when he or she wrote this little aide-memoire for Australia's newspapers:

The Melbourne Age is read by people who run the country.

The Canberra Times is read by the people who think they run the country.

The Sydney Morning Herald is read by the people who think they ought to run the country.

The Melbourne Herald is read by the wives of the people who run the country.

The Australian is read by the people who realise that no one's running the country.

The Financial Review is read by the people who own the country.

The Western Australian is read by the people who think the eastern States run the country.

The Hobart Mercury and the Melbourne Sun are read by the people who think the country ought to be run the way it used to be run.

6 THE PITCH

The Adelaide Advertiser and the Brisbane Mail are read by the people who think it still is.

The Sydney Daily Mirror is read by people who don't care who runs the country as long as she has big breasts.

Everyone needs the great Chinese clockwork fly-trap

You can teach almost anything these days, even salesmanship.

The gift of the gab, as it used to be called, has been broken down into its separate elements by motivational analysis.

When you put them together in the right combination, they make people buy things they never suspected they wanted or needed.

Or so the left-wing academics would have you believe, which is absolute nonsense.

People only buy things when they perceive a self-interest in doing so.

In our Western society we've left basic needs way behind and been brought up to expect material trappings.

Occasionally an important, but unpalatable, idea needs to be sold.

But, in most instances, salesmanship is only important when one is selling something that isn't important, except perhaps in the mind of the buyer.

This is the most important selling reason of all: selling and the good life, as most people perceive it, are one and the same thing.

I recently returned from China where the Government had invited me to conduct a three-week lecture tour on the free enterprise system and its extensions into advertising.

Queer food indeed for a system that has fed its people for two generations on a fare of single-product, single-source supply. The Chinese want to share the good life.

They were effectively asking me to teach them the principles of selling in a free market.

Chairman Mao brought the free enterprise system in China to an abrupt halt in 1953.

Now, 33 years later, it is semi-okay to buy and sell on the free market.

So the Chinese peasants took up where they left off in 1953.

The cars and the clothes, the clocks and the pots and just about everything else for sale looks as though it has been trapped in a 30-year time warp.

8 THE PITCH

Being back in 1953 is rather nice, once you adjust to it. Lots of things hadn't happened then.

For instance, they hadn't invented aerosol packs and in particular, fly-spray.

The great Chinese clockwork fly-trap was in use in 1953. This was an ingenious machine, which had been whirring away trapping flies in the better class Chinese homes since the time of Marco Polo.

It wasn't the advent of aerosol fly-spray that put an end to the great Chinese clockwork fly-trap, but Chairman Mao himself.

He was soon to initiate his fly extermination program where every schoolchild got red stars for bringing dead flies to school.

The great Chinese clockwork fly-trap played an important part in the decade or so that it took to eliminate the flies from China.

When every fly in China had been trapped all the great Chinese clockwork fly-traps came to a halt.

All this happened behind the bamboo curtain in the mid-60s and only one man in the West was aware of the demise of the great Chinese clockwork fly-trap.

His name was Jim Spratt, a cockney who had failed at several things and spent his life sweeping up his failures and moving on to the next idea that would make him a million.

Spratt had been given my name by someone who obviously wasn't fond of me and he called me at the agency.

He had imported the last 2000 great Chinese clockwork fly-traps and so far he had not been able to sell even one.

Would I see him? "No." I replied. 'I don't know what a clockwork fly-trap is and, besides, we've got the Mortein account and can't accept competing products."

"I'll be around in five minutes and if there are any flies in your office, keep them," he said, hanging up before I could reply.

He arrived carrying a camphorwood box from which protruded a large brass key.

He placed the box on my desk and removed a panel to reveal a wooden cylinder.

He then wound the box using the great brass key. Slowly the cylinder began to rotate.

The principle was engagingly simple.

One spread something attractive to flies on the cylinder and when they came down to feed, they were drawn by the cylinder into a death chamber inside the box.

"This truly elegant great Chinese clockwork fly-trap is designed to catch 20 flies every hour, on the hour, and that's absolutely guaranteed." Spratt said, launching into his sales pitch.

As there were no flies in my air-conditioned office on the 11th floor, I had to accept his word.

We agreed that he would leave the fly-trap with me and return the next day with a few sample flies to demonstrate the machine.

By the following morning, the creative department of the agency had come to a halt.

Spratt arrived promptly at 11am carrying a jar holding what appeared to be several thousand flies.

The creative staff were jammed into my office as he unscrewed the lid to let six flies escape.

"Got these little beauties from the CSIRO, they're bushflies," he said.

He lifted the lid a fraction too high and several thousand bushflies emerged from the jar like a black tornado.

By the time I had managed to climb over the bodies of the creative people trying to get through the doorway, I had already received half a dozen nasty bites.

We sealed my office, leaving it to the bushflies and the great Chinese clockwork fly-trap, which was whirring away, its cylinder spread with vegemite.

"At 20 flies an hour, there's about three weeks' work in there," a senior copywriter, Arthur Hankin, said.

An hour later I was forced to go back into my office to retrieve a file and there wasn't a bushfly in the room.

"Good God, the great Chinese clockwork fly-trap has done it," I shouted.

We were all experiencing the salesman's euphoria when one comes to believe in the product one is selling.

If you can believe in your product, the road to success is invariably carpeted with flowers.

We all crowded around the marvellous contraption. Hankin pulled out the death chamber to see how many flies it contained. Alas, not a single bushfly lay within. Not one.

The air-conditioning outlets had sucked the flies into the ducts, where they had spread evenly throughout the building.

For days we would pass closed doors from which loud ouches and sudden slapping sounds emerged.

Days, then weeks went by, but no copywriter could come up with a surefire angle for the great Chinese clockwork fly-trap.

Our small advertisements produced a zero response.

"It can't be sold," said Hankin.

"Rubbish," I said. "Anything can be sold."

Arthur Hankin, who had a face like a chewed-up Minty and a mind like a Swiss watch, put $50 on the coffee table.

"Fifty dollars says you can't sell one personally," he growled.

It was on for one and all.

Jim Spratt bet $100 against me and bets amounting to several thousand dollars were laid one way or another during the next two days.

Even Sim Rubensohn, the chairman, laid $50 against me.

Time to slot more women into the top positions

It is difficult to write about women's rights without putting your great big male foot in it.

The women's movement has become so sensitive to nuance, so wide awake to the slightest sign of inappropriate male response, that male comment has largely gone underground.

Pretty bottoms, long, slender legs and front bits that take your breath away have to pass without comment in the office.

Even the tiniest touch on the bony uninteresting parts is kindling for the axe.

Sex-based office banter is banned and I'm not sure the majority of ladies entirely like its demise or that it is even to their ultimate advantage.

The boor with the wandering hands has always been with us and always will be.

But the average bloke, showing his not always beautifully expressed response to a nicely turned ankle or well rounded rump, is as common in the office as paper clips—and as harmless.

Men are, I fear, beginning to feel a little crowded by the women's movement.

After all, we are not individually very well equipped to fight a determined movement or, for that matter, a determined woman.

Perhaps the women's movement might give us a few pointers on how the two sexes should behave with each other in the workplace?

We now know the do nots, but what are the appropriate dos? The question is not intended to be flippant.

Absolute neutrality in the workplace is no more practical than it is elsewhere. Women and men are different.

The corporate male is genuinely feeling threatened and doesn't quite know what to do—which almost certainly means he will begin to gang up.

All the signs sent to top management from middle female management suggest that the young female executive on the way up wants all the privileges of management, while retaining all the traditional cop-outs.

These cop-outs have, in the past, been the unspoken compensation for the less important positions women occupied in the workplace.

Female middle-management executives, it is contended, have more days away sick.

They tend, more often than males, to be late for meetings and appointments, take longer lunch hours and want to get away before the traffic gets too heavy.

Of course, this is a generalisation. There are many exceptions, but as a general comment it seems female executives try to modify the working environment to suit themselves.

I accept that the above comment comes from half a dozen phone calls and has no statistical basis.

I also accept there may be a perfectly good reason for wanting to modify the working environment.

The workplace, at the middle- and top-management levels, has been traditionally organised to suit males. It is largely their paddock and so they choose the game and the rules by which to play it.

The problem is that the men still occupy the high ground. They still make the decisions on promotion from middle management.

When they see a reasonable excuse to postpone or overlook the promotion of a young female executive, many of them grab it like a lifeline.

A great many men in management have always been awkward in the company of women. It has something to do with the private school system and being Australian.

The idea of sharing the boardroom with an aggressive female is simply too much to contemplate, so the middle-management male, whom management can be persuaded is almost as good as the middle-management female, gets the promotion.

The point is, the women's movement is winning the war at the reception desk and losing it in the boardroom.

One managing director of a multinational group told me his organisation had 18 product managers, 15 females and three males.

He claims that 10 years ago there would have been no females and went on to say the female recruits sitting for company entrance exam were simply brighter and better than the males.

I asked him whether this meant females would be at the top in the future. He agreed it was possible but unlikely.

"The three males we've got are also very bright," he said.

It may be time for the women's movement to go underground to forsake the high profile they have gained from protesting every little twist and turn of the heavy-handed, largely male-run corporate machine.

It is time to concentrate on getting more women into the top slots.

This year, the prestigious European Management Forum rated the business acumen of 27 countries. Australia rated 16th overall and a dismal 23rd in management talent.

There never was a better or more important time to give management a bit of a shake and to bring in a fresh point of view.

The battle for the bosom in the boardroom may be one of the most important to win if this country is going to keep abreast of our competitors.

We are a young country groaning with goodies for an entrepreneurial managment to exploit.

So far, all we've managed to do effectively is dig things up and ship them out to smarter nations to develop.

Our management structure is reactionary, the men in it are too often under-qualified, over-cautious, too complacent and hierarchical in the structures they build to perpetuate themselves.

The business of Australia is, with a few exceptions, managed by men who see no need to change systems and whose attitudes to the workforce are defensive.

They are unwilling or unable to compete. They lack originality, drive, determination to succeed and they are prepared to blame government or the unions, or both, for failures which are more often than not compounded by their own shortcomings.

The average Australian businessman in management does not have a lot to boast about.

The concept of a female-led business revolution could have a lot going for it.

Female management would not feel obliged to perpetuate the structures we've built between management and the workers. They are far more willing to embrace change. They are used to taking risks and are generally more open to new ideas.

They are much more likely to have a constructive dialogue between labour on the one side and their customers on the other.

Having spent their lives negotiating and planning every career move in a hostile, male-dominated business world, they will be tough, tenacious competitors on behalf of Australia.

But there is a price. You can't go around shouting unfair every time you don't like the rules.

Like the America's Cup, before you can change the rules to suit yourself, you've got to win using the other side's rule book.

If you will continue to demand the rights you believe are due to you by proclaiming them to the world, then you are condemned to remain in middle management.

You are scaring the pants off the average, conservative member of management. You are invading his comfort zone.

If your call is too strident and your tone too demanding, you keep winning the battle and losing the war. In an unequal world, you have always won when you used your wits and tiptoed into a situation.

It is pointless warning the opposition that you're coming. They will pull up the drawbridge and prepare to defend.

Remember, a well-planned defensive position is very difficult to beat. Do not try to storm the citadel.

The walls are too high and the collective prejudice too strong. Win from inside the castle; you're good enough to do it, if you keep your cool.

The real spirit of Christmas Day

Christmas. That's the six hours on December 25 when the family clan gets together—and goes to where the celebration is being held this year—in an attempt to be nice to each other.

The day begins on the drive over when your wife forces you to make three solemn promises.

First, that you won't disgrace the good name of the family by threatening to punch all its left-wing members for coming to the defence of Paul Keating; second, that you won't attack the Labor-voting, shop steward, teachers' federated, maths teacher brother with the charge of having turned Australia's children into mental cripples, particularly as this year he is the host; and third, that you will abstain from alcohol except for a glass of white wine at lunch and a beer on arriving and just before leaving.

By the time you arrive you need half a dozen beers just to calm down. You discover the maths teaching pinko bastard only has a brand of beer that you wouldn't drink in a sand storm. What's more, one look at the smug expression on his face convinces you that it's a deliberate revenge for having refused to lend him your Range Rover last August to drive down to Victoria to rescue stranded whales.

Two hours into the day your wife nudges you and points to a couple of kids, thankfully not yours, who are tearing each other in half. You know that at the end of the day she will be totally smug about how her kids out-behaved everyone else's.

Or, if your kids didn't exactly conform to the seen-but-not-heard school of juvenile behaviour, you'll have to undergo a two-hour dissertation on how your sister's splendidly behaved kids are suffering from creative frustration because she turned Catholic when she married Bruno, who started life with a fruit and vegie shop and now owns three blocks of flats and the building the TAB is in.

By the time lunch is ready you're already delirious with boredom. You face the prospect of nibbling, plucking, picking, tearing, stabbing and masticating around 8kg of the sort of heavy-weather fodder which lands with a splash in the litres of warm beer swishing around in your stomach and plummets straight to the bottom.

By then it's about time for the family altercation to begin. Everyone is tired of being nice. Overstretched gut linings, light heads and boredom are a deadly combination. It's time to stoke up one or two of the generic quarrels that have been smouldering away all year waiting for the six hours of Christmas Day to set the tinder-dry thickets of intra-family malevolence alight.

The first signs of the furore come when politics is introduced. The family dichotomy is complete with workers on one side and capitalists on the other. This year I'm prepared to wager 100 to 1 that Keating features again, and the FBT is a blow-torch to the inferno to follow.

The Pope's tour sponsorship by a beer company may get a look in, as may the decline of Australian cricket or the pros and cons of Alan Jones taking his Kiwi mashers over to South Africa to prove who is the real boss of rugby union.

With my luck I will be forced by my wife to leave just at the point where I've got the maths teacher to admit that the undermining of the national juvenile brain is a deliberate plot by the pinko, nay scarlet, Australian Teachers' Federation.

In his latest Mackay Report—Australians at home—Hugh Mackay shows that the concept of family, both singular and expanded, is very important to most Australians.

The transition from the traditional family to the nuclear family is proving to be a far from smooth one and few younger families admit to an ideal family environment today.

While most adults who are raising families look back on their own childhood environment with almost mawkish sentimentality, they are far from convinced that their children are blessed in the same way. The contradiction faced by many of today's working mothers is that, while they enjoyed the warmth and security of a selfless and attentive mother occupying a fixed, disciplined and loving home, they are unable or unwilling to supply the same environment for their children.

In an attempt to compensate for this serious shortcoming, they have replaced the calm certainty of a mum-dominated home with an often over-frenetic environment which is child-centred and dominated.

Both parents are becoming involved in a more or less equal sharing of domestic chores and child-raising duties and children see their parents in a neuter or ambivalent way. Today's parents seem to be spending more time carting their children around to child-oriented events, such as shows and sporting or cultural activities, in an attempt to compensate for the lack of a sustained maternal presence in the home.

From a marketing point of view, guilt, particularly parental guilt, is an open sesame to high ticket-item sales. The watering down of the mum-dominated home has turned it into an entertainment centre.

A small child steps off its tricycle into video games. Suburban houses are wired up like mission control with electronic knick-knackery intended to keep today's child amused. Eight year olds have computers in their rooms and use them for playing space invaders, war games and electronic ping pong.

Outside, the back lawn bristles with the kind of amusement furniture good councils used to boast about and young parents will go into hock for a decade to pay off the backyard pool.

Christmas this year promises, more than ever, to be a silent and expensive apology to their children from parents who feel guilty for having denied their kids a maternal doormat.

It seems rather a shame that the role model today's mother nostalgically admires is one which in so many ways depreciated the life and times of her own mother.

Love has a way of conquering all and it is the quality of love that counts, not the servitude it traditionally imposed on everyone's dearly beloved mum.

1987

The trendy's sandwich proves hard to swallow

Those of you who were kind enough to read this column two weeks ago may recall my declaration that henceforth, I would not accept the slip-shod, the badly done or the rip-off; that, as Australians, we have grown much too tolerant of the mediocre.

I vowed to fight back, no longer would I swallow my gall. If Australia is to become competitive again, we will have to demand much more from ourselves and others. I thought you might like to know how my personal campaign is going.

On January 2, after waiting 45 minutes to be served at a trendy Sydney coffee shop, where they art-direct your sandwich so what looks like a 10-minute chomp turns into a 30-second mouthful, my order arrived. It was flounced with lettuce leaves, teased with tricky swirls of grated carrot, with an orange peel ring to further add to the illusion of food.

The bread base on which it sat, made from chook feed and a slice of smoked salmon so thin and opaque that it barely tinted the butter showing through underneath, was pinned to the bread by the toothpick topped with a small cocktail onion dyed green.

SPOILAGE

I immediately sent the waiter with the torn T-shirt back with a message for the proprietor to present himself. He turned out to be one of those failed interior-decorator types who had been sitting at a nearby table talking to five patrons, all of whom fell into the same category.

He looked none too pleased to be summoned and the ankle nearest to my wife was already beginning to bleed from impact with the toecap of a Charles Jourdan shoe. I pointed a finger at the heap of paspalum in front of me and said:

"That is described on the menu as a generous helping of smoked salmon on a thick wedge of country-baked bread, topped with spring salads in season and a large pickled onion," I said.

I paused to look him straight in the eye. Next to this very creative description it says $11.50. He arched one eyebrow until it receded into his hairline.

"Smoked salmon is $33 a kilo," he said, as though that explained everything.

I did a rough calculation based on the 8cm transparent square of fish prevented from the toothpick from flying away. "On that basis, you would be turning it over for roughly $600 a kilo," I said.

"You exaggerate," he said. "Besides, in the food business you have to cost spoilage."

"The bloody stuff's smoked," I yelled.

"The salad, you can't get salad things at this time of the year," he said.

"I see, because you can't keep the promise you make in the menu," I said, "you hand-craft two lettuce leaves, a tablespoon of grated carrot, a twist of orange peel and a coloured cocktail onion into an $11.50 special, but you don't downgrade the price with the growing season do you? $1.50 would be a generous offer for that excuse for a sandwich."

"We like our food to look nice. We get a nice type of person in here generally," he said archly, his look clearly indicating there were occasional exceptions.

I then gave him my lecture on picking Australia up from its knees by giving service and value.

"Who do you think you are," he said. "Leo-bloody-Schofield?" He grabbed the plate from in front of me and stomped away.

Then he stopped and, turning back to me, said: "Why don't you and your bourgeois wife just piss off."

The table of look-alikes cheered and clapped and beat their well manicured hands on the table surface.

"Game set and match to your opponent, sugarlips," my wife said grimly, taking a hasty mouthful of blueberry muffin (not a blueberry in sight, $3.20) and reaching for her handbag.

Well, I guess it won't be all plain sailing, but then I've never had to pick a country up from its knees before. Service and value for your money is the name of the marketing game. You can do everything right in the book but if you leave your customers feeling they didn't get full measure for their money, you've failed. Simple as that.

I was recently invited to chair a marketing case-history seminar at which Mojo MDA, among others, presented the marketing case history for Australian Airlines. What a splendid and creative job they appear to have made of the task. At the conclusion of the presentation, Don Morris, a partner in the Mojo MDA, emphasised that the staff of Australian Airlines had contributed and how they had turned the airline around to make it number one above the clouds and under the sun.

I had flown to Perth to deliver a talk the previous week and the Ansett first-class service had been splendid. I had been asked to do another in Hobart, so I asked my host to book me on Australian Airlines. Again they were kind enough to send me a first-class ticket, so I was in a position to make an immediate comparison.

Australian Airlines had booked three people into the same seat, my seat, and I had to stand in the aisle with two other people for nearly 15 minutes while they sorted it out. It was the bleary-eyed special and I hadn't had breakfast so prior to boarding had gone to the Australian Airlines first-class lounge for a cup of tea and a biscuit.

PERCOLATOR

The urn wasn't boiling yet and all the bickies had been snaffled. On board, no orange juice was served once the plane got away, though I must say the aircraft was brand new, the wider seats very comfortable and the hostesses looked terrific in their new uniforms.

Breakfast was the usual cocktail sausage, bacon and ham omelette, but as I had neglected to tell them that I was a vegetarian, they can't be blamed for that. In Melbourne I was off-loaded to wait for my Hobart connection and fronted up to the first-class lounge.

A rather pretty hostess reading a book looked up, looked at my ticket and said, politely, sorry sir, this is a GO or something like that, you can't use the first-class lounge. But this is a first-class ticket and I used it in Sydney. The lounge was almost empty and I could see there was coffee in the percolator.

"I'm sorry sir," she said. "I don't make the rules."

She seemed anxious to get back to her book. The return flight was 20 minutes late taking off. Dinner wasn't a patch on the smoked salmon and lobster and fresh fruit plate I had enjoyed on the Ansett flight from Perth.

Finally, my baggage did not come rumbling out first, which happens with Ansett first-class passengers, but very close to last. So much for the new improved Australian Airlines. That's roughly 25 flights they won't be getting from me this year.

Because them's the rules I'm playing by in my version of the new, improved Australia.

America's Cup is no excuse for a handout

We were done like a dinner in the America's Cup. The better man, the better crew and the better boat won and all the rich little boys had a lot of fun.

I thought it was terrific television. The nation now knows more about 12-metre sailing and sailing in general.

While I can't quite see why that's important, getting to know a little more about the sea and the things on it may lead to eating more of the things in it.

Fish is said to improve your brains and with improved brains we are unlikely to consider seriously the sort of silly suggestions Mr Parry made in *The Australian* last Wednesday about the 1990 defence of the America's Cup.

Mr Parry, it seems, wants to have another go. Well, that's alright. As long as he uses his own money and that of sponsors who are able to convince themselves that associations of this sort lead to sales and not simply sails.

But that's not entirely how he sees things. He wants a tax deduction for sponsors and he has approached the Government to have the 1990 program classified as research and development, thereby attracting the 160 per cent tax deduction granted to new technology.

I passed a new piece of graffiti on my way to work last Wednesday. It simply said: "$1.40 for a vegemite sandwich is going too far and you, Mr Parry, are also going too far. That's my money you're talking about."

If the entire space program could only produce the non-stick frypan as a commercial by-product, then the scientific configurations involved in perfecting the 12-metre hull shape or more puff in a spinnaker is unlikely to be of lasting benefit to mankind.

I am prepared to accept that scientific breakthroughs come about in strange ways, but I don't enjoy being conned and you may not have my money for what amounts to an exercise in self-indulgence.

I loved the America's Cup races, the way the Kiwis came from nowhere, the fact that the logical and popular challenger, Mr Alan Bond, was beaten by a crew and a boat which simply tried harder and sailed faster, that the race was won by the most professional skipper, crew, taskforce and boat.

That's the stuff from which free enterprise is made. Business in the free world is based on doing something better, winner take all.

If the only way we can achieve it is to beg for concessions from a mob of politicians who are likely to underwrite our effort because it is yet another opportunity to distract the nation from the real issues confronting us, it may be better to step aside.

The last exercise in tax concessions and government largesse gave us our film industry.

This was a sort of cultural America's Cup, where our film was supposed to win the national heart and mind from the preoccupation with and mental abuse of American film.

All of which is very nice and, if you believe Phillip Adams, essential to the cultural integrity of the nation.

It has led to Actors Equity deciding who can and who can't act in our films and who can and can't work on them.

Costs have gone through the roof and most of our best directors are working in Hollywood.

We've made a couple of hundred films, most of them hugely self-indulgent flops, perhaps half a dozen have been modestly successful overseas.

The only Australian film to make it big, with perhaps the exception of Mad Max 1 and 2, has been Crocodile Dundee.

The producers replaced moral integrity with entertainment and completely ignored the local film mafia, tax and handouts to compete head-on with all comers using money borrowed from small local investors.

If we're going to contest another America's Cup, let's do without a handout or a research subsidy or any other euphemism for getting something for nothing.

Thanks for a terrific series Mr Bond et al, you seemed to enjoy yourself enormously and the spin-off is that we all know and like you better and that includes Mr Parry.

But if you want to play big games, don't expect me to pay for the practice kit.

I'm already paying for unwed mothers, minority groups of doubtful sexuality, minority groups dedicated to tearing down business, minority groups camping outside parliament, people on the dole, subsidised industries, big government waste, a bicentennial celebration which doesn't look like planting a single seed that will add to a blossoming future, free medicine that is using more and more money to employ more and more people to treat fewer and fewer of us in an increasingly ineffectual manner and a school system that's telling our kids that business is a basically dishonest way to make a living.

The car I drive to work is being taxed and if I forget to pack enough vegemite sandwiches for my client as well, I get taxed 100 per cent for buying him lunch. I don't need a goverment-sponsored sporting contest against the United States.

I just want Mr Bond and Mr Parry and Mr Fisher and all the other big boys playing with their toys to understand that this isn't war.

Our pride hasn't been destroyed, it doesn't mean we have a national emotional emergency.

All it means is that Mr Conner's 10,000 hours and his boat were the better combination, until next time. Mr Connor got his bottom spanked last time and he came back for more.

He didn't call out the marines or solicit the US Treasury. So pull your pants up and get on with it fellas. Ask Mr Bond how it's done, he knows how to come back and win after taking a good spanking.

Stimulating talk worth all the hot air

Last week I gave an address at a marketing seminar which seemed to go quite well.

The audience were kind enough to laugh in the right places and gave me longer than simply polite applause.

The following day I received an anonymous note which expressed the writer's disgust at having to sit through a lecture laced with obscenities.

Now I am apt to get a little excited in a talk of this kind and have been known to drop the odd expletive.

These are not written into my talk, they're verbal gremlins built into the Australian vernacular which, in a moment of excitement, make the odd appearance.

Had the writer given me a name and address I would have written to apologise.

After all, polite convention dictated the language we use from the podium must not contain the expressions we use on the pavement, even though Shakespeare did it all the time.

This got me to thinking about the conventions of language and of social habit.

Running alone with a friend of mine at the weekend, he related an incident at a dinner party the previous evening.

He had been invited to one of those perfectly ghastly affairs where you are asked to wear a dress suit to dine.

Apart from a casual acquaintance with a well-known surgeon, he knew no-one else at the 12-person, 14th-century oak refectory table.

The small talk was as stiff and awkward as the starch on his winged collar and all the signs of a long tedious evening to come were manifest.

Without warning, the doctor let go a tremendous fart which immediately warmed the atmosphere and in no time at all a good time was being had by all.

I happened to be glancing through a book by Eric Newby called A Book of Travellers' Tales, published by Picador.

As I flicked through the pages a tiny sub-head leapt up and hit me between the eyes.

It simply read: On farting. I defy even the person who wrote me the indignant anonymous letter to pass such a headline by.

No more than a paragraph, this is what I read: "Farting anywhere in public is usually embarrassing for the perpetrator, but there are countries where it is treated as a disastrous breach of manners.

"There is a man in Lamu, Kenya, who is known as the man whose grandfather farted, and I have heard of a traveller being forcibly ejected from a shop in Afghanistan on account of an involuntary fart."

However, it hasn't always been a serious faux pas in every part of the world. I quote again from another travel writer who recounts an episode at a Chinese dinner. The writer was astonished at the individual next to him indulging not only in loud sounds from his mouth but by explosions of a different nature.

The writer looked at him in disgust, much to the amusement of the perpetrator, who excused himself by saying that unless guests showed their approval for the repast in this way, the host would fear that he hadn't given them a good dinner.

I guess convention has it that a speaker is expected to leave his expletives, fore and aft, at home.

I have listened with pleasure to a great many talks where the verbal dish was reasonably well salted.

All these talks had one characteristic which most talks at marketing seminars lack—they were invariably well worth listening to.

The speaker spoke with conviction and with a burning desire to reach out and touch his audience with a message or point of view which was never dull or pompous.

While this does not excuse me or anyone else from using less-than-the queen's lingo, nor suggest there are no spellbinders who do it according to Fowler's, it does suggest that excitement, a single man's or woman's excitement, is the most infectious and stimulating thing that can happen to an audience.

If the price we are made to pay for a stimulating and rewarding message is a lack of couth, then it is, in my experience, well worth paying.

The average marketing or business seminar becomes remarkable if three out of 10 speakers are reasonably articulate and have something valuable to say.

Let me use another example over which a lot of people with breath like fresh strawberries are getting very het up.

I sit in a great many conference rooms where the air-conditioning has no hope of coping with the cigarette smoke.

I don't smoke and I find the acrid smell of a room filled with smoke very unpleasant.

But I accept that people have a right to smoke and that smoking while they talk and work is, for them anyway, a stimulus without which they would become nervous and twitchy.

To send them an anonymous note after the meeting to say that while the meeting was very successful the smoking during it was enormously offensive—an unthinkable way to behave.

Conversely, sitting opposite a chain smoker with a stimulating point of view is a hundred times better than sitting opposite a non-smoker with nothing to say.

Is it simply that convention still allows us to smoke in a captive situation, whereas we should not use expletive vernacular in the same situation?

Of course it does. If it didn't, I guess conventional good manners, one of the cornerstones of civilised behaviour, would soon be lost.

I mean, we couldn't go around farting away all day in public could we?

I mean, that would be disgusting, wouldn't it? So I called a doctor friend of mine and asked him about flatulence.

It seems the average person farts three times every half hour, that's the national average.

So I guess we're doing it anyway and it isn't the act that's bad manners, it's being discovered.

Thou shall not be found out. You can swear like a trooper at home, or with your mates, or in bed with your wife, but thou shalt not be found out.

That's what cements the cornerstone of civilisation.

To save you working it out, my talk to some 150 people took just on an hour. That's six farts a person, making a total of 900.

I want you all to know that, while I am deeply offended at this reaction to my talk, I won't be sending you any anonymous letters.

THE AUSTRALIAN MONDAY JULY 20 1987

When hamburgers were made with love

There was a time in Australia when we made the best hamburgers in the world.

This may still be true of some of our smaller towns where McDonald's has counted the mouths, calculated the mince masticated per head of population and left the local Greek cafe to carry on.

If this is so, then I encourage local shire councils to declare the cafe on the corner a part of the national heritage and a Bicentennial gift to the nation.

The Greeks may have brought us civilisation, the modern alphabet and the Olympic Games, but in Australia, their gift of the perfect hamburger transcends all of these in importance.

On every Greek island and in all the remote mountain villages, every generation produces a son in a peasant family who, unbeknown to anyone in the village, has the gift.

The gift only manifests itself when the young man hands the goats over into the care of his younger brother and migrates to Australia.

The moment he steps ashore and ties a greasy apron round his waist, the gift manifests itself and he instinctively understands the magic combination of wristwork over an iron hotplate which changes half a pound of coarsely ground Australian beef into a sizzling patty, browned on the outside, slightly burnt on the edges and a deep, succulent pink in the centre.

With this miracle of metamorphosed mince goes an ability to cut an onion just right so it frizzes into a nest of slightly burned onion snakes which give forth an aroma which makes you dribble like an old labrador.

The urgent wristing of the jumbo-sized aluminium salt and pepper shakers and the authority with which the hand tumpts the bottom of the tomato sauce bottle borders on arrogance as exactly the right amount of crimson sauce blurts on to the beef patty. And that's only your basic burger.

If you've requested a hamburger with the works, the egg is tapped on the edge of the hotplate with a carelessness that threatens disaster but it always shirrs and clouds white instantly into the perfect shape to top the patty.

The surgeon-like flick of the spatula as the yolk is broken and the bubble, splat and plop as the flattened egg is marbled white and yellow is a study in professional disinterest.

Then comes the snarl of steam as the egg is flipped to reveal its flecked, brown underside aproned with burn at the edges.

In the meantime, the pink, streaky bacon can be seen sizzling away on the edge of the hotplate, ready to crown the egg when the time comes to build the final, perfect acropolis of bun, beef, tomato sauce, egg, bacon, tomato, beetroot and shredded lettuce.

Wow! There may be more lasting monuments to Greek genius but the all-Australian hamburger has to be a contender. When you've been brought up with a hamburger ritual such as I've just described, it's a bit of a letdown to enter a franchised, sanitised, Americanised hamburgery and ask for a quarter-pounder.

You're handed a foam box containing a paper napkin and a bun, into the centre of which is placed something looking as though it's been cut from the fluff coming out of a vacuum-cleaner bag.

You count the sesame seeds on the bun and hope they're not made of plastic and shed a tear for the legendary hamburger of your salivating youth.

Sadly, the franchised hamburger simply cannot be translated adequately from the original Greek.

Now that Bob, the sporting captain of Australia, and his offsider, the clockwork sleazebag, are back, we are likely to see an even greater proliferation of prim-faced, tight-lipped committees and minority groups trying to impose on the remainder of us their particular view of what Australian society ought to be.

As certain as sunrise tomorrow, fast food will be one of the subjects most often tied to the public whipping-post to be flogged.

Fat thighs on teenagers, the escalating crime rate, police aggression, neighbourhood pollution, families in crisis, the divorce rate, impotency, cardiovascular disease and teenage drunkenness will all be laid at the feet of the Colonel and his mate Big Mac, as well as all the other deep-fried franchises which dot the suburbs and which supposedly empty the pay packets of the poor.

The assumption is, of course, that before fast food there was slow food. Slow food is supposed to be the sort of real food a non-working mum prepares with infinite love and a knowledge of calorific intake and essential vitamins which could earn her a PhD in nutrition.

If my mum was your average cook, her slow food was so named

because it was slowly cooked to death with the vitamins thrown out with the pot water.

Steak was pan fried until it had a cholesterol count as high as our national debt, chips deep fried in saturated fat and wheatgermless white bread was in large supply to fill up the holes in your appetite.

By today's standards, we consumed enough saturated fat to have the arteries of an old man by the time we were 13. I'm not at all sure that fast food may not have added something healthy and good to the extraordinarily horrific diet of your average white, Anglo-Australian family.

Advertising may well be praised by future and more rational generations for the universal spread of the fast food outlet. In a generation or so, they may well look back and talk about how advertising helped to get the English-speaking Western world out of history's most destructive eating rut.

Already we begin to see mass food marketing deliver food straight to the mouth which embraces almost every conceivable taste, fad and fancy.

What I object to isn't fast food, because your Greek hamburger was never fast food, but style, anticipation, a sense of occasion and the fact that the love has gone out of the hamburger.

Feminist talk more thunder than enlightening

My wife, who 27 years ago held the position of manager at McCann and who resigned a nanosecond after she was declared pregnant, never fails to remind me that she was once a senior executive when women executives were very thin on the ground.

She is apt to wonder what all the fuss in the feminist movement is about and I notice that the two Chanel suits, designed for a woman considerably smaller than the one to whom I am at present married, still hang in her dressing room.

In her mind, I imagine, she feels that if she could lose three stone, the years would fall away and she would be instantly transformed to her former executive status. But then, she is an incurable romantic.

Several days ago, when she once again broached the subject of work, I checked the balloon bubble above her head and saw her dressed in a little black-and-white striped Yves St Laurent number she'd admired at the NSW Art Gallery several weeks ago.

She was reading a slim report placed on the desk in front of her beside which stood a steaming glass of cafe au lait. Somehow she was answering both telephones at once, while at the same time dictating to two rather plain, flat-chested secretaries.

As with her hot flushes, which have been going on for about four years, and her pre-, during and post-menstrual pains which have been going on for 28, I have learned to mumble the appropriate concern without breaking concentration.

"Sure," I said. "It will be good for you to work again." But then, in a moment of pure insanity, I added: "After all, you've read all 75,000 books in the Woollahra Library."

"How is it I always dreamed of marrying the handsome prince in Snow White and I ended up with one of the seven dwarfs?" she spat, her invective so acid it made the grouting between the handmade Mexican tiles bubble.

Not daring to meet her eyes, I concentrated on the bubbling grout.

"You don't think I can do it, do you?"

"Well, I mean, you may need to start at the bottom again, don't you think?"

"The bottom? You mean typing? Well, yes, good typists are hard to find. I never was a good typist," she spat again.

"Well, there aren't too many jobs where you walk in and they give you a huge desk, two telephones, two secretaries and your very own cappuccino machine."

"I'm prepared to share the cappuccino machine," she said generously.

"Well, what I mean is ... don't you think you ought to take a course or something?"

She looked at me with one of her withering heights looks. "Radio hasn't changed, people still turn it on and don't listen to it, so what's to learn?"

"Well, it's tough out there. The token women have been replaced by real live hellcats. You'll have to learn to kick and scratch your way to the top."

"Token women. Me? A token woman? You pompous bastard."

I am writing this column free of interruption as all sound other than footfalls on the Mexican tiles has ceased around the place. I don't know what it is, but this column seems to offend feminists rather a lot. About six out of every 10 letters I receive contain abuse from feminists who feel I have wronged them and the cause.

Last week a Ms pointed out that having babies was a lot harder than writing a book. "Madam," I recall saying, "from my point of view making a baby was a lot more pleasant and certainly easier than writing a book. My wife, who isn't speaking to me, agrees with you and lays claim to three babies, all of them best sellers, to my as yet unpublished book."

A great deal of noise is being generated by the feminist movement, a lot of it more thunder than enlightening. I sense a lot of the girls are finding that being one of the boys in the boardroom isn't all beer and skittles or chilled wine and happy families. As a male, it's hard enough minding your ps and qs around the new militant feminism, but as an angry female executive it must be almost impossible trying to do the same thing around your male counterparts.

Can't we make peace? As a series of sweeping generalisations: I'm becoming accustomed to sitting in meetings where none of the males smoke and all of the females do. I accept your right to have more sick days than your male counterparts. I accept your right to longer lunches and less after-five stay-behinds. I accept your right to spend more time on the phone making personal calls. I happily accept that your intelligence and common sense often makes a refreshing change, and I am more than happy to grant you equal status and equal pay.

What I can't accept is the constant whingeing and your expectation that I will treat you as though you were neuter. I happen to believe that women, like flowers, have a special magic. I can't apologise because my wild and woolly brain has the odd carnal thought during office hours. I admit a whiff of perfume leaves me weak at the knees: all the tricks of make-up women use work wonders on my daily psyche.

I know this is all wrong. In the brave new world of business I'm supposed to go dead from the waist down. But I am an Australian male and John Turnbull, the poet copywriter, says this of us:

So narrow is his mind,
His ears very nearly touch.
So lowbrow are his tastes,
His brains are in his crotch.

Turnbull wrote another small poem which is going to land me, as usual, in the proverbial:

Behind many a successful man,
A successful woman you'll find.
Behind many a successful woman,
You'll find a successful behind.

Food for thought on a dog day mourning

Last week our dear old dog died. She was 14 and well past the time her pedigree are expected to live.

In fact, she was so old and worn out that every time she farted she knocked herself over.

I arrived home and she gave me what was unmistakably a goodbye kiss and I took her into my study and we sat in the dark together and at about eight o'clock she gave a deep sigh and that was that.

My running partner for 10 of her 14 years was dead. I had a bit of a sniffle and wrapped her in an old blanket and then in a large sheet of plastic. The idea of sending her to the dog crematorium seemed inappropriate.

I decided I'd bury her under her favourite tree in the garden.

This wasn't quite as easy as it sounds. I am building a new house where the old one stood and living in a flat. The next morning a howling nor'-easter was blowing and the rain fell in buckets; it was as miserable a late winter day as Sydney can turn on.

Carrying the plastic-wrapped bundle across my shoulder like half a side of beef, I dumped Lana into the boot of my car.

She was a big dog and I'm a little bloke and it was heavy going across the rubble on the building site where a bunch of Australians, new and old, laughingly called builders, have been playing around with the erection of my new home for nearly a year.

By the time I reached Lana's favourite tree I was soaked, exhausted and knee deep in mud. It occurred to me that there was probably a law against burying anything bigger than a canary in the garden so I decided I'd dig a deep trench.

After an hour of digging only my head protruded from the hole. I buried Lana and, while I was soaked through to my underpants, I felt good, the way one does when one has done the right thing.

That's when I heard the police siren. Funny, you don't expect to hear that sort of thing at 7.30am in the quiet suburb I live in.

Then the siren stopped alarmingly close to what will one day be my house. Suddenly I was looking into the barrel of a police revolver.

"Freeze!" a young constable said, and I could see his hand holding the gun was shaking. An older policeman shone a torch into my eyes even though it was completely daylight. So I froze.

"Dig!" the older one commanded.

"It's only the old bitch," I said. "She died last night." I was probably breaking the law by burying her in the garden but surely it didn't merit getting my head blown off.

The older cop waved the torch at Lana's grave. Half an hour later Lana's second coming to earth was witnessed.

It seems new people have moved in next door and reported a weirdo burying a suspicious-looking bundle about the size of a child in the building block next door.

The police left chuckling and I, weeping from fright and fatigue, gave Lana her second burial in two hours.

If dogs were eliminated from our society the world would be a vastly more screwed up place.

I guess this goes for pets in general, though dogs seem to be the animal humans care about the most.

ATAVISTIC

The point is: you can love a dog in the open. Nobody calls you an old idiot if you show affection for your dog and mush up its ears and even give it a bit of a kiss in public.

All of us need to let off emotional steam, and while it is permitted to show anger in public, spontaneous affection for each other outside a so-called meaningful relationship is generally frowned upon.

So pets are used by humans to satisfy this atavistic need. They become the willing and, in the case of a dog, delighted recipients of all that bottled up love. A lolling tongue with a pair of floppy ears, and a constantly wagging tail attached, has put a great deal of love into many a previously empty and lonely life.

In one of those meaningful statistics which are not meaningful at all, it is claimed Americans spend enough money on pet food to feed, clothe and educate every child in the Third World.

Knowing this, it is doubtful that we'd give up Rover for an anonymous though starving child. While this sentiment may lack humanity, it is nevertheless very human; our need for the giving and receiving of spontaneous love is paramount.

The marketing of just about every kind of manufactured food is frequently the target of social criticism and tinned food in particular is considered the bad boy on the supermarket shelf.

Yet I cannot recall having heard any complaints about pet food commercials. This is curious, because to those who believe in the insidious and corrupting influence of television the pet food commercial is one of the most emotionally manipulative.

While parents are reasonably sensible about the demands of children who may have been tempted by a commercial advertising lollies, toys or soft drink, they show absolutely no common sense when it comes to selecting the brand of pet food for Fido.

Australia spends $461 million on pet food a year, which makes it one of the major food items in the supermarket.

Of all the branded foods on the market you would expect pet food to be swamped by the generic brands. No such thing has happened.

The reason is simple. The emotional appeal isn't to the pet, who would probably make quite a sensible decision; it is to the love the owner has for a pet. No cat ever demanded Dine, the superior cats' food.

But I know the owner of two Siamese cats who felt terribly let down when her cats rejected Dine for a generic brand of fish.

On Australian television annually, $25 million is spent on advertising pet food. The branded products own 90 per cent of the market.

This is a prime example of love for sale which is demonstrated every time you open a can of pet food and give it a thump or two to make the jelly-like mould plop into the dish to be mashed with the edge of the can just the way they do it in the Pal commercials.

THE AUSTRALIAN MONDAY OCTOBER 12 1987

Did you know that? Facts of absolutely no consequence

I have long admired the letterists in *The Australian*, most of whom seem to think better than I do.

Not always a serious lot, they do tend, on the whole, to address themselves to the more important issues.

When I asked for contributed trivia in return for a very modest prize I expected a small, high-quality return.

Instead, the response was generous in the extreme and took the North Sydney post office somewhat by surprise.

Thank you for proving once again that facts of absolutely no consequence have a place in the rat's nest we refer to as our minds.

So much trivia arrived that I have decided not only to announce the winner in each of the three sections but to print some of the almost-wons as well.

That way you can drop a dozen or more interesting "did you know thats?" around the office and boardroom, and if no one else, impress the hell out of the switchboard operator.

I regret I cannot print every contributor's name for lack of space.

Because this is fondly regarded as a marketing column by the high priests and oracles who dwell in the temple in which I labour, I shall begin with marketing trivia.

Except for the very beginning of each category, again in the interests of the dreaded word count, I shall omit the mandatory preface "did you know . . ." Please add this essential ingredient as you read each delicious piece of trivia.

Did you know that when he is depressed, stockbroker Rene Rivkin, alias "The Lamington" because of dandruff-sprinkled shoulders on his dark brown suits, spends up to 24 hours at at time under his doona hiding from the world?

Sir Peter Abeles, boss of TNT and Ansett, sold detective books before buying a truck to begin Alltrans?

Leon Fink, boss of Kolotex and Hoyts, began business in Australia by driving around Melbourne clothing factories collecting rubbish and offcuts?

Phillip Adams' first job was as a film critic for the Communist Guardian?

The Lord's Prayer has 56 words, the 10 Commandments 297, the Gettysburg address 266, the US Declaration of Independence 300 and an average 300gm packet of breakfast cereal 1300?

When a startled Lee Iacocca, former president of Ford Motor Co, asked his boss, Henry Ford II, why he was being fired, Ford answered: "I just don't like you very much"?

Business Review Weekly estimated Robert Holmes a Court's income during 1986 at $2604 per minute?

A sign on the coffee machine of a large Perth corporation says: "If it looks like coffee, smells like coffee, and tastes like coffee, then it didn't come from this machine"?

HOW TO IMPRESS HELL OUT OF THE SWITCH OPERATOR

A Sydney second-hand bookseller advertises himself as a pre-owned book re-allocation consultant?

At an ad industry lunch in Chicago, the great Leo Burnett made his entire speech with his fly gaping?

The winner of the first of the three Reader's Digest How To Write and Speak Better books for the marketing categories goes to Owen Denmeade of Sydney with the following:

Did you know that in 1959, completely frustrated by repeatedly making errors using her new electric typewriter, Texas bank secretary Bette Nesmith made up a little pot of water-based white paint to cover her mistakes.

In 1979 she sold her corporation, Liquid Paper, to Gillette for $50 million?

The next section is for Australian trivia. It seems that the nation isn't in much of a mood for trivia at the moment as there were not too many entries in this section. Pity.

Did you know that one of the reasons the kangaroo and the emu were selected for the Australian coat of arms was that these two, from a very small number of species, cannot physically move backwards in retreat?

The first rhinoceros in Melbourne Zoo was landed by cable from the wreck of the Bancoora of Bream Creek in 1891?

The Qantas machine flying Queensland's first regular airmail service was an Armstrong Whitworth, FK8 bearing the identification G-AUDE?

There are no alligators in the Alligator River, Northern Territory?

OF GENERAL INTEREST 41

The second Reader's Digest book goes to Wyn McLean of Mentone, Victoria.

Did you know that the Macquarie Dictionary contains at least one spelling error.

"Summer pudding" is defined as "a cold sweet sponge cake, the centre of which is filled with stewed fruit as berries or *currents*"?

Most of the mail was in the general trivia section, and I laboured hard and long to find a winner.

My criteria were simple.

To be a worthy winner the trivia would need to be unusual and be something which once heard would never be forgotten:

Did you know that as the amount of oxygen on earth is finite, the atoms of it you breathe in now could have been inhaled by living things from Confucius to Christ?

The mouse population of New York's Central Railway Station revolves in four-year cycles, reaching its peak in presidential election years?

The last words entered in Hansard in Fiji before Parliament closed on May 14 were "what the f--k are you doing here?" spoken by the Speaker of the House to his nephew, who had come to arrest him?

Surveys throughout the world show that girls would rather be pretty than brainy? Is it because they know men can see better than think?

Only one word in the English language has five consecutive vowels—queueing?

Medieval anatomists poking around in a cadaver asked: "What shall we call this bit. How long is it? About 12 fingers? Let's call it duodenum (12)"?

Italian dictator Mussolini once received a hero-worshipping letter from a young Austrian man and replied by berating the young man for wasting his valuable time? The young man vowed that he'd make Mussolini suffer for his arrogance.

The young bloke was, of course, Adolf Hitler.

The word trivia comes from the Latin words for three roads?

At the crossroads was where the local Romans used to meet, to pass the time of day and discuss . . . well, trivia.

In 1980 the Lapps postponed their annual migration to see who shot J.R.?

The third Reader's Digest book goes to Reg Barry of Melbourne with this splendid effort.

Did you know that when Orville Wright made the world's first flight in a powered heavier-than-air machine about 85 years ago, the distance he flew, from takeoff to touchdown, could have been made within the length of the passenger cabin of a Boeing 747?

That's a piece of trivia you'll never forget.

As they say in the cartoons, "that's all folks!"

Winners, congratulations, your prizes are on the way.

A big thank you to all, published and unpublished, who wrote in.

1988

Even big companies need pleasant party manners

It was still dark as I left home and ran up the hill to meet my mate, Owen Denmeade. Together we ran to Hornsby lighthouse on the tip of Sydney's South Head.

We'd only just made it in time to see a fingernail paring of gold rise above the horizon out to sea.

In no more than two minutes the sun was up over Down Under.

"Happy birthday Australia!" Owen shouted. Around us dark cotton cocoons stirred and groaned and coughed; some sat up: bent worms sticking tousled heads out of the top of their sleeping bags.

Empty stubbies and tinnies lay everywhere and it was painful to observe how last night's fun had turned into a cacophony of bongo drums behind a hundred pairs of bloodshot eyes.

"What do you reckon you'd get for a crate of ice-cold Coca-Cola right now?" Owen whispered out of the corner of his mouth.

We turned and started back down the bush path which runs along the harbourfront.

It was not yet 6am and already it was people-dodgem time as families puffed up the path struggling with enormous Eskys and all the other paraphernalia of a picnic.

Sydney's version of Australia's birthday was a beauty. Everyone seemed to be in a good mood.

We had something of our own to celebrate and, while we understood how rotten our Aboriginal brothers and sisters must be feeling, we didn't much want to listen to their righteous whingeing.

Tomorrow maybe, but not today; today was for blowing out candles, not blowing up issues that promise to be with us for a good while longer. For a few hours it was party time.

Charlie, in a slouch hat, made a good speech, and Jill Wran, among the celebrities, wore her Bicentenary baby-to-come with great aplomb.

For once, the sight of Bob squinting into the sun, er-ing and ah-ing, didn't prompt me to punch the "off" button on the remote control. Let him have his fleeting moment in history.

I stood on the roof of a block of flats in Kings Cross looking down the harbour, my binoculars trained on the biggest small-fleet escort possibly in history.

In the far distance I could see the First Fleet re-enactment coming towards me.

I picked out a brilliant red topsail, a bright pinpoint among the white canvas sails.

Then I saw it.

Oh no! Tell me I'm wrong, it simply can't be? That topsail can't possibly have the words, Coca-Cola, emblazoned on it? But it had.

It was quickly followed by another majestic ship wearing the Telecom logo.

Somewhere, among the two million people watching, were a couple of advertising agency managing directors inwardly congratulating themselves for having conceived the idea while at the same time pumping the hand of their respective marketing managers from the Coca-Cola company and Telecom who were, no doubt, busy taking the credit and basking in the glory.

One expects Telecom to be stupid, but not the Coca-Cola company, who spend millions of dollars every year making friends around the globe.

Australia's birthday was a private party: a small nation huffing and puffing and feeling rather grand in the process.

GREEDY

To gatecrash in the way Coca-Cola had done leaves a nasty taste in the mouth.

Corporations are no different from people. They are judged by their corporate manners.

Tens of thousands of feet of red sail in the sunset had been shot and shown before the ship made its birthday voyage up the harbour.

The Coca-Cola company had already received excellent value for its money, but they were greedy and couldn't help slurping the last drop from the bottom of the bottle.

Perhaps you think I'm making too much of what could be thought of as a simple publicity gaffe, but alas, it doesn't end there.

Coca-Cola, in another flush of Bicentennial exuberance, has sponsored a splendid exhibition at Hyde Park Barracks at the top end of Macquarie St.

Splendid, but for the noisy and continuous playing of the present Coca-Cola commercials, which was hugely offensive to the nature of the exhibition.

Don't take my word for it. The Visitors' Book contains hundreds of irate statements and cryptic messages which quite clearly indicate the disenchantment people feel for the soft drink manufacturer.

There was a time not so long ago when this kind of crass behaviour would have gone unchallenged.

Australians are, by nature, fairly easygoing, but the mood has changed of late.

The cynical disregard the Government showed for the wishes of the people over the ID card made us all realise that government, any government, wasn't in the least interested in doing the right thing for its people.

The same eyes that were opened by the ID card con trick, which so nearly came off, have observed the behaviour of the Coca-Cola company and of Telecom, its rapacious corporate cousin, and they are not amused.

How do you suppose Americans would have felt if Coca-Cola had replaced the torch in the hand of the Statue of Liberty with a Coke bottle during that country's bicentenary celebrations in 1976?

I've never heard of a multi-national corporation apologising to a nation for its lack of good manners and unseemly behaviour.

As for Telecom, it should apologise for just about everything it does anyway. Business has always paid for its mistakes.

Now I think it would be an appropriate Bicentenary gesture for the Coca-Cola company to say it is sorry; that in its anxiety to be invited to the party it got overexcited and spoilt things for the other guests.

For my part, in a small and probably meaningless gesture, I shall refrain from drinking the company's product and shall drink Pepsi, the drink for a new generation and one which, hopefully, has better corporate manners.

Modify us if you like, but don't change us without our consent

Have you ever heard the expression, an idea whose time has come? Of course you have.

One moment we hold quite firm convictions about something and the next we've modified them to embrace a fashion or a trend that would not have had the remotest chance of succeeding with us even a week or two previously.

For instance, at the local rugby club where I join several of my colleagues most lunch hours for a 10km run I am known as lucky legs (lucky they don't break off).

Last week my wife, who seems to sniff change like a camel sniffs water, asked me if I could come home before eight o'clock so that we could walk along the beach. She added that she had a surprise for me.

I arrived home to find a pair of pants, neatly spread out on the Yves St Laurent sheets, which I figured must have been designed for some bloke roughly two metres high.

"Try them on," she said. "They're the latest. I can't stand those things you wear that come right up to your crotch."

Those things I wear are your normal khaki pants such as Australians have been wearing for roughly four generations.

My mouth fell open. "You're bonkers," I exclaimed.

She stroked the pants lying on their bed of sea island cotton. "You'll look gorgeous."

I put them on and they ballooned out away from my waist and ended somewhere between my shins and my ankles.

I looked into the mirror. I looked like a potato with two matchsticks poking out of it.

My wife cocked her head, pursed her lips and squinted. "Absolutely divine!" she said. "I just knew they'd suit you."

On the beach we met a mate of mine who gleefully sniggered behind his hand as he approached us. When we returned home one of the kids dropped around, saw me and fell to the floor clutching his stomach.

"That's enough," I said and went into our bedroom for a pair of proper khaki pants.

"I gave them all to the Smith Family," my wife yelled from the kitchen.

I was stuck with an idea whose time had come. Fashion is only the obvious tip of the iceberg, but all around us we see modifications to old habits that seem to arrive from nowhere.

CATACLYSMIC

But of course they don't. People don't basically change their ideas. In fact, it is almost impossible to change a socially established habit.

In advertising we rather grandly talk about changing a consumer habit, whereas, in fact, we haven't the remotest chance of doing any such thing.

Habits are changed only by cataclysmic occurrences and not simply by a few bucks thrown at the television set.

But modification is a different thing. It seems that provided we establish a basic uniformity, we allow ourselves, from time to time, to experiment with it.

Hairstyles are a perfect example of this. There seem to be about five traditional gender fashions in hair to which a woman can always return.

Modification is therefore possible because escape is not cut off permanently.

So my wife walks around in a hairstyle which four years ago caused exclamations in the street as a punk passed, and I walk around in baggy pants which make me look like a refugee from Changi and it's okay, because it's only a modification, only a temporary aberration.

The advertising man or woman looks for these modifications constantly and jumps aboard when they've gained just enough momentum to begin to stick.

This is what is known in the business as being trendy.

Trendy advertising people always act as though they've invented the change of pace, whereas, at best, they timed the climb aboard perfectly as the modification came cruising by.

With the intrusion of television into our lives we have become accustomed to being accosted with the banal and the bizarre, so that our entire society has been conditioned to constant modification.

What was right for yesterday isn't the look, feel, inclination or trend for today.

People have become essentially superficial, even whimsical in their daily lives. This apparent superficiality has been picked up by politicians, who mistake simple modification for change and assume that people are an easy mark and will allow radical change without equivocation.

The cynicism this implies leaves me breathless. The ID card was a perfect example of someone trying to ram change through without understanding the principles which keep a society intact.

People, any people, are by nature highly conservative. They will tolerate almost any amount of superficial or cosmetic tinkering but they won't allow basic habits to be denied.

Anyone who is foolish enough to attempt to alter the basis of how people regard themselves is in for a lot of trouble.

Governments generally, and this Government in particular, seems bent on making sweeping changes to how Australians act and see themselves.

REFERENDUM

This quite clearly involves removing a great many freedoms and choices which the people have traditionally regarded as belonging rightfully to them.

Government today believes that if it can obtain enough power to employ any initiative it desires, it will be able to cure the nation's ills. Which is, to say the least, arrant nonsense.

I have been waiting to see what the people would do in reply and I begin to see the emergence of an idea whose time has come.

It's called "citizens' initiated referendum" or, given its street name, voters' veto.

Put simply, legislation is passed whereby any person objecting to a proposed piece of legislation, such as the ID card, can collect 100,000 signatures from like-minded people—whereupon the government is forced to hold a referendum so that all of the people can decide whether they want the legislation or want to throw it out.

This simple idea would mean that politicians would be forced to obey the will of the majority of people. Voters' veto has been at work in Switzerland for 100 years and it's hardly a coincidence that the Swiss are the wealthiest and most peaceful nation on earth.

Watch this idea: its time has come. Australians will reassert the old and cherished habit of democracy, for like all habits, it's just about impossible to kill.

The art of selling . . . from every perspective

After reading last week's column in bed, my wife strolled into the kitchen where I was buttering a slice of burnt toast.

"This column is no more about marketing than my cooking is about food," she said, tapping her copy of *The Australian*.

"It couldn't be that bad," I said.

"It's too early to be funny," she snapped. "Besides, they're going to catch up with you. You're supposed to write about marketing and you're writing about whether it's better to fall in like than in love. By the way, do you like me or love me?"

"Right at the moment, neither," I said. The toast broke into 17 pieces as I added pressure to it with my butter knife. My wife swapped a perfectly good toaster, one that left the toast crisp on the outside and soft on the inside, for this one, because this one looks prettier.

"Everything is marketing when you look at it from a certain perspective," I said. "Well, I mean, everything has to be sold—ideas, opinions, lifestyles, religions, even lovers have to sell themselves to each other."

"Pray tell?" she said. (I hate it when she says that.) "Pray tell! What does that mean?"

I think she heard it in a television series called Love in a Cold Climate, where all these silly little girls with toffee accents began practically every sentence: "Oh do, do pray tell!" Except that there is nothing breathless about my wife's "pray tell". Hers is imperious and superior and looks down my nose.

When she's "pray-telling", you learn to press on regardless.

"Well, when it's all boiled down, marketing is all the steps you take to sell something," I said.

First, it entails the gathering of information about the product type, then about your own product and then about the expectations of the end user; your weaknesses and strengths and the weaknesses and strengths of the competitor.

"Armed with all this, and lots more, you formulate, modify, package and present your product in a form most likely to appeal to its most likely buyer.

"Well, a young bloke in love does much the same thing. He plys his troth using very much the same principles. In other words, he markets himself to his prospective end user."

"You know what I've always hated about you?" she asked. "You tap-dance. You can tap-dance yourself out of anything. Last week's column has nothing to do with marketing and you know that as well as I do."

"Well they printed it didn't they? I've written 140,000 words on marketing for that column—that's more than the average novel. Every once in a while, you're allowed to stray from the centre."

"This isn't straying, this is a massive migration way from the subject. Do you mean to tell me that in this theory of yours about falling in like with people instead of love, you can see the salvation of the world? That if we learn to like each other, everything will fall into place?"

THE PRINCIPLES ARE THE SAME

"Well yes, as a matter of fact, I do. You see, liking isn't threatening."

"Oh I see, love is? What I've been practising on you for nearly 30 years is suddenly threatening? You're saying that if I'd liked you for the past three decades instead of loved you, we'd love each other more?"

"Yes, that's precisely it! You can't love all the time can you? Well not intensely anyway. But you can fall in like and stay that way. Take a product—if you allow people to love it too much their relationship with it becomes too precocious," I said.

"For instance, I went into David Jones the other day and asked them to show me a pair of brown Crockett and Jones shoes. You know I love, not like, love Crockett and Jones, it's simply the best shoe made."

"Sorry sir, Crockett and Jones have gone broke," the salesman said.

"Pray, make it short, it's 8am and I have a luncheon appointment," my wife said.

"Well, I loved my Crockett and Jones shoes so much that I kept them forever, repairing them long after I would have contemplated doing so for any other brand," I said.

"Everybody must have done the same thing, you see. They loved their Crockett and Jones so much they all boasted about wearing them forever and in the process sent the company broke."

"I think that's a rotten analogy—more tap-dancing—loving a man isn't like loving a pair of shoes," my wife said.

"But you're wrong, the principles are the same," I protested. "If I'd merely liked Crockett and Jones shoes, I'd probably have had three pairs in the period these old clodhoppers have been with me and so would everyone else and Crockett and Jones wouldn't have gone broke."

"Oh I see. So if you'd liked me instead of loved me you'd have had three wives by now instead of one and your marriage wouldn't have gone bankrupt. Is that what you're trying to say?"

"Look, why don't you go back to bed and start at the beginning of the paper. By the time you come to my column, which is hidden in a far-flung corner of the paper, it will be time for your luncheon appointment and I won't mind one bit if you haven't read it."

"That's a horrid thing to say. You're my husband. I'm very proud of you. I'm proud that you write for *The Australian*.

"I love you, don't you understand that? I don't want the editor to fire you because you're writing about love instead of important things like baked beans and toilet paper.

"There really isn't any point in thinking you're a proper writer like Phillip Adams and can write anything that pleases you. Sooner or later, they're going to catch up with you, and when they do, what is laughingly referred to as your journalistic career will be well and truly over.

"I only say this because I love you. I mean if I merely liked you, I wouldn't bother telling you, would I?"

THE AUSTRALIAN MONDAY AUGUST 1 1988

The fountain of youth runs dry

I think the biggest problem I have as an advertising man in my mid-50s is constantly reminding myself that I'm probably a poor judge of what's happening out there on the street.

How easy it is to assume that nothing has really changed and that you can use the same value judgments today as you did 30 years ago. After all, you don't feel much older or behave much differently, nor do your friends.

It is difficult to admit to yourself that changes to our society have been so sweeping that the business of communicating effectively to some target audience is simply beyond you.

That's the trouble with growing old, it sort of happens invisibly. You don't feel it and you don't even see it. The image you see in the mirror changes so fractionally each morning that the bags under your eyes and the grey in your hair seems always to have been there. Before you know it, more than half a century has passed. And what a half century!

When you were very young, the model T Ford was not an uncommon sight on the roads. The jet engine hadn't been invented, nor had television. The calculator, transistor and the personal computer would have seemed a little far-fetched even in a science-fiction story. Even the atom had yet to be split.

Yet it seems like yesterday, and you kid yourself that nothing much has changed when, in fact, just about everything has.

It's not that the things that motivate people have changed. We are still driven by roughly the same fairly crude motives: love, fear, security, sex, money and power.

It's what these things represent in terms of symbols that may have changed. I can remember as a schoolboy looking lustfully at a B-cup bra suspended in limbo on a magazine page and allowing my imagination to do the rest.

My pubescent equivalent today watches a soft-core porn video or examines a full-frontal in any of a dozen magazines he can flick through at the newsagent.

My imagination, on puberty control 40 years ago, would have short-circuited had it come across anything as wonderfully wanton and exciting as the centrespread in any Playboy magazine.

While it was commonly used in the schoolboy vernacular, I can remember seeing my first four-letter word on the page of a novel and sharing it gleefully with my mates at school.

By definition, I had discovered that greatest schoolboy treasure of all—a dirty book. Made dirty, not by the story, but by the presence of a single four-letter word in a book, which otherwise contained 150,000 innocent ones. Today, this word, when written, is simply character dialogue and passes unnoticed.

YOUNG PEOPLE APPEAR MORE, RATHER THAN LESS, CONFUSED

It is here where the problem begins for me. Why isn't the effect of these radical changes apparent for all to see? Why aren't young people so different in their outlook as to be unrecognisable to someone of my generation? Why aren't they tougher, ruder, colder, harder and more worldly wise than I was? Why aren't they infinitely smarter and more sophisticated? Or even more cynical?

They ought to be as far removed from where I was as a teenager as a rote-learned multiplication is from the calculator. Sexually, with all the explicit information available to them, they should be totally casual in their relationships, hopping from one bed to another like amorous fleas. But they don't. Instead, the opposite seems to have happened.

As a generalisation, they are more shy, uncertain and ingenuous. They seem to have very little idea what they want to do with their lives.

In fact, they appear more, rather than less, confused; more, rather than less, conservative; less, rather than more, inclined to dare their personal genius to walk the wildest unknown way; and amazingly, less promiscuous than my generation. They have more of everything and are less inclined to use it.

Media hype tends to present today's youth as a drug- and grog-corrupted mob of totally promiscuous unrulies. And some small part of it is right; just as it was in my time or at any time in history. But what concerns me is not that youngsters are too street-smart and worldly wise, but that they are not sufficiently so.

Young people talk to me about being uncertain about their futures, unwilling to take chances, to change jobs to seek adventures. They dance to a more frenetic beat and mouth lyrics that are tough and street-wise, but like the way they dress, it seems to me, this is simply a way of camouflaging a timid soul.

A young person I was talking to some days ago told me that my generation was to blame for screwing up today's kids. "How?" I asked, expecting the usual line of non-caring, self-centred, career-preoccupied parenthood.

"You were too good to us," was his reply. "You gave us everything, more than we could ever hope to achieve on our own. Every generation before mine improved markedly on the lifestyle and the affluence of the one that preceded it.

"Mine is the first to regress. I come from a very middle-class family, yet, as an adult, I cannot hope to duplicate my affluence as a child. By comparison, I'm going out backwards."

If he is right, then certainly my business has been making several wrong assumptions when it talks to the youth market. Life is not really drugs, sex and rock 'n' roll.

We, who so happily pontificate on behalf of youth, naturally assume that the serious side of kids is all about standing on the starting blocks of life, muscles tensed in anticipation, waiting for the starter's gun so that they might compete joyfully and eagerly for the glittering prizes life has in store for the bold and the enterprising.

Whereas the truth may be that behind the cacophony and hype, is a bunch of ultra-conservatives in search of security and continuity rather than adventure and opportunity.

It may be that we've read the symbols incorrectly—that the full frontal of everything hasn't made them smarter and tougher, but that by leaving nothing to their imaginations, they no longer see the need to employ their imaginations.

That too much in the beginning has proved to be too little in the end; that the speed of achievement and change around them has left them feeling inadequate and unable to compete; that by giving them everything we've left them nothing to do for themselves; that the only thing left for them is to attempt to maintain the status quo.

Now, presuming the status quo is worth maintaining, the only way to maintain it is to strive to change it. That's the message, but how the hell are we going to get it across to today's panic-stricken kids?

That's the trouble with being an ad man with bags under your eyes and grey in your hair: you start to question the cliches. And when you do, you become unsure of what to say out there on the street.

THE AUSTRALIAN MONDAY AUGUST 15 1988

The new, improved Constitution

We are going to be a part of that most precious right a democracy has to offer—a referendum—and, like every other Australian household, we have received a large, black and white booklet with "yes" and "no" in bold, black words on the cover.

It has always concerned me that I am obliged to vote for one party or another just because it roughly coincides with my viewpoint.

Most often I vote for a party because it promises to do the least damage to the beloved country and not because it represents my personal opinions.

Therefore, for me, the referendum is a perfect idea. We should have them for all the important issues that concern the long-term welfare of our country.

Going to the people directly to ask them what they want done is the perfect system.

Perhaps this is why we hold referendums so seldom. In my experience, politicians are less than interested in what plebeians think ought to happen.

Referendums are presented to us as emergencies—critical decisions that have to be made to allow governments to function properly.

The suggestion is that times have changed and that old and cumbersome parts must be cut from the body of the law and new, efficient parts welded back in their place.

The booklet calls our Constitution "a blueprint". We are being asked to change the blueprint.

I guess it's a little like renovating an old house. You get the original plan and you modify it to put in a new kitchen and bathroom, knock the wall out between the dining room and the lounge and generally tart up the old place.

For the time being you're happy, convinced that you've improved the old mansion.

But one day you sell it and the new people don't like the way the renovations have been done.

They proceed to change the house to suit their taste and it is another step removed from the original blueprint.

I don't suppose there's too much wrong with this if the old house is consistently improved in the eyes of everyone.

Of course, this is impossible. People have different expectations of the houses they live in.

The analogy I have made is not precise but becomes more so when I add that some modifications to the original old mansion may have been sensible.

GOING TO THE PEOPLE DIRECTLY...
IS THE PERFECT SYSTEM

I approached the four questions involving the referendum with this question in mind: "Which of the changes involved essential issues such as kitchen, loo and bathroom and which were issues which were there to enhance the egos of the present owners of the House of Parliament?"

However, it occurs to me that it may be interesting to see how a referendum compares with a product on the market.

There is a law in marketing which says change is a difficult process to bring about—that well entrenched products enjoy loyalties and habits which carry their own momentum.

From a marketing point of view, the Australian constitution is a well used product which has served the day-to-day needs of its users for nearly eight decades.

Once in a while, the product has been slightly modified but basically it has remained the same.

Now the management at present responsible for the product wants to change it quite dramatically. If they were in a competitive market, they would be taking a big risk.

If the Australian Constitution were subject to the conditions of a normal market and people decided they didn't like the changes, then the product would lose market share, which, in turn, would threaten the welfare of the incumbent management team.

In the real world, when change is contemplated for a successful product, the manufacturer, naturally, is very careful to seek the approval of its customers before doing so.

The manufacturer knows how people hate change and is reluctant to upset the status quo.

If test market results show that the changes to the product are overwhelmingly approved by the people, the manufacturer goes ahead and implements the changes and in doing so strengthens it against the competition.

In theory, a referendum seeks the customers' approval to change the product and, of course, this is how it should be.

But the customer in this instance is put into a very difficult position. The new, improved product cannot be personally experienced to see whether it suits the users' needs and in addition, the product enjoys a monopoly and owns the whole market.

Once we change the constitutional product we cannot choose a competitor's product if the changes we make prove to be unhappy ones.

We are stuck wtih the reformulated product. So we are forced to ask ourselves why the present management of the product wants to make the changes.

Is it to make their lives easier, to give them more power or security and more opportunity to make changes to the product without consulting us next time?

Or are their intentions honourable and their desire only to enhance our lives with a new, improved product?

Only you can decide whether this is so. But if the analogy is even half correct, it is my observation that management which controls a product that has a market monopoly seldom acts out of the need of its customers.

It is for this reason that most referendums do not succeed. The changes are not predicated out of the needs of the people.

It is not that people are necessarily conservative, it is that they are suspicious of the motives of management.

How comforting it is to know that our founding fathers were smart enough to leave the decision to the shareholders rather than to the management team of the day.

Book sales business needs a really good dose of salts

This week I boarded a plane for Melbourne and spoke at the Australian Booksellers Association breakfast session, where about 50 bleary-eyed booksellers made the supreme effort and came to listen.

I was grateful. Breakfast talks, much loved by Americans in particular, are a horrible intrusion into a time of day when men and women should be left to themselves to pick up and arrange the mental equipment which allows them to face another day.

It was the first time I'd been exposed to book marketing, a fairly gentle business, conducted by rather pleasant people.

I am used to people showing enthusiasm bordering on aggression for their products, men and women who are sales driven, bonus driven and career driven.

What I seemed to sense here were people who liked books, who wanted to work with books not simply for the profits but also because the making of books was important work that did something for their self-esteem and egos.

They talked about writers and the making of books as though they themselves were a part of the creative process, as I guess they are.

Many of the booksellers at breakfast spoke to me afterwards, promising to stock my book and, more importantly, to push it.

The book trade is still one where the proprietor's recommendation carries a fair amount of weight.

They seemed genuinely delighted that an unknown Australian might have one of the big international books for next year and clapped spontaneously when they were told that the book would appear in six foreign languages simultaneously with the English version.

This is a first for an Australian book and a rare occurrence in the world of books, where foreign translators quite reasonably wait to see how well a book does in English before parting with an advance.

After my talk, which was an attempt to try to explain what I was writing about without telling the story of the book, I walked around the publishers' exhibition, where the new titles for the Christmas market were on display.

Again, there was no hype. You looked, you touched, you discussed in what passes in Australia for a cultured accent and finally you left with a handful of publicity blurbs, mostly photostats of what the critics were saying about the more important books.

Books, it seems, bring out the nicer aspects of the competititve instincts in man.

Despite the old-world feeling of continuity, of being a part of a process that has been going on since Gutenberg invented the printing press and, more than anything else in history, freed man's mind and shaped his vision, I felt that here was a business that might well benefit from a really good dose of marketing salts.

THE NICER ASPECTS OF COMPETITION

In the end, a book is a product like any other and must compete for the expendable dollar.

Standard, hardcover books of fiction sell for $29.95 and even the humble paperback has crept up steadily to about $15.

Both are well beyond impulse items and must be seen as considered purchases.

The first rule of a mass-produced, considered purchase is that it must be actively sold.

It can't simply sit around hoping that sufficient buyers will take the time to work their way relentlessly through the racks and shelves and hundreds of competing books to get to it.

However, the dilemma is that too many books are published in relatively small numbers to make it affordable to promote them.

The writer's constant lament is that the publisher "didn't get behind" his or her book.

Publicity is the key to sales but the machinery is expensive to crank up and sustain, so that most books have to rely on word of mouth.

The dream, of course, is that Maggie Thatcher will come along and ban your book, as happened with Spycatcher.

This moderately interesting book, about Britain's once mole-ridden, communist-infiltrated and therefore largely inept MI5, contains no surprises and is so conventionally written that you vaguely feel you've heard it all before.

It sold 300,000 copies in Australia.

Malcolm Turnbull's Spycatcher Trial, a much more interesting book, where Mrs Thatcher's high-blown legal eagle gets downed by a local sparrow in the form of the clever, but hitherto unknown Turnbull, is already a best seller.

It seems to me that the dust-jacket is an opportunity for the publisher to be much more effective without having to spend a large amount of money.

The average book has nothing but its dust-cover to defend it in the bookshop environment.

To the dust-jacket goes the job of beckoning a potential reader from across the shop, enticing her to lift it from among the surrounding plethora of books and, when this small flagging-down miracle has taken place, getting the reader to read the blurb on the inside front and back flaps and the back cover of the book.

By advertising standards, this area is quite large and, in the hands of a skilled art director and copywriter, the dust-jacket could become a powerful medium.

The job is simple enough and has two distinct tasks.

The first is to catch the potential reader's attention and, having done so, get her to read a couple of hundred words of well written copy.

In all, a three-minute opportunity to get a potential reader to take the book out of the literary orphanage and give it a good home.

Stuff the panda—how about a cute koala?

The pand(a)monium is over; the two black-and-white diplomats from China have gone home via New Zealand.

One cannot help wondering whether they'd have been quite as popular if pandas were as common as chooks in China. The fact that they're practically extinct has made them the best promotional and marketing tool China has ever had.

With the two animals went the results of months of overtime in Chinese factories turning out every conceivable panda artefact.

These near-extinct creatures have become big business. There must be some sort of vicarious pleasure in standing in a queue for hours to get a glimpse of an animal who may not be around for very much longer.

Today's kids will one day tell their grandchildren what real pandas were like. They will expand the two or three minutes spent viewing into a proper adventure, telling of the day they went panda-gawking.

Now pandas, I must admit, are pretty cute, but compared with koalas they're really nowhere. A koala, next to your actual teddy bear, is the most lovable of the "bear" clan. But, as usual, we haven't marketed them properly.

Nobody would think to stand in a two-hour queue to view a koala. People don't pay good money to take the kids to see a stupefied koala, drugged to the eyeballs on eucalyptus leaves, snoring away on a branch, although we have managed to market imitation koalas pretty well.

There are several factories in the orient, mostly in Thailand, turning out synthetic koalas with plastic button noses.

This is obviously an appalling state of affairs! Why should nimble oriental hands turn out our koalas when clumsy Australian ones can do the same thing more expensively?

What we obviously need is a koala marketing board. I'll be the chairman of the board and we'll send a government-sponsored trade mission to China to see how they knocked the panda into shape for export to the world. After all, anything a bunch of Chinese marketing unsophisticates could do for a panda, we'll be able to do in spades for the koala.

We pick up the panda technology halfway through the first official, 30-course banquet held in our honour by the Chinese People's Panda Protection Program.

After exchanging a toy koala made in Thailand for a toy panda at the gift-swapping ceremony after the giant nosh, we are ready to come back and get stuck into koala marketing.

We're not a stupid bunch, and we know that a good marketing man or woman must know the product in great detail. So we set about learning all about the Australian koala.

The first thing we discover is that the koala has a lot in common with a great many Australians. It spends an average of 14.2 hours asleep, 4.8 hours resting but awake and 4.7 hours eating. It moves as little as possible—often for no more than four minutes a day.

In marketing, it's always a good idea to see what has been done before for the product. There's no point in reinventing the wheel, and many an opportunity can be rediscovered by looking at the product's past.

We find that koala-marketing is not new. In 1924 alone, almost two million koala pelts were sold for about 15c each, and this sort of sustained marketing effort has been going on for about 50 years.

For a product that only moves around for four minutes a day and is usually fast asleep when you creep up on it, this was money for old rope.

It was about this time that we got very excited. We suddenly realised that, if you combined this factor with another we'd discovered, they added up to the perfect marketing situation.

Here we were, thinking that the koala was plentiful and therefore going to be a real marketing problem and now, thanks to the previous koala bear marketers, no such situation existed. Added to this was the bushfire factor.

The bushfire factor was a big marketing plus. Our animal-testing laboratory told us that the part of the koala's brain which controls motor function is very small. Clearly, koalas were never created to run and, while they can swim in an emergency, they'd be a lot better with a pair of floaties.

IT'S A BIT MUCH TO EXPECT THE KANGAROO TO BECOME EXTINCT

They cannot out-distance a bushfire. Putting a koala against a leaping flame is like racing Russ Hinze against Ben Johnson. Even if a koala survives a bushfire, it lives only on certain kinds of eucalyptus leaves which, of course, have been consumed in the fire, so the koala simply dies of starvation and disease.

Now you can't get luckier than that, and every marketing exercise needs a fair amount of luck.

Here we were with the perfect marketing climate handed to us. Like the panda, the koala was fast becoming extinct. Man, God bless him, had done what was expected of him with guns, cars, dogs and bushfires. What an efficient lot those previous marketers had been.

Well, I'm happy to say we are just about to launch the campaign. Just imagine the queues when Australians think the koala is about to become extinct. Never mind the Australians, think what it will do for Japanese tourists. If they went ape over our frill-necked lizard, imagine what they're going to feel about our almost extinct koala.

We've even decided to be very brave and make our own imitation koalas—a cash crop to augment and capitalise on the foreign tourist dollar. We're going to make proper ones, not that synthetic rubbish we import from Asia.

Our imitation koalas will be made from genuine kangaroo skin. It's a bit much to expect the kangaroo to become extinct, but every bit helps.

If only our ancestors had thought like that, by now we'd probably be positively overrun or, rather, overslept by koalas.

On Monday, November 7 the first Koala Summit will be held at Sydney University.

The koala is in serious danger of becoming extinct. Can you imagine that? The last dozen or so koalas are being paraded around the world's zoos. Kids are standing around to see a koala before it's too late.

Send your donation to the National Parks and Wildlife Service in your State. Please.

Mediocrity Rules in the Race to be President

The last time I was in the United States, things weren't going all that well for Ronnie and so he invaded Grenada.

Grenada, in case you don't know, is a tiny island in the Caribbean, of absolutely no consequence to anyone.

Ronnie sent in the marines, two of whom managed to shoot a couple of their mates, during the invasion exercise.

If the US had really needed to invade Grenada, they could as easily have sent a squad car from the Bronx, which could have done as good a job.

For the next week, Americans were beside themselves with joy, they had won something and they had shown everybody who was boss.

It's pretty easy to laugh at Americans when they do dumb things like that. It's as well to remember that Thatcher, when things were not going too well for her in Britain, started a nice little war in the Falklands, which soon had everyone in Britain jumping up and down, waving flags and shaking their fists at the world.

Kennedy, having been given a good lesson by an upstart named Castro, thought he'd gain a little face by starting a war in Indochina. He would show the Frogs how to go about beating up a handful of Vietnamese.

Menzies thought it might be a nice way to keep Australia's youth off the streets and went along for the ride; things were a little shaky for him at home and he wanted a bit of a diversion to keep the people's minds off politics.

History will probably write it all down differently as each nation tries to justify the inexcusable in the name of patriotism. What, in fact, happened was that a bunch of politicians did not want to lose power and were quite prepared to bomb, rape, lie, pillage and cheat to maintain their place at the helm of the nation.

Last week we saw the election of another US president, a pretty ordinary guy whom nobody seems to care a lot about. I can't imagine there are too many Americans willing to die for George Bush. Why is it that a country with such obvious brilliance can only manage to field a couple of candidates of such obvious mediocrity?

Such plain, dull men. There must be 10,000 men and women in the US who are much better qualified to be president. People with brains, charisma and the leadership qualities to take a great nation and make it respected in the eyes of its people and the world.

Imagine, if you will, the following scenario. The phone rings one dull, rainy Monday morning. The voice at the other end describes herself as a concerned citizen who, together with a lot of other concerned citizens, wants your agency to look at creating a marketing program that will attract the right type of candidates for the presidential campaign in 20 years' time.

THERE IS NO CREAM IN A BUCKET OF SKIMMED MILK

"Find the right natural talent and train several candidates so that whoever gets in, on whatever side, is remotely capable of leading America and presumably the free world, or whatever remains of it in 20 years," she says.

Well, there could be worse briefs. Better start by doing the usual background into the product type. What sort of training have past presidents had? Well, you are soon forced to conclude that the answer is none.

There are no schools for presidents, no degrees, no character training and leadership courses. You can't even conclude that being a politician is training to be a president, there are hundreds of politicians but none suitably trained to be a great, charismatic leader.

Perhaps an analysis of some of the more recent past presidents could help. Maybe a look at their jobs before they became the boss of the nation. This doesn't tell you much. While a bit of acting may be handy for a president to have in his bag of tricks, it can't be taken seriously as a real qualification.

While there have been a few peanuts in the job, being a peanut farmer does not give you the potential to be the head peanut.

A lawyer, a crooked laywer? Well it's probably better than an actor or a peanut farmer, but then is it? A lawyer would have to be the very worst type of person for president. Lawyers are men who are paid to take no sides, to defend the guilty, never to allow morality to stand in the way.

So it becomes clear that no training system exists which can hope to produce a proper president. Okay, that's tough but there is always the natural system where the cream rises to the top.

Among all those hapless politicians there has to be some raw material. But you are mistaken. The young Turks are given no say in the running of the system. All they are required to do is to sit like stuffed dolls on benches and say aye or nay when directed to do so.

There is no cream in a bucket of skimmed milk, the young guy who is going to get anywhere is the one who does the most crawling.

Eventually, he has enough old pros in his stable to wield influence, to make them scared of him. It's called having the numbers. If you have the numbers, you have all the qualifications you will ever need to become president.

The bright young politician soon learns that being president has nothing to do with integrity, honesty, loyalty, a burning desire to serve your nation, a lifetime spent training for a job where your brains and nerve and character and determination can lead your people to happier lives.

If you want to be the president of a great nation, then you have to learn how to get the numbers. That means you have to start making promises to mediocre men in return for favours, promises that will leave you compromised, your nation compromised, the system compromised.

Now it's not hard to see that any man worthy of being president is not going to want any of those things. Which means the job is left for the mediocre men who need power and are prepared to buy it without glory.

So you make a reluctant phone call back to your client. "We have looked at the marketplace, it is ready for your product, but the factory has not got the machinery to make it," you say sadly.

THE AUSTRALIAN FRIDAY DECEMBER 16 1988

How to beat the tradesmen rip-offs

In the back yard of the jumped-up worker's cottage in which I live is a small pool. So small that if you splash under your armpits too carelessly the pool half empties.

The pool is of the cement hole-in-the-ground variety favoured by the not so rich in the 1960s and my wife decided to tart it up into a sort of oversized bidet.

This clever exterior decorating ploy called for a single row surround of aqua Italian tiles, each of which cost more than the original pool would have cost.

The inside of the pool, she decided, would be given a pebble finish. We contacted a poolman to do the job and once he had a 50 per cent down payment he forgot about us for a couple of months.

I called him every day but he was already used to that. He had an answering service operated by a Filipina who asked me 67 times, which was every day I called: "Cornee, how you spell that name please?"

I could hear her sucking at the pencil as she wrote my name down and then she would always say the same thing: "Oh, I don't know why you always call, he never answers. He never even calls in for his calls."

But every once in a while he would call: "Can't get tradesmen, tilers are impossible, still trying, got to run, urgent job, see ya," click, brrr.

Finally, I got mad and called one of those franchised odd-job do-anything places. A very smooth-looking bloke came around in spotless white "foreman-material" overalls with a brand new expanding tape clipped to his belt.

He hummed and hawed and took measurements and tut-tutted. "Not an easy job, mate, these designer Eye-talian tiles." He picked up two tiles and butted them together. They fitted perfectly.

"Lucky," he said, "lucky I got two the same. Very bloody difficult, these dago tiles."

I pointed out that there were exactly 75 tiles and that I didn't mind if a few of them stuck out a couple of thousandths of an inch. After all, this wasn't the Roman Bath we were building.

He looked at me with a hurt expression. "We only employ good tradesmen, we don't like to do a sloppy job," he said.

Now, I've been around long enough to know when I'm being worked up to a price. "Just give me the bad news," I said. "Two thousand one hundred dollars," he spat out, so fast I thought I hadn't heard it. I looked at him stunned.

"There are 75 tiles, most in a straight row, in this overgrown bird bath," I screamed. He shrugged. "Eye-talian tiles, mate, very bloody difficult."

I told him where he could stick his quote and went back to making my daily call to "Cornee, how you spell that, please?"

A week passed and I had driven out to a nursery to get a bougainvillea to cover the trellis my wife had caused to be built (eight weeks wait) to cover the unsightly two-car garage, which along with the swimming pool takes up the rest of the backyard.

The nursery was in one of those suburbs I originally came from and have absolutely no intention of returning to. As I got back to my car, two kids of about nine stood one either side of my 10-year-old Porsche. "Nice car, mister," one of them said. "Like a ride?" I said.

In about two seconds flat they were seated, arms folded and ready to go. We did a few fancy spins and varooms around the place and skidded back into the nursery to be met by a big bloke who didn't look too happy.

"Where you . . . been?" he demanded of the two boys. I explained and then, you're not going to believe this, it turned out their old man was a tiler.

"I'll do it for you Saturday, sparrow fart, five o'clock start, got to be gone by 11. Saturday is me racing day. Sorry, but I have to charge youse time and a half, mate."

Wary from my recent encounter with Foreman Material, I swallowed hard and asked him to give me a vague sort of estimate after I described the job to him. "Sounds like a standard pool. Done thousands of them . . . 75 tiles, high quality. Eye-talian tiles. They're easy to work with for a start. What do you reckon about $350?"

I don't think he liked being kissed in front of his two boys.

Now, as usual, you'll be wondering what this has to do with marketing. So let me explain.

LET THE OLD FOLK KEEP THEIR RESPECT AND EARN A FEW BOB

This country is definitely in need of skilled tradespeople. A tiler makes $250 a day cash-in-the-hand, a bricklayer up to $500 if he's good. Buildings are going up like mushrooms and are siphoning off all the tradespeople. That leaves millions of jobs, such as my own, with nowhere to go.

It's nothing to wait two months for a tradesman to come. What he does when he eventually arrives is what you get. No comeback and damn little pride in doing a decent job any more.

So why not create a new class of tradespeople? Call them Grey Power. All the old blokes who spent their lives handling a trowel or doing carpentry or whatever, bring them back into the work force.

It doesn't matter if they're a bit slow on the job as long as they get the job done.

Anyway, it's a damn sight better than waiting six weeks for someone to arrive and then watch him screw up the job thoroughly because he's only using one hand to do the job because the other one is in your pocket.

It could work quite easily through the local CES. Senior tradesmen or Grey Power would simply register for work and the Government would allow them to keep all the money they make and still keep the pension.

The Taxation people would be no worse off because they know that if you don't pay a tradesman cash in the hand for a casual job you don't get him to come, so we might as well let the old folk earn a few bob without hounding them.

The extra money would circulate in the community anyway, which would be good for the economy. This idea would achieve several things. Older people would gain a lot of self-respect and would get out into the community where they could work at their own pace and whenever they felt inclined.

I'm prepared to bet that result would have a telling effect on the hospitals and clinics, as fewer old people would suffer from depression and a feeling of hopelessness, a feeling that they've been thrown on the junk pile.

It's a simple thing to do and the CES could easily organise it. We could even have old people with a trade taking young people without a job out with them and teaching them how to lay tiles or bricks, or build a stone wall, a patio, or tile a pool.

Well, what do you reckon? It's a damn sight better than sitting on a park bench feeding the pigeons.

1989

Kermit takes a back seat to the call of the wild frog

I read all the usual columnists last weekend, those literati and glitterati among us who are chosen to sail in the pride of the fleet, *The Weekend Australian*, and can write about anything they please instead of having to write about marketing.

In a frenzy of creativity, they all chose to write about the Bicentenary. Most seemed to think it wasn't quite what was wanted but few had any suggestions as to what might have been done instead.

In my opinion, those readers who managed to plough deeply enough into *The Australian*, where I now lie buried between the stock exchange report and the list of appointments of marketing people lower than chief executive, should not have to endure another word on the bloody Bicentenary.

So, as my New Year message to the faithful handful who read The Pitch, I have decided to thrill you with a column about frogs. How this will end up with a marketing twist is, as yet, unknown to me, but it will, even if I have to croak in the attempt.

THE LAST TRULY REWARDING PRESENT WAS A COMPOST MIXER

I am the original guy who has everything. I do not mean that I have a lot of things. I'm just not the sort of person who needs a lot of things.

Buying Christmas presents for my kind of bloke is very trying. I've got about three million books and the last truly rewarding present I received was a compost mixer.

So I always end up getting socks, ties, hankies and occasionally, if someone has a sudden rush of blood to the head, which forces them to the outer limits, the teetering edge of their imagination, a couple of pairs of underpants.

This year, at the major skirmish which passes in my family for a Christmas get-together, I got two great presents from entirely unexpected sources.

My boilermaker cousin gave me a light that you strap to your waist to shine down on to your toes. It's supposedly for seeing where you are going when you jog at night. But as it only lights up the tips of your toes, you are already there when it shows you where you are.

The other really good gift was from that destroyer of children's minds, my pinko, left-wing, teacher, brother-in-law. In an attempt to find a gift which would thoroughly annoy me, he got me a tape of frog calls. To be more precise, it is titled Frog Calls of SE Australia, by Gordon Grigg and John Barker.

Not it just so happens that I'm very fond of frogs. I mean, I don't go around telling people that I love frogs, so there is no way this dumb child-intellect molester, whom I have the misfortune to count on the periphery of my family, would have known.

There he was, sniggering behind his cupped hand as I unwrapped this tiny, really mean-looking parcel, which used the recycled ribbon and paper from the gift we gave him last year.

As I tore up the paper so he wouldn't be able to use it a third time, my face muscles were poised to turn into a look of disdain. Instead, they twitched upwards into a grin. Frog Calls of SE Australia. Bewdy!

Frogs are very much to my liking. Frogs are nice people. In a secret drawer in my study, I have lots of frogs collected over the years. Alabaster frogs, ivory frogs, stone frogs, jade frogs, crystal frogs, bronze frogs; wooden frogs but absolutely no plastic frogs.

Despite the fact that I quite like Kermit, I draw the line at cuddly frogs and plastic frogs.

Frog Calls of SE Australia was a big hit with me and beat the pants off the socks, ties and underpants brigade.

Shortly after Christmas, the trumped-up workers' cottage my wife calls "Courtenay Residence" on the phone, had house guests in the form of the delightful English editor of my first novel (the Power of One, out March 1, all book shops, $29.95, demand a copy), who is holidaying with her barrister husband in Australia.

So, with the frog tape primed to go, I hid the kitchen radio-recorder in the geraniums beside the bidet we call a swimming pool. As the sun set over darkest Woollahra, mixed with the police and ambulance sirens and other inner-city cacophony came a series of sharp, quacking notes, irregular at first, then building to a rapid climax.

"My goodness! What was that?" asked my editor.

I looked casually into my drink. "Oh that's *Litoria latapalmata*, quite common in SE Australia."

The noise died down but was almost immediately followed by

a series of long wails, followed by low-pitched trills and then a whole lot of mixed-up froggish sound as the whole bloody swamp got going on the tape.

"Yup, probably be rain tomorrow. That's old *Litoria chloris* starting to get excited ... listen to that chorus. I do believe I can hear *Mixophyes balbus, Lechriodus fletcheri* and the whole *Litoria* family, *dentata, peroni* and *verreauxi*. You're lucky, it's not often you hear those three together. Shall I see if I can find a couple of specimens for you?"

I strolled into the backyard and, scrunching among the geraniums, I switched the tape off and returned.

"No luck, frogs are clever ventriloquists, they could be calling from several houses away," I said.

"Just as well," the barrister said. "I like my frogs, legs only, on a plate with a garlic and herb sauce. I say, you do know rather a lot about frogs."

Mrs Courtenay Residence gave me one of her I'll-get-you-later looks before burying her face in her Pimms.

My editor looked up from her glass. "You know, it's such a shame really. I can remember the frogs in the village pond from my childhood," she said.

"Now that I think about it, it's such small things that add up to a proper childhood. Frogs, bird calls, fishing for minnows, the hoot of an owl on a snowy night when the moon paints the countryside silver.

"There's nothing like that in Pimlico and here I am, in an inner-city suburb of Sydney and children can hear all this and grow up with it. What are the bird calls like around here?"

I panicked inwardly, where the hell was I going to get a bird-call tape over the Christmas break?

Our guests left two days later for Queensland, after being warned about the Queensland cane toad, which I assured them had none of the charm of *Limnodynastes dumerili insularis*, commonly known as the delightful Pobblebonk frog.

And then I had my marketing idea. FROG TAPES TO THE JAPANESE! If they could go ape about frill-necked lizards, imagine what they'd do for Frog Calls of SE Australia.

I can see it now, a honeymoon couple returning to Osaka to live in a stacked shoe-box with her mother-in-law and when things get really bad, on goes the tape featuring the opening chorus of the Hylidae family led by *Litoria aurea*, the Great Golden Bell Frog, followed by the random "bonking" from *Ranidella signifera*, mixed in with a background of birds and insects.

I mean, would that not be something? Then right at the end of the tape, to tell the old cow what she thought of her, we would hear the maniacal cackle of old *Litoria peroni*.

Now, even if I say so myself, that is a helluva good marketing idea. Phew! I knew I could make this into a marketing column. Happy New Year. God bless. Rib-bitt! Rib-bitt!

Glowing result from the potting shed

My eldest son, who thinks I have an anal fixation because I am the greatest living bore on the subject of dog poo on the pavement, came rushing in the other day.

"Have I got news for you!" he cried, brandishing the latest copy of The Economist. This, by the way, he reads for pleasure, which will give you a pretty clear fix on him. He sat me down and commenced to read.

I suppose, in the interests of accuracy, I ought to quote the article, but as it went on a bit I'll give you the main drift. It seems that the world's second great bore on canine pavement defecation lives in a small, not very well lit, village some way out of London. Each night he arrives at his village station after dark, which of course you know is any time after 3pm in the winter. In order to reach his home he is obliged to negotiate his way along several badly lit lanes, unable to see the pavement in the dark. He generally arrives home not very nice to be near and has to leave his shoes at the back door.

Now I know exactly what he has been going through. As you already know, I do a fair bit of running at night and arriving home and having to find a stick just the right size to fit into the tread and then having to hose off my running shoes is not a lot of fun. Besides, I haven't run in a dry pair of running shoes for years.

Now, the Pom's family, it seems, was as bored as mine is about hearing what he was going to do to the poodle next door. You know what the Poms are like about their pets. I can understand his frustration, as appealing to the council would be a joke—the mayor probably breeds corgis and is patronised by the Queen.

So, angry and bitter, he went into his potting shed. All Brit homes in villages have potting sheds. Potting sheds are to them what the outside dunny used to be with us, a place to put the lawnmower and old copies of the Women's Weekly. He began to mix things deep into the night. What was left of his love life went to the dogs as he worked at a feverish pace.

One moonless night, which is any one of 352 nights, he emerged with a bowl of dog food. Creeping up to the hedge he made dog-enticing sounds and watched with glee as the poodle ate every scrap. Now all he had to do was wait. The next evening on his way home along the dark lane he was rewarded, he saw it from about 50m, glowing in the dark, a green mysterious looking sausage-like shape glowing softly. "Eureka!" he shouted, dancing in delight. "I have invented the poostep!"

Now The Economist didn't exactly tell it like that. All of the minor details like the potting shed and the poodle next door were invented by me. But if you know anything about the Poms you'll know that an eccentric and determined Pom who gets it into his head to do something is unstoppable and the action always takes place in the potting shed. So I have simply added a bit of needed colour to a magazine that worships fact and cannot tell a lie.

CITIES WILL LIGHT UP AT NIGHT WITHOUT ELECTRICITY

Anyway, what the Pommy genius has invented is a compound that is harmless, but when mixed into their pet food makes their poo glow in the dark. Now can you imagine what this is going to mean for mankind?

Cities will light up at night without electricity and you'll see them for hundreds of miles glowing in the dark. Planes will no longer need expensive navigational systems to guide them home. Tourists will come from far to learn the poostep. Hobby groups will be formed to go poo-typing, with high prices paid for rare breeds. Sotheby's will auction a splendid specimen authenticated as once belonging to the Queen's corgi for $1 million to a private American collection, believed to be the Paul Getty Foundation.

Soon the Japanese will be marketing imitation poosteps that smell and look like the real thing, play a poostep tune but don't eventually crumble. The Russians will score a major ballet so that the poostep becomes culturally acceptable and puppies will be sold to the rich together with x-rays of their major intestine to denote length, thickness and pootential.

Finally, people like me will be able to come home and fall exhausted in the kitchen without having to spend half the night with a stick and a cold hose.

So you can see I got pretty excited about the invention. It was undoubtedly a marketing breakthrough and certainly worthy of a place in this column, which some people have often referred to in terms not too far removed from the subject of this week's column.

But then, being a realist, I started to think about what was really going to happen to one of the 20th Century's most significant inventions.

Our intrepid Pom will take it to a major pet food manufacturer, who will see the potential immediately. Here is a marketing edge that doesn't mean chunkier pieces of soya meal cunningly contrived to look like chunks of ox heart which is worth its weight in offal. This, they will conclude, is unquestionably a major breakthrough in the canine diet scenario. A genuine benefit you can see even if you would rather not touch it.

Trials will begin using every size of dog from Sydney Silky to St Bernard. Millions of dollars will be spent testing to see if there were any after effects.

Miles of poostep will be laid out on race courses specially hired as test tracks. Leading athletes will be paid to wear dark glasses at midnight and break world records running avoidance on the track, missing the glowworms laid out in every degree of difficulty and glow rate.

At last the perfect cost-efficient glow co-efficient will be found. By this time clinical tests would be run to show the dog actually thrived on the additive, were less aggressive on the pavement and more aggressive inside the yard. The ad agency would be sworn to secrecy and would not be allowed out of the Glow-works compound for three months before the launch in case they got drunk and talked in the pub.

Finally the Department of Health certificate will give the all clear and "Meatyglow" "Let your dog be a shining example in your neighbourhood!" will blanket television with a $6 million, all capital cities, prime time, six week saturation campaign.

Alas, just as our capital city pavements are beginning to develop a warm and happy glow at night and the first poostep dance academy is about to open its doors for Japanese tourists, the bomb will explode.

Additives! Meatyglow has an additive and the food additive lobby will get going. The non-commercial stations will run three-hour documentaries about food additives and what they are doing to the unborn. Television promos will be aired for weeks showing the three-week-old glowing foetus of a Woolloomoloo rat which accidentally ate Fido's food. Scientists will be called upon to speak as dog lovers and before you can say "Oh no not again!" and look down at your shoe, Meatyglow will be taken off the market by a frightened government bowing to the wishes of a minority group.

So I just want you all to know that the marketing idea of the decade may never see the dark of night.

Another example of English genius has been locked forever in the potting shed of life.

How to turn a case of Delhi belly into a ball in Lahore

I have just returned from Pakistan where, by default, I represented Australia at the Adasia Advertising Congress. The bloke originally invited found it convenient to be away elsewhere and my name was dredged up from somewhere as a last-minute replacement.

Now I want you to close your eyes and think for a moment. You are allowed to visit any one of 30 countries and among them is Pakistan. Place Pakistan on your mental list of preferred countries in any position on a scale of 30.

Well, I feel the same.

Those of you who read this column from time to time will know how I feel about most conferences, seminars and industry get-togethers. Add a location such as Pakistan to this feeling of antipathy and my attitude to nomination as the principal speaking Australian delegate can only be described as one of white-hot apathy.

But as I get older and realise that I have got less time left than I've already had, I've learned to think of experiences in three ways. Those I definitely want. Those I most certainly do not want. And those which when offered can be turned into something else.

I hurriedly consulted a map to find out where Pakistan was. I mean precisely; I already knew it was somewhere above India. I discovered that if I did a sort of dog-leg flight I could go via Nepal.

Kathmandu, like Timbuktu, is one of those places that has a certain ring.

If you can picture a commercial for a cigarette, before they were banned of course, you would have this terrific-looking guy, tough but not cheap, the sort of bloke women know instinctively is going to be a bastard but cannot wait to find out.

You'd show him in various situations, all of them amazingly macho and chauvinist, like the ads they had before feminism struck its blow for womankind. On a raft up the Amazon, Chinese junk up the Yellow River, on a camel in the Sahara, mustering wild horses on a black stallion, and on elephant back in the jungles of Nepal.

There would be a jingle which would go something like this: "I've ridden the rapids on the Amazon/ run the New York Marathon/

fought pirates on a Chinese junk/ learned to meditate from a Tibetan monk/ a camel train is not new to me/ I've taken breakfast with the Shah/ hunted tigers with a maharajah/ From Timbuktu to Kathmandu/ let me tell you, folks/ best flavour by far is an XYZ rum-tipped cigar."

It has been some time since commercials were quite as bad as this, and thankfully the women's movement has stopped all this kind of jaw-grinding, sweaty-armpit stuff. But the names still ring like romance and there was Kathmandu and tiger country just a flying dog-leg away from my grasp. So I agreed to be Australia's speaking representative at the Adasia Advertising Congress.

Because this is a marketing column I can't tell you about the terrific three days I had in the jungles of Nepal, or about the elephant safari or the fact that I actually saw a tiger make a kill.

But I can tell you that I ate something dubious on the Royal Nepal Airlines flight to Karachi and arrived in Pakistan with the north and south apertures in my frail body doing overtime. Those old been everywhere, done everything commercials never mention about the trots or the things a crook curry can do to your constitution.

There was only one toilet on the plane from Karachi to Lahore and I nearly caused a riot by commandeering it for most of the trip. "This is very, very ungracious of you," one gentleman kept shouting through the toilet door.

Finally we arrived in Lahore where, to my consternation, I discovered that the totally enfeebled delegate from Australia was to be given the royal treatment. Garlands of welcoming blossoms further bowed my head, red carpet appeared under my tired feet and a military band umpa-umped as I was whisked off the plane, slid through customs without a backward glance and placed into a limo and delivered to the Pearl Continental Hotel.

Banners, even in the poor part of town, proclaimed Welcome Delegates to the Adasia Advertising Congress. Through the rumbles of Delhi belly and eyes misted from throwing up I was beginning to realise that in Pakistan they were prepared to take an ad convention pretty seriously.

At the hotel desk, where they festooned me with further flowers, which now draped like a heavy python around my sagging shoulders, I ordered a doctor. Like everything else for the next four days, my wish and the wish of all other delegates was their command. A nice-looking old gentleman with a genuine doctor's bag arrived just as I sank exhausted, shoes still on, on to the double bed.

The old bloke didn't muck around. He had my pants off in a

flash and shoved a great needle into the pale flesh of my posterior. "You pay me 400 rupees now," he said. I indicated my wallet and he helped himself to a 500-rupee note and made the change.

"Will I live, doc?" I asked, my bum still quivering from the vicious needle.

"I am coming again tomorrow morning and you pay me 400 rupees, and again tomorrow night and you pay me 400 rupees, and then I think we are making you better very very soon after that." It was true—1200 rupees later all openings finally shut down.

The conference was no different from any other. Long and tedious. But the hospitality shown to us by the people of Pakistan and in particular Lahore was unbelievable. The organisation was superb and the local hosts couldn't do enough for us.

A banquet for 2000 people set on a polo field outside the Governor's residence was a shimmer of silver and crisp white linen. Attentive waiters in magnificent turbans served 18 exquisite dishes to the other delegates and a plate of boiled rice to me.

Margaret Fulton would have chomped out an instant glossy cookbook of new and hitherto unknown Eastern dishes, and Leo would have ten-starred every nosh-up.

The banquets held outdoors in the cool spring evenings were a festoon of a million tiny lights, with each evening's event more impressive than the last. Bands played, military tattoos tatted and rapped and piped and fifed. Dervishes whirled and dancers in ribbons and bells and sharp brilliant colours leapt and gyrated.

The final banquet, held in the gardens of a Moghul palace, ended with a fireworks display which made the Opera House on New Year's Eve look like a match-striking competition.

The Governor opened the conference and four days later the President of Pakistan closed it with an intelligent and perspicacious speech, a lot better than most delivered by speakers from Asian and other countries, including Russia. Pakistan was in the full flush of a brand-new democracy and was delighted to be playing host to Asia.

What can I say? Perhaps it would be different if I had arrived alone. But I doubt it.

The people are naturally friendly in the bazaars, the glorious medieval bazaars that look like an improbable set for a production of The Arabian Nights. There was never any undue pressure to buy and everyone was helpful.

You have to take a country and its people as you find them. The country is beautiful and the people refreshingly natural and curiously friendly. I am forced to promote Pakistan to a new position very high on the list of 30 countries.

Thank you Lahore. Thank you Pakistan. I had a ball.

Fear—a classy way to fleece fools perfected for centuries in Europe

I was in Venice the other day staying at a hotel on the Grand Canal, which my Italian publisher assured me was the very best hotel in the world.

Now titles like that scare me.

More than scare me, they reduce me to instant wimpdom. Waiters and assorted uniformed people at such places always make me feel distinctly inferior.

Every time one of them moves I'm apt to mutter an apology and press money into his hand.

I have been known to stand up to people who by any criterion are my betters, but hotel staff reduce me to a cringing state simply by coughing politely behind a clenched fist.

It begins at the reception desk where a bloke in a $1000 suit and a grey, perfectly knotted silk tie (how do they get the knot so perfect?) opens a large book to see if my name is in it.

He seems to take an indecently long time to find it and when at last he does I'm convinced he is on the verge of making a decision to reject me anyway.

The phone beside him rings, which saves me from expulsion as, distracted, he turns to answer it. With the phone cupped between his cheek and shoulder (how do they do that?) he pushes a small square of cardboard towards me and indicates a biro pen stuck into a pseudo-marble pen stand.

This part I know. I have to put all my details on the card. I open my travel wallet to get my passport out and the entire contents spill on to the 15th-century marble floor.

I find myself on my knees retrieving pieces of paper from around the feet of other guests who have materialised from nowhere like a rent-a-crowd. Silver sideburns looks up from the phone, peers over the edge of the reception desk and asks me for my hotel booking voucher.

With both hands full of bits of paper, travellers' cheques, cards, onward bookings and airline tickets, my travellers' folder clasped between my knees, I plonk all the paper on the reception counter and start to search amongst it for my hotel booking voucher.

Meanwhile, old perfect-tie-knot is still on the phone shouting something in a foreign language, but he pauses for a fraction of a second to re-tap the small square of cardboard and utter the single word "passeporte".

The hotel booking voucher isn't to be found; the crowd around me is beginning to clear its collective throat and surge impatiently. The booking voucher was definitely there when I checked it prior to departure, it will no doubt reappear later wrapped in a dirty sock.

I leave the collection of paper from my travel wallet scattered over the reception desk and reach for the pen to complete the registration card.

The bloody pen doesn't work. I look helplessly around and old phone-face raises his eyes heavenwards and, digging into the folds of his Georgio Armani suit, produces a gold Du Pont pen and proffers it while he continues yakking down the receiver.

My heart sinks—my passport isn't in my bag. I beat my breast, desperately seeking it in the pockets of my jacket.

It's gone! I've lost my identity.

The concierge leans forward, phone still cupped into his shoulder like the avenging wings of a bird of prey. He points at my papers scattered over the reception desk. Protruding from under a concertina of airline tickets is my passport.

Finally I complete the form and, capping his pen, I absent-mindedly slip it into my breast pocket. This causes him to say "ciao" hurriedly into the phone, which he recradles. Then he sticks his hand out for his pen.

I hand him the registration card and my passport. He takes it, puts out the other hand and says "penne!" He has not lost his cool, it is 9.30 in the morning, idiot peak hour. If he can last until lunchtime the worst will be over. Wearily he hands me a key.

I go to take it and a hand shoots over my shoulder and grabs it. I look around and it's a bloke in a white jacket who is carrying my bag. I follow him to a brass lift which looks like an elaborate birdcage and we jerk upwards.

By this time I'm willing to pay any amount of tip money just to be locked away alone and safe in my room. But that's the other thing about European hotel staff. No matter how generous you are, their manner suggests that you've only just reached the minimum expectation.

So, there I was in Venice stepping off the 80-bucks-from-the-airport water taxi, up the gangplanks, on to the pontoon and into the world's best hotel, an ex-prince's residence on the Grand Canal known as the Gritti Palace.

Thousand dollars a night for a small room with bath and juice, roll and black coffee thrown in for breakfast.

Even though I wasn't paying, I was reduced to a state of abject terror.

I can tell by the decor when things are going to be really bad and this place had twice as many of the worst signs as I'd ever seen.

Worn Persian carpets on the concave marble tiles, faded tapestry drapes and old dark paintings of gloomy potentates in chipped gilt frames hanging on ancient hand-decorated walls.

Worn leather couches squatted in dark corners and huge 6ft Murano vases and assorted old-fashioned bronze statues lurked in unexpected places.

Finally an elaborate brass birdcage lift you could hear coming for 10 minutes jarred and clattered to a halt.

I knew I was in terrible trouble. Silver sideburns at reception gave me the usual hard time and I responded by cringing disgustingly.

Having forced the registration card confession out of me and having confiscated my passport—so I couldn't escape without paying, he leaned over to me, drawing me closer with a well-manicured conspiratorial forefinger, and whispered: "The customary gratuity for all staff is 15,000 lira, sir."

Panic-stricken, I reached into my wallet and produced three 100,000-lira notes and shoved them into his hand, where they disappeared so quickly and discreetly he hadn't appeared to move a muscle.

By the time I got to lock myself into my perfectly ordinary room with worn imitation antique furniture and cold bathroom it had cost me sixty bucks in tips. They had me well and truly by the short and curlies.

Now I know you're wondering what this has to do with marketing. Well, everything really. Fear is a major marketing tool in the tourist business. The Europeans are the best at it. They work on the marketing principle that the more they can unsettle clients the less they are likely to demand and the more they can charge for increasingly diminished services.

They have discovered the world is filled wth cowardly snobs who will pay almost anything to be subjected to a bit of really high-class confidence undermining.

An arched eyebrow, a clearing of the throat or a slight pause when a price is queried is standard procedure.

The Gritti Palace in Venice wins the European Cup hands down for fear marketing. I mean, who else could sell you a damp room in a crumbling, tired and badly furnished building situated beside a noisy and smelly canal for a thousand bucks a night plus a breakfast roll and a cup of bitter black coffee?

/ THE AUSTRALIAN FRIDAY MAY 12 1989

A bird on the ground is worth more as PM

Clive Robertson, a popular radio and television personality who operates from Sydney, interviewed me several weeks ago on the subject of a novel I have recently completed.

Mr Robertson had obviously not read my book nor did I expect that he would have. Life is much too short on radio and television to wade through a 500-page book in order to evolve a decent five or six-minute interview.

People in Clive's job have to tap dance and, indeed they get very good at it. Starting with very little, they can work up quite a decent sort of interview.

Robertson is quick, intelligent and lively, even if his style appears laid back and seemingly uninterested. The first question he asked me was whether my name, Bryce Courtenay, was real.

It's too perfect for an author, you must have invented it, he challenged.

Mr Robertson isn't the first person to ask me whether my name is real; in fact I've had people tell me to my face that it wasn't, that they know someone who took the trouble to check up and found that I'd invented it.

They say Bryce Courtenay was just too perfect a name for the creative director of a multi-national advertising agency.

Names often do conjure up pictures of people and it is surprising how they also seem to affect their owners. Every advertising man knows that names have feelings attached to them.

Dunhill chips and Smith lighters are not interchangeable. We do look into names and see things.

Hawke, for instance. If you wanted to name a prime minister, you'd have to go a long way to find a better name. It suggests all the right things, a fighter who sees things clearly from a distance, is brave, ruthless, brilliant, a leader.

Now I'm not saying that a bloke like Bob Hawke didn't have to fight for all he got, but I am saying that his name didn't get in the way.

If two young blokes with almost identical talents were to line up for a Rhodes scholarship and one was named Cuthbert Fuddlepenny and the other was named Robert Hawke, the committee might just be swayed Bob's way without being conscious that they had been.

Last week we saw a change of names in the Liberal line-up and as everyone in Australia now knows, we again have a Peacock opposing a Hawke. It's a tired joke I know. But there still may be something in these two names.

As I know neither of them other than from their public personas, like everyone else I am forced to judge them by what is said about them in the media. Both of these men have been in the public eye for a long time and there is an accumulation of truisms about each which might be called popular knowledge.

The fact that much of this may be distorted or highly coloured or simply untrue makes no difference whatsoever. If asked to talk about either man, this is the sort of information the average person in the street might be able to deliver.

Hawke is a brilliant bloke who won a Rhodes scholarship to Oxford where he played a lot of cricket and drank a lot of beer. He returned to Australia and became the boss of all the trade unions where he continued to drink a lot of beer and opened his mouth in other ways as well.

Sometimes the combination of beer and brag got him into trouble and sometimes it got him into women. Anyway, he was a pretty strong sort of bloke and did a lot of good things for the working man and Israel, which he loves second only to his fellow Australians.

When Gough took his tumble Labor was in the poo and somebody offered the job to Bob, who despite the booze and brag was a pretty popular and dynamic sort of bloke. He could have the job if he cleaned up his act, the party said.

"If you promise to give up booze and women, the big one's yours, Bob," was more or less what they said.

Bob, who had honestly never met his intellectual match, showed what he was made of and did exactly that and even a little family disappointment did not prevent him from becoming Father of the Year.

He then became captain of every sport in Australia except of the teams which wanted to play against South Africa and, in his capacity as the ultimate representative, he is always on hand when Australia wins and away on urgent business, mostly with tycoons, when we don't.

He seems to make an awful lot of promises which his offsider

Keating ignores so that voters hate Keating and forgive him. And when you put it all together he's a dangerous opponent, who knows how to fly high, can see a victim a mile off the ground, strikes without warning, devours his prey and likes to perch on high places.

If you had to give the perfect name to this bloke you'd have to conclude that it was Hawke.

Now, if you use the same method, this same conventional wisdom, and you apply it to Andrew Peacock, this sort of thing happens. Here is a bloke who could only come from Melbourne, rich parents, rich school, rich accent.

A very good looking politician who probably uses one of those lamps to give himself an all-round suntan and who knows which is his best profile on television. He's a man who seems to marry and divorce women who are not as good looking as he is, but who end up with money, real estate and media personalities of their own.

His political life has been spent being groomed for something which would inevitably lead to his becoming prime minister. He doesn't seem to have botched up any of the jobs given to him other than the challenges to and for the leadership of his party, where his timing was always too something—too soon, too late, too inconsistent, too often.

He seems to understand nearly as well as the incumbent that television is a powerful medium and so he has had the bags removed from under his eyes and any controversial opinions held by his party removed from under ours.

He has a lot of political presence and is hard to ignore. If you had to sum up what we know about him you would have to conclude that he was a pretty good looking candidate for PM and that Peacock was the perfect name for him.

But if you conclude that Hawke is perhaps a better name for a prime minister than Peacock just stop and think for a moment.

Would you not agree that what this country desperately needs is a prime minister who can be clearly seen with his tail up and his feet planted firmly on the ground rather than one who seems to be wafting away with his head in the clouds?

Fire of enthusiasm can revive that flickering candle

In the past few months, two of my friends who are also past business colleagues have died.

Both had lived relatively passive corporate lives and their particular candles had burned brightly, but always sensibly at one end. Suddenly in their early 50s they were snuffed.

"Okay," we all say, "it could happen to us any time."

We pick up the phone, order a wreath, call a few mutual friends interstate who may now know the bad news yet, feel bad together on the phone as we share a few recollections, then we tuck away our memories in a safe place where they won't interfere with our own expectations of living for decades yet. We call home and ask our wives to send the dark suit to the same-day cleaners and momentarily wonder what we did with the black tie we bought just the other day.

Even death has a nice, polite routine.

Because we are Australians with a dash of Irish, not much is said at the funeral—in fact, it takes several beers at the pub afterwards to loosen tongues and bring out the memories.

I stood at the bar looking at my contemporaries, those of us who had belonged to the ambitious generation where hard work, drive, energy and only a modicum of talent were needed to succeed.

Some looked sharp and glossy but most of us had a rather tired, strained look that went with the 10 or 15 kilos we had gathered on the way to getting the Mercedes with tow-bar, double garage, pool, boat and outdoor entertainment furniture.

Golf was the early subject. It seems that around your mid-40s and roughly the male menopause period, golf replaces women, business and even the horses. Golf becomes the new passion. Men who never came nearer to a ball game than the television set are suddenly driven into a frenzy over a little white ball.

Men whose total previous weekly exercise consisted of crossing the parking lot from the lift to the car now get up at 5am for nine holes, happily trudging through dew-soaked grass, chasing the little white pill of utter frustration.

There must be a reason for such strange behaviour. Why would a man in his late 40s spend a fortune on golf clubs and lessons when it is patently obvious that he is neither a gifted ball player nor likely to improve his utterly hopeless status significantly?

The only thing he would seem to gain is a new topic of conversation, which to the non-golfer is about as interesting as watching the grass grow—although even watching grass grow is part of golf.

I heard two disciples talking about the US Open and noting that the players who teed off last had to contend with a fairway on which the newly mown grass had grown in three hours!

Now I got to thinking about this propensity for golf at an age when real sporting heroes are about to lay down their clubs and it seems to make some sort of sense.

I have this theory that we all ought to have two lives. The first is for kids and mortgages, double garages and tools, sticking it up the neighbours and messy divorces, then finally when we have shown the kids the front door, hopefully for the last time (why is it that they keep returning?) we ought to have a second life. The second one is for ourselves.

Now this second life is not retirement. It's a whole new life, carefully planned with all the expectations of success but, even more importantly, for fun.

The point is that most people start their working careers in Australia in their late teens. At this time they have almost no idea what they want to do or even what they might prove to be good at.

Because the work ethic is deeply ingrained, most of us spend our lives working at something we find difficult to feel any passion about. We work to eat and play our allotted part in the dreary system and we seldom have fun.

Then one day we retire, mostly to die a quiet, harmless death. Our candle, far from being lit at both ends, has never done much more than flicker at one. That's not what I mean by a second career.

Now, I think golf may be a sort of compromise between shaping a new career that is fun and about which you can become passionate, and dying of boredom. It supplies some of the goodies.

It is difficult to master at any age, least of all when muscular atrophy is beginning to set in and bones begin to creak. It has a sense of getting closer to nature and reality. It stops you having to think about getting old.

It keeps some old friends and makes new ones. It even seems to be fun, though perverse, for those people who take it up.

Best of all, it gets you out of a rut and out of the house and attempts to fill that part of your personality which asks as you approach the post-menopausal part of your life: "Is that all?"

But there is another way. It's called planning what you really want to be while you are busy beginning who you have to be.

Hopefully, as we grow a little old we get a little wiser. We begin to sense those things we might like to do and even be good at doing. So why not do them?

If you work as a clerk in the Department of Main Roads but always wanted to be a landscape gardener, why not go to tech for a few years, then take out superannuation in your mid-50s and buy a second-hand Toyota, a shovel and a chainsaw and launch yourself upon the unsuspecting landscape? Why not?

Most people in their 50s have learned something about themselves—they're not complete fools. Your chances of success are much higher than at any other time in your life. All it takes is a dream. Have we lost that talent as well? Are we unable to dream? Has life been that compromising for us?

Think of it this way. You can only eat three meals a day and sleep in one bed. The kids are grown up and the mortgage just about paid. Provided you've got the rice ration and the inner-spring covered, the rest is a bonus.

One of the paradoxes of life is that our greatest fear is fear itself. The fear of failure keeps us from launching our spirits and energy and our love and enthusiasm into something.

I have never met anyone yet who has decided to do the thing they believe they would love to do the most and failed. They may well have come unstuck a few times on the way, but in their own eyes they have not failed. And your life is for your eyes only!

The point is that you can only succeed through failure. How the hell are you going to learn anything if you do not fail? Success is the business of failing, learning why, picking yourself up, dusting yourself off and having another go.

Eventually you know the whole game and it leads to fame and fortune or, better still, an enriched and prosperous life.

People doing what they like to do cannot fail, because what they're going through isn't failure—it's a learning curve and a pathway towards the thing they really want to do and find they are happiest doing. Any of us can walk the well-known way; the trick is to dare our genius to walk the wildest unknown path.

I cannot help feeling that with this one life we have been guaranteed we ought to use it for happiness. We ought to use it all up, every little scrap, so that when we get to the end we can say: "I did it my way!"

And if your way is hitting a little white ball in an erratic fashion all over the landscape, I guess that's also okay. It's just that some of us want to die without having turned our lives into a handicap.

THE AUSTRALIAN FRIDAY SEPTEMBER 29 1989

Forget the kid gloves when educating hoons

If you've been in advertising for a while, you begin to realise there are a whole heap of invisible communication rules, things you don't do or are not done.

Call them conventional wisdoms. Like a lot of rules which hang around for a long time they become set in stone, no longer questioned and passed on from father to son.

In fact, if someone does question one of these truisms they are regarded somewhat as amateurs, people who obviously don't know their business and are not acting professionally.

Here are two such rules. The first is that you never show the blood and bone of an automobile accident.

Conventional wisdom has it that people become so upset when they see gore that they miss the message and the mind goes into neutral or wipes out, like a wet sponge over a blackboard.

The result is that for the past 20 years we've seen road accident campaigns carefully skirting the blood and gore and exalting us with slogans which seem to do very little for the statistics.

Now I'm perfectly willing to concede that this "no blood, no gore, no broken bones" philosophy is perfectly right when it's addressed to little old ladies or, for that matter, the average driver who's been on the roads for a couple of dozen years.

But then he or she is not likely to get drunk and drive all that often, or to speed just for the thrill of it.

If we took all the fatal accidents in Australia for which drivers aged 40 or older were responsible, we'd have the safest driving environment in the world.

The fatalities occur overwhelmingly in accidents involving drivers—most of them male—who are under the age of 25.

They have three things against them.

Even when they're sober they know with a certainty that they're immortal, after they've had a few drinks this knowledge is totally confirmed and besides, young guys like to take risks and go fast. In their opinion, that is the reason the car was made.

Traffic lights are not for stopping at, they're a race track starting line and they judge the car they buy by the time it takes to reach 100km/h from a standing start.

Some of them spend thousands of dollars and hundreds of hours hotting up a Holden to improve this ability by a few seconds.

These blokes are also the people who turn up in their souped-up Holdens and Falcons at the drive-in to watch movies of people in fast cars killing themselves.

They see more gratuitous blood and gore in a week than most people see in a lifetime. It's a language they understand, it makes them scared, they go for the thrills and the vicarious horror. They actually pay for it.

Now it may just be that the conventional advertising wisdom that the corpse is never shown is a nonsense to this group of drivers. It may well be that the only way to make these guys take note is to scare the bejesus out of them. To let them see the carnage and to make them identify with it.

Right now, what's being shown on the media and in the commercials are shots of broken cars.

If you came down to Earth as an extra-terrestrial television viewer, you might just return home with the observation that Earth could not be invaded because the people on it were invincible—for fun they drove around in capsules running on four wheels, which smashed into each other at 150km/h willy-nilly without anyone ever getting hurt.

The evening news shows a head-on collision caused by a young bloke with a blood alcohol content of 0.300 heading up the freeway going the wrong way.

Six people are killed and all the viewer sees is crumpled metal and broken glass.

How does that relate to the average under-25 goose-head who thinks he's immortal behind the wheel of a turbo-charged panel van?

Or the young bloke in a leather jacket and two day's growth who leaves the pub and mounts the 2000cc motorbike absolutely legless, when he can't really handle that amount of power safely when he's stone-cold sober?

Slogans and platitudes and art-directed accidents have got Buckley's.

Pictures of old blokes blowing into bags on the side of the road do not leave these young guys trembling in their Rio underpants.

A 20 year old doesn't think of dying as real. When you write the words "speed kills!" he reads them as "speed thrills!"

But there may be a way. A 20 year old can understand not ever being able to walk again. He does understand what killing his girlfriend would be like. He does comprehend what losing a couple of limbs would mean to him.

But, again, there is no point in showing him a bloke in a wheelchair exhorting him to drive carefully or the grieving parents standing beside the tombstone of their daughter in a carefully art-directed cemetery.

Perhaps, with this kind of young killer, you have to show him the real stuff. You have to make him dirty his Rios with the fright you give him.

Perhaps the conventional wisdom of mental wipe-out at the sight of blood is not the turn-off to him that it is to you or me.

Perhaps you have to talk a different kind of language to a young bloke who takes a tonne of steel and hurtles it at another tonne of steel at a speed of 150km/h.

Perhaps you should show him, graphically and specifically, how such an incident in his life can further scramble the mashed potatoes he already has for brains.

And just to finish up, another one of the cherished wisdoms of this business concerns the cake mix the housewife won't buy unless she is compelled to add two eggs of her own and a fair amount of elbow grease so that she can face her family without guilt and reap the rewards of warm-scone motherhood with a clear conscience.

Any advertising man who still believes this kind of junk should add the two eggs to the mashed potatoes he has for brains and beat vigorously.

Beware the conventional wisdoms of your business because they may just be a conspiracy of the hacks and the reactionaries who are trying to keep progress down to the same pace at which their minds are working.

THE AUSTRALIAN FRIDAY OCTOBER 27 1989

When a pregnant thought leads to a womb with a view

I arrived home last night to receive a message to call a medico running mate of mine, a research associate at Sydney University, who runs a flock of sheep upon which he performs gynaecological experiments designed to study infertility in women.

He's pretty big time and is always off delivering papers in exotic places, getting awards and accolades for his work.

I'm only telling you this so you'll understand that his credentials are pretty impeccable, so when I tell you what he wanted, you'll take what he said to me seriously.

It seems that, in conjunction with another researcher from the Argentine, he is interested in the impact of television on the unborn child.

The other doctor, it seems, is pretty convinced that television can have an effect on the foetus.

The contention is that in a study conducted over some 20 years, pregnant women who watch violent shows on television seem to have children who develop anti-social tendencies.

There may be lots of other reasons for this, of course. The type of woman who habitually watches this sort of show may well belong in the bottom socio-economic bracket and the child may consequently be born and raised in conditions ideal for spawning anti-social tendencies.

All this was explained to me and my mate went on to say, with this taken into consideration, that there still seemed enough empirical evidence that the television theory might still be valid.

YOU CAN'T GO AROUND TURNING WOMEN INTO UNIVERSITIES

He even went on to say that there seemed to be some evidence that the unborn child can "see" the picture.

"Now wait a minute," I said. "I can get my head around the fact that a violent show on television could trigger responses in the mother, which created some sort of chemical change in her body which was picked up or absorbed by the foetus.

"But see? That's going a bit over the top, don't you think?"

His reply was interesting.

The word "see'" is used to explain a phenomenon which a great many people claim to have experienced, in that they feel they've been to a place which they know they are visiting for the first time or they believe they are undergoing familiar stimuli, when it can be patently proved that the experience is a new one for them.

This sense of deja vu may be attributed to the input of a television program that has excited or impressed the mother at some time while the person experiencing the phenomenon was getting their steak and eggs in liquid form through an umbilical cord.

Well, I'm not very big on genetic or human engineering, believing that somehow it all works out in the end and that mankind's imperfections are what makes human beings interesting.

When, 20 years from now, some bloke sticks a knife into an innocent victim and blames it on his mum's TV viewing habits, I'm not sure that's the sort of world I want to be living in.

On the other hand, most knowledge generally leads somewhere positive and I don't want to be guilty of staying the hand of progress.

"How can I help?" I asked.

What he wanted was a series of TV commercials which would never be broadcast again but which were fairly dramatic in terms of noise and action.

These would be played to pregnant women and then in the years following they would be monitored for a reaction from the now born and unsuspecting children.

I can already see what the academics are going to do with this piece of information. Marketing, they will scream, has found the ultimate tool.

TV commercials, they will claim, will be sneakily placed into programs thought to be watched by the unborn, so that children will have this inexplicable desire for all sorts of exotic goods and services.

A consumer society will have finally been programmed to consume without having any choice in the matter.

I'm told that several of the universities are already conducting learning experiments in what is rather revoltingly referred to as The University of The Womb, and that there is a waiting list of pregnant women willing to submit to all sorts of experiments in the hope of giving birth to a kid who can recite the 12 times table before he or she can say "mumma".

So presumably when the foetus goes to university it will be told by pre-natal academics to watch out for the negative influence advertising threatens to have on them in their years on the blue planet.

Now, if you just happen to be born into an ordinary family whose mum likes to watch a bit of action on the telly, you're in a lot of trouble, kid.

You'll have a packet of Arnott's chips, a McDonald's hamburger and a Coke in your lunch tin, and every time you enter the supermarket your hands will develop lives of their own.

Which, when you come to think about it, isn't really all that advanced. Most academics seem to feel we've managed all that without having to flash subliminal stimuli to the unborn.

The most unbearable part of all of this will be the books we will get from American academics.

I can already see the titles which will tell mums how to avoid being foxed by the box: The Subliminal Consumer, The Marketed Monster, The Borrowed Brain, The Maturing Mouth.

There will also be those urging mothers to get their kids on to the pre-natal educational bandwagon: Womb at the Top, The Nine Month Doctorate, The Genius Behind the G-String.

Oh yes! Just wait until the feminist movement gets on to this!

You can't go round turning women into universities!

In the interests of the future of mankind, I warn all mothers-to-be to wear heavy black cotton knickers, to keep their legs crossed while watching television or, if they want to play it really safe, to listen only to Vivaldi on ABC radio.

Only trifles can fulfil a certain need

There is an immutable rule of marketing that goes like this: where a need exists it is filled.

Like most rules in business, it does not take an MBA to work it out.

The problem sociologists have with advertising, for instance, is they believe that the rule goes a little differently: where no need exists it is filled.

In other words, advertising is a want maker rather than a social opportunist, which I think is doubtful.

Needs above the breadline are seldom essential but are inclined to be emotional. Or put another way, very few needs are wrought by logic alone.

However, I must confess that around this time of the year there are some pretty dumb needs on display.

One shop in Sydney, aware that executive fitness is always a good area of need among the soft and flabby underbelly of society, has a skipping rope for sale made from pure silk with sterling silver handles.

I guess it takes all sorts of emotional needs to fill a Christmas stocking, although the spirit of Christmas is kind of knocked around a bit when you open your pressie and it's a silk and silver skipping rope. Whoever is giving it to you is probably expressing their need, which is for you not to be such a fat slob but to get fit so that you don't drop dead from a heart attack and, by doing so, cut off a wonderful supply of income allowing them to give your this sort of silly gift at Christmas.

Of all the needs that marketing fills, the oral gratification need and its opposite number, the denial need, are two of the most common and profitable.

Put into English, this means making and selling something good to eat, which seems always to have too many calories, and then marketing a diet.

Christmas is, of course, a time for these marketing needs to come into their own, with Christmas cakes of every shape, size and colour, from almost pitch black and sticky, to light brown, suddenly appearing everywhere like field mushrooms after rain.

On the run last week Owen Denmeade, who features from time to time in this column, brought up the subject of Christmas cake, pointing out that his mum made the most knock-out Christmas cake in the culinary history of mankind and her brandy-laden Chrissie pudding was only half a millimetre behind.

Suddenly it was on for one and all. "You think she makes a good cake? You haven't eaten Christmas cake or brought a decent, moist, steaming, raisin-and-fruit-laden, pungent and delicious Christmas pudding to your lips until you've tasted my nanna's," someone else yelled.

The great Christmas cake and pudding debate was on! Nanna was pitted against nanna, mum against mum, even the odd auntie got a guernsey. Cake and pudding descriptions reached new heights as runners dug deep to do justice to the Christmas cake and pudding makers who had given meaning to their lives.

And then some silly bugger spoilt it all. "Have you noticed that no one has mentioned the cake or pudding made by his wife?" A stunned silence followed. All you could hear was the pitter-patter of Nike, Adidas and New Balance.

"Not just that," Alex Hamill said bitterly, "what about bread and butter pudding?"

"Bread and butter pudding!" everyone shouted. "Now you are talking."

Then Hugh Spencer described a particular bread and butter pudding his mum used to make, but nobody took him seriously because he comes from New Zealand. Not that anyone running with me at lunchtime is racist, it's just that, well, the bread in New Zealand probably doesn't get stale quite the right way and the butter, with all that green grass, could be just a pinch too rich.

Wayne McCarthy put the conversation well and truly back on the rails when he said: "OK, OK you bastards, bugger the stale bread, what about stale cake, what about trifle?"

ECSTASY

The run came to an instant halt and people collapsed in ecstasy at the mention of the wonderful name of trifle. Trifle stories were swapped and runners nearly came to blows over whose nanna made the ultimate, sherry-soaked, Aeroplane-jellied, custard-covered, jam-laden, tinned-cling-peached trifle.

People argued about the ingredients of the ultimate trifle. However, all agreed, of all the food that ever existed, the trifle reigned supreme and then, after we ran in silence—a three minute silence for the departed trifle—Michael Mooney said: "Why? Why is it that our wives cannot cook any of the proper things?"

We then talked about bangers and mash, with the potato handwhipped with butter, with a dash of creamy milk added, someone mentioning cutting tiny bits of raw onion into the mash.

"That's nothing!" Brian Carter said. "What about when you made a hole in the top of the mash and filled it with tomato sauce and then covered it up and mixed it around until it turned a nice rose color. Yum!"

Now, it seems to me that silk and silver skipping ropes may well be a gift of love but if your wife or girlfriend really wanted to show you how much she loved you, if she really wanted to give you a Christmas present worth having, she'd call up her mum or nanna and ask if she could take a month's cooking lessons, starting with trifle. Talking about marketing filling a need!

It just could be that the real solution to the nation's growing sense of inferiority and general unhappiness has something to do with the elimination of lettuce and mineral water from our diet.

The first nanna who establishes The National Cooking School of Childhood Food will be filling a need both urgent and of great importance.

There is a generation of Australians growing up who have never even heard of a chip sandwich!

Happy Christmas everyone, may your puddings be pungent, and your trifles terrific.

1990

THE AUSTRALIAN FRIDAY JANUARY 5 1990

Electrify visitors with a smile

Christmas was spent at home and my car stayed in the garage unused over the break. Naturally, when I went to start it, the battery was flat.

The second time it's happened in as many weeks, so I jump-started it and drove it to the nearest garage.

The attendant was a young bloke who looked busy, the way some guys do. I don't know, they just look busy even when they're standing around. It's a knack you used to learn in the army, but with no National Service now I guess it must be a natural gift. I asked him to sell me a battery.

"For that," he asked, looking at my car.

I refrained from giving him a smart answer.

"Needs a special battery. I mean, a nice car like that. You wouldn't put an ordinary battery in that now, would you?"

As I didn't know batteries came in anything but ordinary, I agreed.

He returned a few minutes later. "Lucky I had one. Been a rush on batteries over the Christmas break. Look at that, mate!" He placed a perfectly ordinary-looking battery at my feet. "A beauty!"

"How much?" I asked sourly.

He looked surprised, almost upset. "That's an 11-year-old Porsche. They don't make 'em like that any more. You wouldn't put any crappy old battery into one of those." He stroked the front mud guard lovingly, leaving a smudge of grease behind.

"What's so special about it?"

The moment I'd asked this dumb question he knew he'd licked the price objection barrier. "OK, what happened to you this morning? I mean, a bloke like you."

He looked at me in my neat little suit and expensive silk tie. "What's an hour of your time worth? Plenty, eh? Well, this battery is a battery within a battery."

ONE SWITCHEROO—AND SHE'LL BE RIGHT, MATE

He bent down and threw a little yellow switch on the face of the battery. "Next time you carelessly leave the lights on overnight, no flamin' worries, mate. You flick this switch and away you go. That's a battery within a battery, what we in the business call an auxiliary battery. No more wasted time."

I agreed it seemed like a good idea. It also sounded like a pricy one and I was grateful I had my credit card on me.

"Look at that lead," he said, pointing at my old battery with his spanner. "It's practically undignified for a car like this to be wearing a lead like that."

I must admit the lead seemed a tiny bit frayed, but not so you'd notice. Well, I wouldn't have anyway.

"Have to replace that for a start." A new, rather nice-looking lead covered with green plastic was produced; almost conjured up, it appeared so fast. "See what I mean, much more in keeping with the dignity of this German automobile.

"Steady on, mate," I ventured.

"Lead like this will last you another 11 years. Oil? Petrol? See you've got the odd scratch, tiny ding here. We do a classy job on these prestige vehicles.

I thanked him but no-thanked him and produced my credit card.

The cost of the special battery within a battery suitable for a charismatic car like mine came to roughly four times what I seem to remember paying for the last one, though I must confess this may have been a while ago. The splendid green plastic-covered lead was an additional 10 bucks.

I drove off happy enough. After all, I'd been well sold. I figured I had the best battery within a battery in Australia. Little yellow switch, no flamin' worries!

Next time I did something dumb all I had to do was flick and look smug. He'd even patted the battery on parting, as though he was reluctant to let it go, but was happy it was destined for a good engine.

As a final remark he assured me it was made in Australia. "None of that s--- Taiwanese," he added gratuitously.

We all like to think we don't like to be sold, but my observation is that most people like to get a little sales talk when they make a purchase.

We feel happier when the sale has been well sealed with a good verbal how, when and why. This is specially true when we have been sold up—when we come in to purchase X and leave with Super-X. The salesman's explanation will be the one we'll take home to justify the purchase.

"Had a lucky break today, darling. Got the very last of those super auxiliary batteries for the car. Guaranteed failsafe, no more flat battery. Simple theory, really. Battery within a battery, little yellow switch. One switcheroo and she's right."

I mean, fascinating dinnertime conversation like this doesn't come about every day, does it?

So I made my New Year's resolution. This year I'm going to sell Australia up.

Not just bash people's cars about the place—I do that already—but sort of put together a sales pitch in my head. You know:

"Want your batteries charged? Come to Australia. You know how when you get up in the morning and turn on the ignition and there's nothing there? Right, time to get on to a Qantas plane and come.

"It's a country within a country. When you're tired of the cities and the beaches, we've got this little yellow switch. You just go switcheroo and you're in the country, a big, calm, restful, battery-charging country. A country with the sky faded like a much-washed and loved blue shirt and at night the stars barely leave room for the dark."

And then, like the battery salesman's final remark, you've got to remember to keep the sale once you've made it.

So, next time you see a group of Japanese looking confused because it's only 11am and they're in their third city for the day, walk right up to them, smile and say, "Au-stra-lia 'ee yo koso", which means "Welcome to Australia".

You just watch their eyes light up. They'll get back to Japan with a lot of confused memories, but the clearest of them all will be of the smiling person who walked up to them and said, "Welcome to Australia."

Now that's what I mean by selling up when it comes to the beloved country.

Happy New Year to you. May your battery remain charged throughout 1990 and never once be flat in the morning.

… THE AUSTRALIAN FRIDAY FEBRUARY 23 1990

The only person who can save the environment is you

The term "sustainable development" is a new one which will soon become very common in the lexicon of business.

The "in" people in Academe assure me that it's been around for nearly two years, but the first time I heard about it was a month or two ago when someone at Sydney University asked me if I'd talk on the subject in terms of advertising.

They were perhaps rightly appalled when I confessed I didn't know what the hell they were talking about. I thought it might have something to do with preventing unions from striking.

As far as I can understand, the term "sustainable development" means developing the environment in such a way as to sustain the material and emotional resources within it. Put into simple English, leaving as much for our kids and their children as we inherited ourselves.

A resource is only sustainable if we leave behind what we inherited in quality as well as quantity.

In other words, not a tree for a tree but the same quality tree we choose to cut down. A great tree that stands 200ft, bursting through the canopy of the rainforest, is not simply replaced by a *Pinus radiata*, or a bit of quick-growth mulga scrub.

Sustainable development isn't only about quantity—so many trees, kangaroos, emus and patches of wild horseradish—but quality.

The nice thing about this idea is that it puts a value on quality of life. On what your ears hear, your nose breathes, your eyes perceive and, finally, the way your heart leaps.

For instance, if a hillside is full of iron ore but is also a very beautiful hill which has a quality humans finds important—if it's a soft dawn purple, a sharp orange midday and a deep cyan evening hill—then we can't simply blast away, dig the hole, remove the ore, fill the hole and pile a heap of rocks on top of it and call it quits.

Things which are beautiful are given a value because the beauty they represent must be sustained for future generations.

But now let's look at the other side of the sustainable development idea.

When God created the mosquito, in his infinite wisdom he decided what your basic mossie had to eat to grow big and strong and multiply. He made the ideal mosquito food but also allowed that mossies could eat other things and stay pretty well.

When God created me he made me the single most delectable thing a mosquito could possibly eat. I am the steak tartare of the mossie world, the antipodean love apple of the anopheles.

Every summer in the Gulf of Borneo a squadron of kamikaze mosquitoes a hundred thousand strong gather. These are the desperado mosquitoes, the thrillseekers who are prepared to die for a single proboscis filled with me.

They reach the Australian coast a little after 2am in the morning, their buzzing setting the window panes rattling. Seconds later I am awake and at war, firing with everything I've got.

The first wave lick the mossie repellant off my skin. These are the old bombers who've led a useful life and are prepared for a glorious death sacrificing themselves for the sake of the species; the next wave devour me so that, often within minutes, I need a major blood transfusion.

But I'm ready. I blast away with the aerosol spray until the bedroom carpet is inches thick in spent mossies. Around 4.30am the battle is over.

I look as though I have a severe case of the measles and the mosquitoes give thanks to their creator for the unique ability they have to restore their numbers in time for tomorrow night.

Now here is my dilemma. The stuff which prevents them from having me bled white and near dead every hot summer night is also causing a hole in the ozone layer.

Those millions of tiny droplets that dance in the air are my bullets designed to knock the squadrons to eternity; it's pure coincidence that the same stuff is hastening the demise of mankind and is definitely not contributing to sustainable development.

So I think about it a bit, then I say: "Bugger the hole in the ozone, what about the holes in me?"

I once met a Japanese businessman who was in the tuna fish industry and I attacked him about killing the dolphins which get caught in the nets.

He looked at me and said: "How many people in the world have actually seen a dolphin?"

Not very many, I was forced to admit. "OK, so not very many people are going to miss what they've never seen!"

That's the beauty of being a great big intelligent human being. We can rationalise just about everything we do in life. We do it personally, business does it, governments do it. It's called the individual exception.

My case is special. I'm different. I should be the exception to the rule. Nobody is going to be hurt if little old me does it just this once. I'll stop tomorrow, honest.

Today I'm too tired. I don't want to be hassled. "Holy macaroni! Look at that mossie on my hand, it's as big as a tarantula. Where's the goddam spray? Cripes! Look at that mosquito-eating tarantula in the corner of the room, where's the spray!" And so it goes.

Sustainable development has only one chance. It begins with you and me. It doesn't begin with business or government, it begins with the individual.

Only you can stop purchasing polystyrene containers, spraying harmful aerosols, using cleaning products which pollute the waters and carrying home the groceries in plastic bags instead of a basket.

Only you can walk or buy a bicycle rather than drive the car 200m to the shops or the kids' school. Only you can stop people cutting down forests, not only by standing in the path of the bulldozer, but also by not buying cotton buds, by using recycled paper, by not allowing your home to be built out of native timber and insisting the timber used is commercially grown.

Only you can stop drift-net fishing by not purchasing tuna and mackerel tinned in Japan or Russia and not allowing your government to grant fishing rights in Australian waters to those people who do use drift nets.

Only you can insist that the price to the exploiter be the replacement with a quality of environment which is infinitely better than the one they would spoil.

Every journey of a thousand miles begins with one step; every movement of any kind begins with one person.

One person caring. One person who wants to leave the world as good a place as he or she found it so that tomorrow's children can breathe clean air and bathe in clean water and sit in a shade of leafy trees under a blue sky.

This one is known as The Power of One. You're the one. It's time we all left convenience at home and went to the market with our conscience.

THE AUSTRALIAN FRIDAY MARCH 9 1990

Good taste is for those who can't have fun

One of the most frequent brickbats thrown at the advertising business is that much of it is in bad taste.

I long ago decided that this was the really good thing about the business.

Taste is a funny thing. You only appear to acquire it when you begin to perceive yourself as a cut or two above ordinary mortals. And, of course, advertising is all about ordinary mortals.

Clients anxious to clean up their act on television should be careful. Good taste, it seems to me, may be nice to have in a wife but it is a very doubtful commodity in most products.

I thought I'd try to determine what it is that gives people the right to claim good taste—the kind with a capital T.

Most things become easier to define by deciding what they are not, rather than what they are. Taste is no different. It's what you don't do that means you have it.

The best way to determine the lack of taste is to examine the magazines your desired target audience reads.

Magazines are a dead giveaway. If, for example, you are a regular reader of People magazine, this is a sure sign that you shouldn't be invited to a dinner party where there is more than one knife and fork on the table.

I often read the People magazine posters outside my local newsagent and am immediately forced to rush in and purchase the latest copy.

How could anyone in his right mind resist a magazine which carries on its cover Dwarf-throwing—Australia v England, and Aussie Spy Scandal: Lesbian Confesses, together with Nasty Gossip, Crazy Trivia, Amazing Oddities and Giant Crossword.

The picture on the cover shows a beautiful, bare-topped, blue-eyed blonde nymph in the process of throwing a live dwarf.

One poster which had me rushing in at a canter read: Mad Mullahs Roll in Poo to Cure the Lame.

People with taste read magazines to see whether they still have taste and to find out what other people with taste are saying about taste.

This is so they can change their taste before someone acuses them of not having any.

I mean, let's be frank, when it comes to hard intellectual stimulation, these so-called "good taste" magazines don't contain enough in them to see you through the first five minutes at a social dinner party.

Now contrast this with People magazine. It seems to me that your average issue of People magazine might be, from an intellectual viewpoint, more rewarding.

Let's take the issue I gave as an example—the one with the beautiful blonde throwing the dwarf.

If you remove the jaundiced concept of "taste" from your judgment, it scrubs up pretty well.

It discusses how Australia has taken its little people to heart and integrated them into the community, even including them in a serious international sporting event.

Then it shows that ASIO isn't the extreme right-wing, ultra-conservative organisation it's frequently accused of being.

Aussie Spy Scandal: Lesbian Confesses shows quite clearly that those who guard our national security are feminists who are quite prepared to allow people to work within the organisation without concerning themselves with their private and personal sexual arrangements.

Next, in Nasty Gossip, the magazine gets down to a bit of serious social engineering. I mean, what's the point of gossip if it isn't nasty? It only goes to show that the gossip reported here is probably quite true and can be quoted freely.

I admit the Crazy Trivia and Amazing Oddities are a bit lightweight for such a thought-provoking magazine, but every good read should have a little bit in it to confound and amuse.

Finally, the Giant Crossword—not just an ordinary crossword, but one for Mensalike intelligence, designed to leave you quietly but wonderfully mentally stimulated.

That's not bad for $1.50 on a dreary weekday travelling to work on the train, is it?

Now just suppose someone with good taste made the mistake of inviting you, an average, intelligent, People magazine reader, to a dinner party.

You wouldn't sit there like a stale lamington brushing off your dandruff, would you? Or chew each mouthful of steak 150 times so you wouldn't have to make small talk with the lady person next to you. You'd be mentally armed and ready to assert your intellectual prowess.

"Did you happen to catch the dwarf-throwing test match on TV?" you ask.

"We thrashed the Poms again. Of course, they tried to cheat, dehydrating their dwarfs after the official weigh-in, but then what can you expect from a Pom?'

Now if that isn't a tasty little opener to a Toorak dinner party, I don't know what is.

So, the first thing you have to know if you want to isolate someone with taste is that taste is obviously something a lot of ill-informed, rather narrow-interest people who are not very intelligent go in for.

I mean, anyone who drenches themselves in Georgio, hides the TV in a cupboard and as a primary occupation reads magazines about curtain drapes, flower arrangements, place settings and the latest in bamboo outdoor furniture is a bit suss in the head department, to say the least.

The next thing you have to know about taste is that people with it obviously don't care about their country and never go to the beach.

Australia has approximately 316 days of sunshine and 6000km of beach and people with taste obviously never go out in it or near the water (which if you live in Sydney is not a bad thing).

The proof of this is that last year the Advertising Standards Council received hundreds of complaints that the beach gear girls wear in commercials is in bad taste.

It's exactly the same clobber you can see repeated a million times on any beach anywhere in Australia on any day of the week.

It seems people with good taste can't abide beautiful young people with long, straight limbs and bronzed skin having fun in the sunshine.

People with taste are definitely against sun. Why else would they have dinner parties or stay indoors on a beautiful sun-drenched day?

So there you have it. Taste has been adequately defined at last.

It's something rather stupid which somewhat narrow people with very white skin acquire because they've forgotten how to have fun.

So if you want to include this valuable private audience into your product profile, now you know who they are.

If you want my personal opinion, I think it's probably a jolly good thing that most advertising doesn't set out to appeal to these fringe dwellers in our society.

Sustaining development without a mess

When I was young and very poor it never occurred to me that toilet paper came in rolls specially made for the purpose.

I received a good part of my education reading the squares of newsprint hanging from a nail on the back of the dunny door, leafing through until I found a complete piece of news on one sheet.

Sometimes I'd get trapped into reading a bit of something which ended abruptly but which was particularly interesting. Whereupon I was forced to go through all the bits still hanging up looking for the run-on.

For instance, I once read about a young couple who decided to drive through central Australia.

I must point out that I am sitting in the dunny in Africa with the door open. The dunny is located about 40 feet up a tiny hill behind the farm house to catch the breeze on a hot day.

Around me the African veld spreads gold and green, rimmed in the far distance by blue and, further still, purple mountains.

Anyway, the young couple in a Morris Minor had decided to drive across Australia accompanied by the mother-in-law of one of them, I forget which.

The old woman did nothing but whinge and got so het up that when they broke a rear axle she had a heart attack and died.

They still had several days to travel, and as it took two days to fix the axle they couldn't very well keep her in the car.

So they wrapped her in a tarpaulin and put her on the roof. When at last they got to civilisation they stopped at an outback police station to report the death.

The local sergeant came out to the car, where they discovered the tarpaulin with contents had been stolen.

At that point the square of paper stopped and no amount of frantic searching revealed the rest of the story.

So to this day I don't know what happened to the young couple.

Was it murder? Did they find their Mum? Who pinched the corpse? That's what comes from having a bum education.

Well, when I went to boarding school I discovered that toilet paper came in rolls made specially for the purpose. These lacked the softness of scrunched newsprint, but at least you didn't go around with editorial printed on your rear.

This was a definite step up in quality of life. Later I discovered that toilet paper, if you were rich, not only came in snowy white rolls, but was soft and strong as well.

I decided on the spot to become rich and never to compromise on essential matters such as softness and strength.

LEFT WITH THE GOOD EARTH

Then last week I went to the supermarket and Doris, who works behind the counter at Flemings, pointed out a stack of toilet paper.

"Recycled, the latest thing! Be Seen To Be Green!" she repeated happily.

I examined one of these toilet rolls, which were sort of off white in colour and pretty coarse to the touch.

No Way! Screw the Green Revolution! I'm not going backwards! I've discovered wet strength. I've been poor once, no more!

Which brings me to the hottest subject on the political agenda, which is of course the Greening of Australia.

Some weeks ago I wrote about sustainable development and I got a whole heap of letters from Greenies saying I was on track and a whole heap from other interests saying I knew not what I was talking about.

The latter proved to be closer to the truth. It's easy to sit down and write about something with a bit of a brief, picking up on what is the flavour of the month. And, of course, nobody wants to see the beloved country turned into toothpicks.

But, like me, a whole heap of people don't want to be poor again. We can remember how it was. Now, if we carry the Green thing through to where the Green movement wants it, Australia, already in a lot of trouble, is going to be knee deep in the proverbial and it's going to take more than double strength, twin-layer thickness to clean up the mess.

We've proved conclusively that we can't compete with our neighbours in manufacturing.

They make shoes and shirts, ships and sheet metal cheaper than we do.

That leaves us with only two things—our brains and our natural resources.

In the brains department we're not keeping up with the rest of the Western world, and the Eastern world is rapidly catching up with us.

That leaves the good earth, the things we can cut from it, dig out of it or grow upon it. Without these resources we're down the plug hole in no uncertain way.

In fact, the entire economic recovery plan designed by the present Government is based on exploiting those resources which the Green movement demands must remain untouched and in a virgin state.

The hole in the ozone layer isn't nearly as big as the hole in the head some of nature's new protectors are sporting.

The point is, Australia must use her natural resources and must exploit them or we're all going to be very poor very soon.

It's how we husband these resources that matters. It is not a matter of unilaterally declaring a hands-off-everything approach.

Britain was once a country which was densely timbered with oak and elm and beech. Today only a very few tiny forests remain. Basically the land has been denuded since about the time of Elizabeth I.

Yet we think of England as a green and pleasant land. We must take care of our environment and our heritage, but not at the cost of our national wellbeing.

Sustainable development is about husbanding the land, not simply leaving it alone.

It is also about leaving our children with a lifestyle which makes living in the beloved country worthwhile, with clean rivers and skies and renewable forests and carefully sustained soil.

Which all adds up to never being poor again.

A mayday call from Mr April

This week I was invited by Portfolio magazine to a breakfast at the Regent to celebrate their yearly male calendar, where I featured as Mr April.

They also asked me to give a talk, along with Professor Ed Davis, the young, terrifically good-looking Cambridge-educated professor of management at Macquarie University.

It was OK for him—his classes are filled with women anxious to sit at the feet of this big-time business guru.

I, on the other hand, represented all those things the feminist movement seems to be against. My heart sunk.

I'd been silly enough to agree to being Mr April and now I was expected to talk to a couple of hundred women who were going to have me for breakfast, for sure.

The trouble is, I always seem to come unstuck on the subject of the feminist movement. Not because I'm against it. On the contrary.

I am positive that business should be free of gender with the top jobs going to the best man ... oops, or woman.

On the publishing side of my career, my agent is a woman, my editors are both women, my publisher is a woman and my publicist is a woman.

No writer could hope for a better set of executives to negotiate, correct, advise, publish and finally to publicise his work.

At work my entire creative group is composed of women and I wouldn't want it any other way.

They're bright, intuitive, hard working and thinking writers and art directors and gender has nothing to do with it, other than I personally believe they're more practical and down to earth, more responsible than their male counterparts.

My past experience with the feminist movement hasn't been good.

This column has attracted a fair number of letters from women giving me a severe ticking off for something I've said.

A couple of years ago I sprang to the defence of a topless waitress who'd lost her job in a pub because the council had decided what she was doing was sexist.

I figured her rights were rather more important than their decision, but a whole bagful of angry mail told me I was wrong, wrong, wrong!

So, as you can imagine, I wasn't all that chuffed about a 7am lecture in the lions' den.

I wrote my notes carefully and read them over, removing anything I thought might be in the least sexist.

The feminist movement is pretty marshy ground—you can sink up to your ear lobes with one false step.

I began by pointing out that it is tough for the ambitious, career-bent woman in business, that she starts with a handicap which is not of her making but nevertheless exists.

It begins with our system of education.

We educate our boys as though they are the natural leaders of the future. We encourage them to take the more difficult subject options, such as maths and science at school.

We allow them to be aggressive and assertive in class.

We even tolerate a fair bit of larrikinism under the assumption that it's all part of the preparation for the competitive environment they will face in the business society.

A girl in the same class who is just as bright or brighter is encouraged to be neat, tidy, responsible, organised, diligent, kind, considerate and often accepts softer subject options.

Teachers expect them to behave and conform, to work and to play by the rules and most importantly, not to be competitive.

TO CONFORM AND BEHAVE

Then I went on to say that unfortunately life in the business world isn't too many of the things they teach girls and rather more about the things they teach boys.

The net result is that the girls enter the working environment with a bit of a handicap, as capitalism is largely about competing and winning—about taking chances.

I expanded on this by saying that many women I have observed work too close to the rules. While they're diligent, hard working, intelligent and capable, they do not seem prepared to take chances to dare their genius to walk the wildest unknown way.

This was the cutting edge in business, the gamble you often have to make to succeed.

Women, I claimed, often lack the single-mindedness and seem less willing to take risks for the reasons I'd begun with, and so they often missed out on the big opportunities.

Well, it went from bad to worse.

I claimed that women, thinking the solution was to ape the male model for business success, had borrowed a whole series of bad habits—unnecessary aggression, hardness, rudeness and a competitive attitude—which weren't leadership-based but the worst aspects of male performance.

If you think that was bad, I then went on to talk about dress.

I asserted that I loved the female gender for what it was and felt that any attempts to make it change sex via dull masculine clothes and the playing down of their undeniable God-given attractiveness wasn't helping them to succeed.

Nothing in business says you can't be pretty, was how I put it, which is perhaps not the best piece of feminist phrasing.

By this time the icicles were beginning to form around the scrambled eggs and the room was very negative and I was getting ready to duck the bread rolls, which I expected at any moment.

But I pressed on, talking about a number of non-gender things which make for success and some of the things that don't.

Alas, while I have used the same points very successfully with males, after what I'd said before, they must have seemed didactic and condescending.

Mr April was in a lot of trouble! I had obviously said the wrong things and in the process upset a lot of very intelligent women. I hadn't meant to. I had tried to be as honest and helpful as possible but I'd only suceeded in alienating them.

When I returned to work, my secretary asked me how it had gone.

"Not great," I replied. "Mr April had a mayday."

"Yeah, I thought so," she sighed. "When I was typing your talk I wanted to brain you!"

"But I love women!" I protested. "I really want the women's movement to work!"

"Sure you love them, but you don't understand them."

Please somebody out there, send me a book or something which teaches me the correct dance steps for the feminist movement.

I promise I'm a potential ally, a basically sound male who doesn't understand the hidden agenda.

How a little love could help remove our iron bars

I can remember a visitor going through the Sydney phone book and being astounded at the help services available to people.

If you wanted to commit suicide there was someone to call; if you'd been raped, taken drugs, been abused by a parent, beaten up by a husband or wife, needed a feed, wanted to talk to somebody about your soul or your psyche, all you had to do was to pick up the phone.

"Either you're a very caring people or you're in an emotional mess," she remarked.

In fact, I have a feeling the latter may be closer to the truth.

If you walk down a suburban street in one of our larger cities you are struck by the proliferation of iron bars.

In Sydney and Melbourne bars across suburban windows are too common to notice but now the habit is spreading into the smaller capitals.

In the inner suburbs of Sydney, not only the windows but the front door now has a steel grid and one of the most common sounds in the neighbourhood is no longer the birds but an errant burglar alarm tripped by electronic accident.

Almost the moment television was born it became the scapegoat for our social ills and the media man or woman the perpetrator of this new virile strain of social mayhem. Research seems to prove otherwise.

It occurs to me that, rather than reject violence in our lives, we actually seek it.

We convince ourselves that things out on the street are unsafe and so we rush home before darkness sets in and lock ourselves behind bars, in effect putting ourselves into jail for the night.

Then we turn on the television, which is a kind of eye to the outside world.

This eye probes the nefarious darkness until it finds a spot of violence, which it then delivers up unto us.

All our suspicions are immediately confirmed—the violence is at our doorstep, we are drowning in a crime wave.

This vicarious crime seems to be very important to us. Why else would the media dish it up on a regular nightly basis?

If we didn't actually turn on to violence the last thing the networks would show would be stuff that didn't increase the ratings.

The blame for all this self-incarceration is put on the increase in drug-related crime.

The new criminal profile, we are told, is no longer the professional who "does" a house, but the young guy in need of a fix who does "a snatch", that is, he or she breaks in and grabs anything they can carry and convert into fast cash.

If you counted the bars on the windows and doors you'd be forced to conclude that about one in two citizens fell into this category, and while crime is undoubtedly up, it isn't anywhere near the upsurge in the house protection industry.

We have clothed our homes in walls of steel in suburbs of paranoia.

What this seems to be saying is that basically we've become afraid of each other, we've lost our trust in ourselves as a community.

The average citizen has come to believe that, after dark, the streets are awash with rapists, muggers and thieves all bent on violence.

So I started to ask around. In a period of a month or so I asked about 300 people whether they'd been mugged in the past five years? One had, though eight years ago.

Handbag snatched? None. Burgled in the past five years? Four. Physically assaulted? One, in a pub.

I then asked them if they had one or two forms of security at home, bars on the windows or burglar alarms. Most had some sort of protection, even if only an Alsatian with a drooling mouth.

From this far-from-precise survey I was forced to conclude that the fear is bigger than the actuality. In fact, the figures bear this out.

Mugging, rape and burglary are up, but not by a great deal, and this, according to sociologists, seems to have something to do with the unemployment figures—the old adage that hands not busy are inclined to mischief.

Husbands without work grow desperate and occasionally violent. Man doesn't like to be rejected by the system and is liable to hit back at it if he believes he is not getting a fair go.

The media, of course, especially television, are also blamed for the upsurge in violent crime.

The media are only responding to a known phenomenon. Violence on the box is not a social experiment; it is feeding a need, not creating one.

VIOLENCE ON TELEVISION

Teenagers and little old ladies all huddle around the set and get their daily dose of violence, the confirmation that life in the big city is a dangerous experience.

Perhaps it all begins with a sense of loneliness.

People seem to talk less and be more suspicious of each other. At work there is a whole heap of new lines of demarcation.

Over-zealous feminists are constantly probing for sexist problems.

Disenchanted males are perpetrating covert aggression against them. Affirmative action, in many cases, is having a negative reaction, a male backlash.

When people become separated into groups they become negatively active within the group and suspicious outside of it.

They become fearful of each other and the office or the workplace becomes an unfriendly place, fraught with tension.

How long is it since you walked around your company or section or office and talked to everyone in it? Not about work, but simple, easy social chewing of the fat stuff?

Do you know where everyone in your office lives, how far they have to travel each day to get to work, what mode of transport they use, how many kids they have, whether someone in the family is ill or out of work?

Do you send the females of your company flowers on a birthday or a card to the males and make a point of going around and seeing them first thing to wish them a happy day?

This is the social intercourse of the workplace—the reaching out and touching of people, not simply by the bosses, but by the people themselves.

People simply can't do without people in their lives and one of the very best ways of increasing productivity in a company is to get the people in it to know, like and trust each other.

At the Royal Alexandra Children's Hospital in Sydney they have started a surrogate mother experiment where babies from the country whose mothers are not present are held in the arms of surrogate mothers for several hours each day.

The results have been staggering, with babies recovering from illness sometimes in less than half the time.

We all need to be held and we all need to be loved. Love is just as much a right in the workplace as equal opportunity.

We are losing our people skills and they are the most important skills we have as a company or as a nation.

This week, why not look at your company or your department

or office and see what you can do about eliminating the fears and anxiety within it by adding a little kindness, consideration, joy, love and understanding.

Then sit back and watch the bars come off windows.

THE AUSTRALIAN FRIDAY OCTOBER 19 1990

The politicians talk but we're not listening

My grandfather, who by today's standard wasn't all that good at being successful but made up for it by being contented and happy, wasn't the sort of bloke who went around telling people how they ought to behave or live their lives.

So he didn't pass on a lot of wisdom, but I suspect he had a bit tucked away.

When I was going away to boarding school he drew me aside and said: "Always listen to what a man doesn't say, that's where the truth lies."

Because he had beautiful manners, in today's parlance he would, I feel sure, have said " . . . what a person doesn't say".

Though, on second thoughts, he may have kept the masculine gender: women in public don't talk half the rhetorical gibberish men go in for.

At the time I probably didn't understand what he was saying, but the idea of listening to what a person doesn't say must have appealed to my imagination and, over the years, it became a habit which has saved me from the odd conman.

I always thought of this skill as something I'd learned, something important to me, a secret of life to be treasured and as my grandfather had done to me, passed on to my sons.

But some days ago I passed the television set and there was Bob giving some high-up cleric, with a purple vest who cares a lot about the poor, half a dozen kinds of hell.

An hour later I passed the set again and Paul was dishing the dirt, pouring it, oozy voiced, on a sober-minded banker.

On both occasions, if you listened to what they didn't say, it was obvious Bob and Paul had been caught with their pants around their ankles and were blasting themselves out of trouble with several lighted sticks of bombast.

"How come, every time I hear those two talking these days, I grow angry?" I asked my wife.

"I don't even have to listen to know they're covering up and that their rhetoric is absolutely garbage!"

"You too," she said. "I thought it must be me."

I started asking around, not just of people whose politics were against those of the present Government, and then I realised that everyone in Australia who wasn't mahogany from the neck up has become exceedingly skilled at listening to what isn't being said.

Not just in politics, but in almost everything.

What those who talk for us in public life are saying is not what we're hearing. What's being put out is not what we're taking in.

Try this test on yourself. See if you're hearing the same things I'm hearing.

The Government says "we care about pollution enormously", and I hear "as long as it doesn't interfere with jobs and therefore votes in the industries causing the pollution".

The Government says "no government has ever cared more about trees", and I hear "just get the green votes and we'll work out something with the loggers later".

The Government says "there is no recession and the country has turned the corner", and I hear "we're Little Bo Peep and we've lost our sheep and we don't know how to sell them or anything else".

The Government says "we're proud of our record of social services and in particular on Medicare", and I hear "this is the biggest screw-up in the history of medicine after the United Kingdom".

The Government says "sure we've got our own oil, but we're tied to world oil-price parity and can't change that", and I hear "we need the tax from Bass Strait oil so we'll just keep screwing the motorist".

Perhaps you don't agree with me and my grandpa got it all wrong and I'm just a cynical person who doesn't trust politicians and spends his life mining the thunderous silence?

Why is it, though, that so very little being publicly said can pass the test of actually meaning what it says?

When Bush spouts his rhetoric on Iraq, do we really believe he's jumping to the defence of honesty and decency and the time-honoured dictum "thou shalt not bully anyone smaller than you?"

Or has it got something to do with oil?

Didn't we all hear something about Britain and France and America and Russia arming Saddam just a few months back, then finding they were left with a handful of irredeemable IOUs for military hardware which is now lined up and turned against the original suppliers?

Wasn't there something way back in the 1970s, during the original

Middle East oil crisis, about the greedy giants, the American oil companies, manipulating the whole thing?

Do we really believe Kuwait before Saddam was a shining example of democracy in action?

That those sheiks in their spotless white burnouses and dark, neatly trimmed faces were the benign and selfless leaders of a happy and contented people?

Or do we hear something else when we listen to what isn't being said?

I am not saying Saddam is a goodie or even that America or Britain or France or Russia or ourselves or the United Nations is involved in a grand conspiracy against the truth.

All I'm saying is that we've all learned to listen to what isn't being said, because the rhetoric is deafening and the progress towards a solution is minimal and our reasons for being there are not convincing, even though we'd like them to be.

To make sense out of the nonsense, we've all learned to listen between the lines we're being fed.

This is supposed to be a marketing column, but what I suppose I'm saying is that governments and politicians have learned to market the untruth.

They've learned how to dress up and deliver the non-answer.

They've learned the technique of bad manners, they've marketed shouting and bombast, and the art of complicating the simple and keeping people in the dark.

The solution is simple.

Let's ban all politicians from saying anything for 90 days. A 90-day moratorium on rhetoric.

There's just a chance, as people begin once again to use their common sense on the nation's problems, that things might start to look up.

But even if they didn't, things couldn't get any worse anyway and imagine the glorious sanity of the prevailing silence.

Who knows? We might even be able to hear ourselves think.

1991

THE AUSTRALIAN FRIDAY MARCH 8 1991

Why do wars make our leaders popular?

It has always amazed me that wars make prime ministers more popular.

How can this be?

Is it that we are basically a warlike people and all a politician has to do is find a war somewhere to send the kids to and instantly he's a good bloke again?

The latest something-or-other poll in the US has just decided that the post-Iraqi President Bush, with a 93 per cent approval rating, is the most popular American president in history.

Bob too was in the doldrums just before the war. Bob has got to be liked or he goes into a state of deep depression.

So imagine how good he felt when the phone went and it was Mr Bush asking him if he could count on him to give a bunch of Arabs a kick in the bum.

All he had to do was park a couple of ships in the Gulf and create one or two photo opportunities with the pretty young wives waving our boys off at the dockside and he was back in the ratings.

I always felt that Margaret Thatcher was about to be hurled out on her ear when the Falklands presented themselves as an election saver.

She could have done two things. She could have paid every British subject living on these bare and inhospitable islands a couple of million dollars and they'd have left happily on the first plane out, whereupon she could have extracted double this amount in a token payment from the Argentine Government for the Malvinas and, in the process, made a 100 per cent profit with satisfied customers all round.

A PRIME MINISTER WHO CAN'T BEAR TO BE SEEN AS A BAD GUY

But it probably wouldn't have got her elected, so instead she extended Britain's fighting forces to just about their limit and created a thoroughly nasty and bloody little war which instantly took her popularity from barely double figures to an overwhelming victory in the polls.

There can only be one conclusion: the human race, those belonging to the English speaking world in particular, loves a war.

Bob couldn't wait to help his mate George to get one started so he could be seen to be just a nice guy again.

This week Bob, blowing the smoke from his gun, is starting to talk about the fat, juicy contracts which would be going around to repair the war damage in the Gulf—in particular, the need for all the stuff we're good at, like wheat and sheep, that the war-torn Middle East was going to need and we were going to be in a position to sell them if we were really smart and quick enough and got off our bums to elbow the Americans and the Europeans out of the way.

Anyone reading this column will know that I'm no economist, so I've probably got it all wrong.

But this is what I cannot understand. We seemed to have been working for some years now to create new markets for our wheat and live sheep and a whole heap of other commodities the Iranians, Iraqis, Jordanians, Syrians and other Arab nations were happily buying from us.

As I recall, this was a pretty good marketing effort, seeing as we were self-sufficient in oil and so didn't really depend on any of theirs to keep going.

As I understood it, the Arabs were proving to be a very profitable market for Australia—they took our agricultural products and we took a few dates and a bit of caviar in return.

The balance of payments was hugely in our favour for once.

So, as a token of our esteem, and to show them what good trading partners we were, we joined America and Britain to beat the living daylights out of one of our best customers and in the process lost not only this market but several other neighbouring markets as well.

We bombed their oil wells and their cities and killed their people and in return they torched the oil wells over which we'd supposedly gone to war in the first place.

So now most of the oil we fought over is either floating across the Gulf or burning up to create the world's worst pollution.

The money they previously made from their oil wells to buy our stuff is no longer available because it's all floating away or going up in smoke.

So how are they going to find the money to pay us for the contracts to repair the malicious damage we deliberately did to them?

Surely they're going to have to borrow a whole heap of money from someone to buy our stuff. That money is going to be subject to interest and pretty soon they'll be so far behind the eight ball that they will never be able to pay us for the stuff we sent them.

I mean, once the wheat has been made into loaves and the sheep have had their throats ritually cut we can't exacly demand our stuff back.

If this war was really about principles, then I can think of half a dozen fairly recent takeovers of small countries by bigger ones where the very principle we supposedly went to war for was at stake.

East Timor, for openers, is one of these. Why didn't we go to war on principle on these other occasions?

So I can only conclude that the Gulf War couldn't have been over a matter of principle and must have had something to do with making money and buying and selling; starting with tanks and bombs and planes and ending with wheat and live sheep exports.

But on the other hand, how could this be? Australia was selling lots of things to the Arabs at a nice profit and buying very little in return, so the prospects were excellent before we started the war.

We'd have to be crazy to spoil a market like that!

Nobody in his right mind would deliberately set out to send a major customer broke so he couldn't afford to do business with us on cash terms and would have to borrow money, which he can't possibly pay back, in order to resume trading with us.

Unless of course our PM was feeling a bit unloved because his beloved people were catching up with him and his Government's dismal performance and so wanted a diversion.

Well, in this department he seems to have succeeded. Nothing makes a better smokescreen than 600 burning oil wells and in the process he has even managed to pour several billion gallons of oil on truly troubled waters.

But then, of course, the PM isn't entirely to blame. It takes two to tango: a people who love a war and a prime minister who can't bear to be seen as a bad guy. It's a very explosive combination.

Dare your genius to walk the wildest way

Sometimes when giving a talk I use the expression, "Dare your genius to walk the wildest unknown way".

Quite often people come up to me afterwards, their arms crossed and their mouths set firm as they proclaim, "Well! We can't all be clever! Some of us have to do the ordinary things! We're not all geniuses you know!"

In fact, they've entirely missed the point I tried to make.

I believe that, give or take a few years of education or, if you like, intellectual experience, we all have about the same amount of brain capacity.

Some people are not born more intelligent than others: they acquire more intelligence on the way.

Intelligence is largely a matter of experience.

To learn something new is to have done something different, to have acquired a new intellectual experience.

Most people are afraid to fail, which is another way of saying most people never gain sufficient intellectual experience to succeed.

Your mind is a natural odd-job man or woman. It can be stimulated to do a lot of things or it can be dulled to concentrate on doing one thing over and over again.

Most of the really intelligent people I have come across allow their minds to wander around, looking for new jobs, new ways to pass the time.

Now if your mind is going to go walkabout or, to put it another way, if you will dare your genius to walk the wildest unknown way, nothing is more certain than that you will fail and fail often.

After all, failure is the essential ingredient in success.

To have failed is the only way your intelligence can truly succeed, otherwise it simply isn't taking the wildest unknown path but simply meandering down the centre of the road.

Walking down the centre of the road is how you get hit by the traffic coming from both directions.

If you're not killed outright, what is learned is never again to venture out of the front door of your mind.

But when you walk the wildest unknown way you fail in an altogether different manner. You fail spectacularly.

First you fall in a bear pit and big, bad bear jumps in after you and mauls and batters you about a bit before hurling you out of the pit.

You pick yourself up, dust yourself off and you're just getting going again when a lion jumps out from behind a bush and grabs you by the scruff of the neck and shakes you about a bit.

You're just about live and knee deep in band-aids when you get captured by a wild man who stakes you to the ground under a bamboo shoot which grows through your body in 18 hours while a single drip of water hits your forehead every four seconds from a rock dangerously perched 20 feet above.

AFRAID TO FAIL

Because your mind is alert you work out that the velocity per square inch of the deadly drip is sufficient to bring the Great Wall of China down into a pile of rubble and dust.

But the nice thing is that after each of these calamities you learn how to avoid angry bears, bad-tempered lions and wild men while learning how to cook bamboo shoots and drink the required amount of water each day to keep your system functioning at optimum.

Before you know what's happened you've got a new way of seeing things. You're not scared of the world and you know that your intellect is bigger than the problems you generally have to face in life.

Failure is critical to success.

Here, for example, is the career of a man of whom you may have heard.

At the age of 22 he'd failed in business for the first time. At 23 he was defeated for the legislature. At 24 he failed a second time in business. But, at 25, a big year, he was elected to the legislature. He was 26 when his fiancee died, at 27 he had a nervous breakdown, at 29 he was defeated for Speaker, at 31 he was defeated for elector and at 34 he was defeated for Congress. Although 37 was a good year and he was elected to Congress, at 39 he was defeated again.

At 46 he had a go at the Senate and was defeated. At 47 he was defeated for vice-president and at 49 he was defeated for the Senate again. At 51, Abraham Lincoln was elected the president of the United States.

Lots of bears and lions, wild men, bamboo shoots and dripping water in Abe's spectacular life.

The point to be made is this: failure is always disappointing and often saps your courage, but its alternative is not to have tried, and not to try means you are doomed anyway, utterly and eternally doomed.

It is a rare person who doesn't sometimes get discouraged, but those people who succeed seem to have two essential ingredients in their lives.

They have a real sense of urgency as well as the ability to persevere, to prevail, come what may.

They are the people who have taught themselves to take the wildest unknown way and whistle while they walk.

The world is filled with more or less equally intelligent people, all of whom are capable of most of the tasks which lead to material success in life.

Why then do so few people actually achieve the pinnacle they aspire to as dreaming schoolkids?

The major reason is that most people have no sense of urgency. They only do the things which are required of them and only then if they are guaranteed payment for the task they perform.

Success is doing things urgently and without having a written guarantee that what you do will be rewarded.

In actual fact, it often isn't. That's where perseverance comes in, and you determine that you will not give up until you have achieved the task you've set yourself.

Then you, who have no more initial intelligence than the next person, will be seen to be the one who succeeds and who does magnificently in life.

You'll be the one they talk about as gifted and talented and rare.

The human brain thrives on experience and dies when it is only asked to perform routine tasks.

That's what I mean when I say, dare your genius to walk the wildest unknown way.

Every time you give up or put off a task or go slow or ask "Why me?" you insult your intelligence.

Every time you take the safe and easy way you take a step nearer to the centre of the road and where the big trucks roar blindly past going in both directions.

Allow your intelligence to dream of mountains to climb and dangerous passes to cross, huge seas to navigate, things to achieve, hard things that hurt a lot and have a sense of urgency and a passion.

Things that make you proud that you can't be defeated by a mauling from the big bad bear in the accounts department or the man-eater in marketing or the wild man who runs the circus in which you are expected to be the clown.

When you dare your genius to walk the wildest unknown way you soon learn to growl like a bear, roar like a lion and frighten the bejesus out of wild men armed with bamboo shoots and skilled in water torture.

You soon learn to flap your intellectual wings, take off and soar like an eagle.

THE AUSTRALIAN FRIDAY SEPTEMBER 13 1991

Dobbing in the profiteers

In Australia we call it "dobbing someone in", and if you were born before 1950 it is something you definitely would not do.

So much so that we have allowed all sorts of people to succeed who should have been dobbed in long before they got to the top or destroyed a lot of lives before they were eventually caught.

In the police force there was (and there might still be) a strong tradition of not dobbing in your mate, with the result that for a long time the police force lost its credibility.

The Fitzgerald inquiry became necessary as a direct result of a lot of guys—from the bottom to the top—observing the honour-among-thieves code.

Not that Queenslanders are so special; I'm sure the circumstances at the time in the other States were little different—are little different.

A lawyer acquaintance once told me that Australia traditionally has and continues to have the lowest number of jury convictions in the Western world. Even our juries are reluctant to dob someone in.

Clearly there are times when it is necessary and any society worth its moral convictions should not be prepared to tolerate cheating and stealing and taking unfair advantage when this is against the law, and your fellow man, in spirit and in fact.

MAIN MOTIVE PERSONAL GAIN

Businesses which are profiting by cheating, often openly cheating, should not be allowed to operate. This is as true of the chemical plant which spills industrial waste into a river or stream as it is of someone selling stolen goods in the pub or overpriced merchandise because they enjoy a monopoly.

Someone who was no doubt in need of a fix broke open my garage door several nights ago, smashed a hole in the side window of the car and stole the radio.

It's hardly a unique story and probably happens hundreds of times in a night, but the cost to the community is horrendous and we pay this through increased insurance premiums.

And there are other costs. Let me take you through them.

The quote for the repair of my car was $1200. That seemed

to me to be a little excessive. It was a small window and the radio was six years old.

I was told the cost couldn't be lowered—the car was expensive and the side window, not much bigger than an open book, cost $400 from the car importer. The radio cost $600 and the work $200. When I queried this, the suggestion was offered that it didn't matter because it was the insurance company which had to pay.

But it does matter! I believe the car importer should be dobbed in. I went to a well-known windshield fitter and had a piece of car window glass cut to the exact dimensions for $80. No doubt they were making an acceptable profit on that price.

I fitted it myself and that took half an hour. I bought a very good new radio for $250 and a mate connected it in five minutes. So I reckon the crash repairer should be dobbed in.

But more about the radio. When I told the story of the theft to a guy who was painting my house, he said: "No problem mate, you're not fussy about the make but want a good radio. I'll get you one down at the pub tonight for $120 cash."

That's a profit of 100 per cent at least, because I'm told the going wholesale price on the stolen goods market for a leading brand car stereo is $60 to the drug addict.

Now I have absolutely no doubt a whole heap of people know the addict who did the dreaded deed. If they'd dobbed him in so that he could start getting some sort of counselling and medical help, perhaps this whole string of corruptions may not have occurred.

The smash repairer, the car importer, and the fence at the pub all took advantage of the original crime—a blatantly unfair advantage taken on the moral majority—all because we believe it is wrong to dob in people who create problems in our society.

There is another area in which we, as a nation, have no problem at all in dobbing each other in. Sportsmen seem to be doing it more and more. In rugby union the charismatic and mercurial David Campese, the idol of every schoolboy who plays the game, produces a book ghost-written for him in which he dobs in a number of people including former Wallaby coach Alan Jones, the man who took the team to its greatest glory.

Campese's opposite winger, Ian Williams, writes a book and in it buckets Campese, in effect dobbing him in as a thorough bastard on the field.

Swimmers are turning on their coaches and other swimmers. Tennis players are turning on everyone; football codes are turning on anyone with a whistle in his hand or boots on his feet. Even in golf, the last bastion of sportsmanship, the competitors are beginning to dob in each other.

At work it's becoming increasingly common and in some quarters is seen as the way to succeed, a legitimate way to climb the corporate ladder. The dog-eat-dog scenario of fiction and the movies is being taken as the proper way to behave.

In the United States, all you have to do is stub your toe on a fire hydrant and you can proceed with litigation, claiming millions. Doctors refuse to treat people run down in a traffic accident in case they die later and their relatives sue for millions.

In some large buildings which house dentists, properly qualified dentists sit in the foyer and accost people who have just had their teeth seen to. They examine the work and if they think there is a chance to claim procedurial neglect they offer to start legal proceedings for a cut of the settlement.

Ought we not to take a closer look at what kind of people we are becoming?

Last week a well-known columnist took the Prime Minister, Mr Hawke, apart (in writing). Now I am not a particular admirer of this particular Prime Minister, but what the columnist said was often deeply personal and hurtful.

For goodness sake, let's all stop dobbing each other in for personal profit and get down to dobbing in those people in who are profiting from ripping us off.

1992

Why we get carried away by our flag

Now that the far from great flag debate has cooled down and has been folded away for some other time when Canberra wants to divert our national attention from some really important issue, perhaps we can have a few unheated words on the subject.

Flags, it occurs to me, pretty well design themselves. A moment in history comes upon us and before you know it someone's mother-in-law has sewn a flag to be hoisted on the day.

What is hoisted to fly on our behalf is either a new piece of bunting or an old one hurriedly modified to include a new element to which we can henceforth swear allegiance and for which we can proceed to die.

Now someone is bound to write in and say that it doesn't happen like this at all, that a prescribed flag protocol has existed since the Magna Carta which requires flags be designed by someone known as a Flag-master, Herald of Ensigns, Pole Protocol Potentate, Keeper of the Colours, Sultan of Silk, or some such person who is reappointed every 10 years in a secret ballot on a wet Thursday in June by breaking three eggs into a brandy balloon and adding malt whisky, stirred and consumed while standing on one leg, blowing a bugle through the nostrils and farting hundreds and thousands.

The real point is that, unless you're a Canadian, it doesn't seem appropriate to mount a national competition for a graphic design that meets written criteria.

Flags are highly emotional ideas born in hope—the moment they're designed they are imbued with a mystical significance and become capable of rendering us misty eyed in a light breeze to the strains of a badly played bugle.

The reasons for all this are pretty simple. We all want to be a part of a whole, to assume a significance greater than our individual selves.

It is difficult to convince a single person that he or she is very different from any other human being sharing the air on the blue planet. But if we can collect together into a homogeneous bunch, for lots of deeply atavistic reasons, we are instantly able to make outrageous claims of potency and power.

It seems this collective force is best focused with a piece of coloured bunting. The older the bunting the more proud of it we become.

So we saw the Serbs and the Croats hoisting their icons only moments after the red one with the hammer and sickle had been lowered. This allowed them to recommence a 1000-year old quarrel about whose colour arrangement flies highest and proudest.

Tradition is just another word for continuity, and continuity is important to all of us—it tells us who we are and where we've been. We cherish our continuity in family, social class, school, race and nation.

The instinct which causes us to do this is important to our survival and is not in the least strange, nor should we think of it as unacceptable.

Had we not behaved in this manner it is doubtful that humanity could have survived.

Therefore the emotional need to collect together into groups is instinctive. It is almost as though the more we maintain our differences as humans the more we remain the same.

So when some Pooh-Bah gets up and suggests we change the collective colours which represent our emotional commitment to each other we tend to get somewhat steamed up.

To make a change to something as meaningful as the emotional colours needs a reason strong enough to change our emotional focus.

Such a reason might be freeing ourselves from the bondage of another group and declaring our independence as a new nation. If a little blood is spilt in the process all the better.

This kind of traumatic gesture can't be symbolic, it must be real. We must be taught to hate someone else or, at the very least, dislike and want little or nothing to do with the old flag upon us.

In an emotional upheaval we must rush to sew up a new piece of fluttering rag to assemble and march behind as we proceed to chase the original flag providers out of our backyard and to throw their colours out after them.

Even the mild-mannered Canadians had a French-speaking component who got pretty worked up about the British-inspired flag, so that they had a highly charged emotional reason to persuade the other half of their people to throw out the old colours as a gesture of national reconciliation.

Now it seems to me that here, in Australia, we're not likely to do any of these things.

We're not angry with our forefathers, we don't feel oppressed by them or in the least betrayed by the European funny farm to which they now owe their allegiance.

The original indigines, who have lots of good emotional reasons to throw us newcomers out, have their own beautiful flag and lack the strength to force it upon us, or even, I suspect, the desire to share it with us. Besides, they seem disinclined to become embroiled in this particular flag-changing debate.

In fact we, as a nation, have absolutely nothing to become emotionally worked up about, absolutely nobody to hate or even dislike unless we're playing football or cricket against them.

If we should become a republic this will be achieved by a simple die-back factor. We will become further and further removed from the activities and inherited influence of the group which represents the roots of some of us, so that our polyglot people and ethnically intermarried children or their children will have no emotional attachment to the English, Welsh, Scots, and Irish.

ADVERTISING AND RELATED SUBJECTS

THE ADVERTISING INDUSTRY

THE AUSTRALIAN MONDAY MARCH 17 1986

Advertising: the words that seduce consumers

In Tom Stoppard's play, The Real Thing, he has Henry say: "Words don't deserve that kind of malarkey, they're innocent, neutral, precise, standing for this, describing that, meaning the other, so if you look after them you can build bridges across incomprehension and chaos."

When you belong at the bottom of the wordsmithing business, as I do, and you love words, as I do, you have lots of opportunity to see them kicked around and generally beaten up.

The advertising business is very good at doing grievous bodily harm to small, defenceless words.

The words that appear on behalf of advertising are meant to be out there in the paid-for pages of the newspapers and magazines locked in mortal combat with the reader's apathy.

Alas, as readers walk their eyes through the pages they are more often met by grammatical Swiss guards standing in columns of copy looking thoroughly bored, apparently guarding no discernible truth.

Advertising is about persuading people to want things. The more they want things, the more the cogs and wheels of capitalism spin out a standard of living to which we, as a nation, are most fortunate to be accustomed.

When the words we use to persuade people to want things fall joylessly onto the page like cold spaghetti or, in a desperate effort to be declamatory, frantically crucify themselves with exclamation marks or, worse yet, when sycophantic, self-indulgent meaty words plop into advertising headlines like fat grey grubs, then we are in trouble.

People don't buy when the words you write don't appeal to their self-interest.

The enfeeblement of words by the body corporate is costing manufacturers and service industries a fortune in lost opportunities.

I'm not talking about the words used in impulse advertising.

Small, glib decisions don't need heavyweight words. They can be subtle so they tap-dance into the mind for beer, hamburgers, soft drinks and all the other miscellaneous candy floss that television carries so well on behalf of our collective self-indulgence.

But the big buying decisions in our lives need to be pounded home with words.

The cars, homes, stoves, fridges, computers, stocks and bonds, banking, insurance policies and hundreds of other goods and services need bold, clear words to make people understand and want them.

Advertising is the mouthpiece of the free enterprise system and right now most of the words used on its behalf are self-congratulatory.

Words that talk about the manufacturer and not the end user. Words that pussyfoot because they might offend some clause or break some rule intended to protect people who have expressed no desire whatsoever to be protected.

The big, bold words bleed to death, while frail inconsequential ones are pumped full of plasma.

A piece of paper is a tree that once stood proud and green and spent its life reaching for the sky. To sully it with a ragged platoon of beaten words should be a punishable offence.

Every day, in too many agencies in this big country, there are writers and art directors who grab handfuls of words and carelessly bundle them.

They then lay them out in small heaps of semantic garbage across a field of pristine white paper. This exercise is called a layout and it's the same thing one does to a corpse.

In my experience, it is not unusual to find an advertising director of a client organisation who thoroughly distrusts words. Using a 10c ballpoint pen like a blunt instrument, he wanders over the snowy surface of the page bludgeoning beautiful, small defenceless words to death.

These people blunt the vigour of words honed sharp by a caring agency because they may offend some imagined sensibility or say something vigorously meaningful to the end user of the product.

Just in case I'm beginning to sound precious, let me assure you that advertising is not an art form.

Advertising communicates not because it is well written, but because people see a self-interest in reading it.

In the tough marketing environment of today, competing products are similar in most respects, so the words that carry your message must dance or cajole or reason or sometimes even smash their way through several layers of tough, invisible scar tissue built up over a lifetime.

A defence against the continual barrage of advertising bombast.

To do this task, words have to be robust, well trained and superbly disciplined.

Words are the shock troops of advertising. More an undercover operation than a trooping of the colour.

To the average reader, advertising is about as exciting as a head cold. This is because, for the most part, it is composed of empty words, tired, lightweight, husk words long past any capacity for verbal nutrition.

Words are just naturally inclined to be fanatical and they love to have a cause to carry. Your product or service is that cause.

Any fool knows that to sell a cause, you have to have a proposition. Words gather around a good proposition like bees around mimosa blossom.

Once you have a good proposition, you lovingly fashion it, with words, into a promise.

An advertisement without a promise is like a fart without smell. It passes into the environment unnoticed, causing no reaction whatsoever, serving only as a relief to the farter that he got away with it.

Samuel Johnson said more than 200 years ago, "The soul of an advertisement is promise—large promise."

Nothing happens in an advertisement without a promise. Only copywriters like myself read ads to get their jollies.

If you can get the right words to push a good promise, the momentum your advertisement gains will make you rich.

For some years now an advertisement about the size of a matchbox has appeared regularly in a Kentucky newspaper.

The copy says: "Send $10 and get rid of your piles. Don't send $10 and don't get rid of your piles."

As you can see all it takes are the right words.

Production values *aren't* everything

A memo landed on my desk on Wednesday from the Federation of Australian Commercial Television Stations announcing that henceforth their commercial acceptance division could no longer accept commercials in the u-matic format.

From now on all commercials must be submitted in either VHS or Beta.

Thus ends what must be one of the longest continuous equipment specifications in the history of modern electronic wizardry.

Electronically speaking, virtually everything we use in business and the home has changed in 20 years but the dear old u-matic cassette has been the standard in the advertising industry for nearly 20 years: and now the old darling has gone.

I can recall when the agency projection room was equipped with a 35mm projector lit by a special magnesium flare and a 16mm unit that wasn't as sophisticated as the 8mm movie projector people kept at home.

The advent of the u-matic took the showing of commercials out of the horse and buggy era, and electronic editing with video tape revolutionised the commercial film business. The best commercials are still shot in the old way on 35mm and transferred to videotape which, it is claimed, still cannot match the sublety of 35mm film.

This subtle difference is known as the production values. These production values have become an industry in themselves and are largely the cause of the tremendous increase in the cost of the humble television commercial.

As the average carefully made commercial costs around $100,000 for 30 seconds, an escalation of roughly seven times in seven years, film remains the most expensive thing a client can undertake in an agency.

It is not uncommon for half a minute of sell to cost in the region of 300,000 smackeroos and $500,000 is not unknown.

Film—that is, the TV commercial—is still the most glamorous aspect of advertising both to clients and to writers and art directors. Creative people can only command the really big salaries if they have what is commonly referred to as an award-winning reel.

The reel is, of course, a u-matic cassette of commercials to which they can lay some, though often tenuous, claim. Writers and art directors will do almost anything to make a TV commercial.

To gratify this need, the film industry has been quick to understand this deeply mercenary emotion and has developed a support system which allows for someone of absolutely no talent to make very expensive commercials which are completely devoid of an idea but which are greatly enhanced by these often mysterious, though deeply meaningful and essential, production values, which end up costing a fortune.

The box is cluttered with this expensive over-produced crap.

Let me show you how this works. Let's say for instance the client is trying to flog a low-calorie chocolate drink and has enough money to choose any medium.

The agency will choose television and the choice will probably be justified, although it is not unheard of for a writer or art director team, desperate to make a good TV commercial, to spend two-thirds of the budget on production, thus leaving no money over for anything like an appropriate schedule on television.

Clients are often beguiled by the prospect of having their product appear on television and some seem to believe that exposure on television, no matter how brief, will create truckloads of sales.

Well, in the absence of an idea, low-calorie anything means beautiful girls.

These are purchased at a premium as the model agency hastily points out that the models are now excluded from doing drink category commercials for at least a year and must be hugely compensated for this loss of potential earnings.

Next comes the location. As Australia has several thousand kilometers of white beaches and rolling surf as well as an average of 320 days of sunshine, location shouldn't be a problem. But it will be.

The director will point out that the combination of light, water, surf and sunshine he must have to get the right production values only exists on an island in the Barrier Reef which is so remote it must be reached by executive jet to Townsville and from there by 50m launch ($20,000 a day and the big game fishing is free).

Two jets will be needed as the location kitchen staff cannot be fitted into the first one with all their pots and pans.

Nobody has the courage to point out that all of this can be done on Cronulla Beach or a similar beach within a taxi ride of any capital city.

You see, production values have become everything. In fact, in the absence of an idea, production values are everything. I won't belabour the point.

It is also true to say that, in most instances, the agency isn't trying to get a free holiday on the client's budget.

The insecurity of a lot of agency creative people, who are desperate for an award-winning commercial to put on their reel, is such that they allow themselves to be bullied by directors and film houses who look at agencies and only see dollars.

Writing for film is a difficult and exacting task. It requires a strong idea and great attention to detail. It is every bit as difficult as writing good copy.

But, unlike copy, the mistakes are very sensitive. Bad copy can be seen on a scrap of typed paper, but a poor film idea, usually heightened by hyperbole and the promise of things to come, is only exposed after the money has been spent.

I believe that if the advertising industry put a ceiling of $50,000 on all television commercials made for the next two years, the standard of television commercials would improve immensely.

This would weed out the opportunists in the production houses and get rid of the self-indulgent directors and the small-talented and untrained people, many of whom reside in advertising agencies where they are allowed to step on to a TV set with the right to spend a small fortune of someone else's money for the major purpose of advancing their own careers.

Pep up your sales with spontaneity

Like most people, I deplore the idea of a pristine white wall desecrated by a rude and inane pressure-pak-graffiti four-letter word or, worse still, the seemingly popular three-letter "sux" borrowed from US ghetto language.

But I wouldn't be honest if I said all graffiti should be banned. Just as it is depressing to realise that the bulk of mankind seems only capable of scrawling arcane and obscene messages, there is some graffiti which is worthy of the bridges, walls and doors on which it comes to rest.

We all have our favourites and among mine are four, each in a different category. In the protest category: among appeals against apartheid, refuseniks, Nicaragua and all the other ills that beset an imperfect world my favourite is a rather sad and homely appeal against the cost of living: "$1.75 for a vegemite sandwich is going too far".

In the lavatory-door humour section, the graffiti I remember best occurred in a toilet at San Francisco airport. I was waiting for my connection to Hawaii seated on the oval porcelain with my pants down around my ankles when I saw the single word "masturbation" written in a small, neat hand at the very top of the door. From the word ran a thin red line to the very edge of the bottom of the door. I was forced to vacate my seat and get down on all fours to read it. The words at the end of the line read: "stunts your growth".

In the sad and plaintive category the most eloquent and telling for my money was a three-word message I read on a wall the day after John Lennon was murdered. It simply went: "oh, oh Yoko". Finally, in the political put-down category: "Tammy has one, Malcolm is one" is about as cutting and rude as the Australian idiom can get.

I was talking to a group of owners of hairdressing chains at a seminar in Sydney last week and I suggested to them that, with multiple outlets in the same city, they might think of using billboards. Billboards are, if used correctly, the nearest thing there is to graffiti and can be just as effective.

Nobody passes a piece of good graffiti, and the same is true of a good billboard. All it takes is a contract painter of the kind who does the butcher's window and you can make a new offer every week. Instead of a whole bunch of dreary institutional messages for margarine or cigarettes, the billboards could be made to come alive, the way good graffiti does.

A billboard is simply a surface and the message can be spontaneous and have a sense of urgency.

Spontaneity is a virtue most humans appreciate and trust, and more and more, as we appear to tidy up our act, it is lacking in our business.

SAY IT THE WAY GRAFFITI DOES

The hair salon which is designed by an interior decorator, or the bank or business premises or even the chain restaurant or fast foodery where a manual is prepared to tell staff or owners where the bowl of chrysanthemums go, is intended to set a standard of excellence. Often it simply leaves the customer nervous and unconvinced.

The car rental business is among the most competitive there is and among the most competitive of all the outlets must be William Street, the 1km strip that leads up to Kings Cross in Sydney. Avis and Budget eye each other off and Hertz plays no-speak.

Half a dozen cheaper operations also set up their shingles and all of them want the tourist dollar. To get it they shine up their name plates, dress in immaculate uniforms, sink customers into deep Italian leather chairs and serve freshly brewed coffee. Smiles are sweet.

Why, then, is it that people on holiday and, perhaps, in particular the Japanese, are very timid about renting a car? I have a theory. It's only a theory and I'm sure I'll get half a dozen letters from the rent-a-car industry decrying it. My theory is that people on holiday want to do things spontaneously and happily but, alas, they're also on a budget.

When you go into a car rental business the special offer, if there is one, has a whole bunch of strings attached and, while the operator is smiling, she or he isn't over-helpful or enthusiastic about getting you something you reckon you can afford. The environment smacks of businessmen renting cars on company credit cards.

My theory is that these outlets need to be messed up. Paint the week's offer in garish colours on the outside window in English and Japanese, play a little loud music and get into a holiday mood.

Change the offer every week. If you haven't got an offer paint: "Hi, come in, have we got a car for you."

Peggy Levy, a friend of mine who runs a chain of boutiques for working girls in the less trendy suburbs, writes lunch-hour specials on paper bags and hangs them all over the shop. Spontaneity, a sense of urgency and a feeling that the buck in your place has not been too carefully calculated at the customer's expense could just be a way to pep up flagging sales.

People love to buy, but they don't like to be made to look or feel foolish. Environment is everything, and when it isn't personal and doesn't appear to be making an offer, the customer becomes wary.

Figgins, in Melbourne, billed as the ultimate shop, went broke in six months because it intimidated everyone except my wife. People, thank God, are human all over and they still respond to a warm environment, a sense of urgency and spontaneity.

God, after all, completed the world in seven days; that's why it's such a mess but also such a terrific place to live.

Louie de Fly, a fluke idea that became a legend

This week I pulled up rather abruptly when someone angrily accused me of claiming to have been the author of Louie de Fly when he had it on absolute authority that I was no such thing.

Advertising is a strange business. Louie de Fly was first presented to the homes of Australia some 27 years ago and has, if nothing else, endured.

That it should be of importance who conceived of the character in the first place is an illustration of how brittle the creative person's reputation can be in this business.

Louie de Fly has endeared himself to Australians as the little Aussie battler who, despite being zapped a million times by the dreaded Mortein, always comes back for more.

At least one doctorate degree has been awarded based on a thesis which used Louie de Fly as the archetypal symbol of the little man who keeps coming back despite the knockdowns and the frustrations of life.

I recall the earnest young man who interviewed me at length about the psychological implications of Louie de Fly and who wondered out loud at the brilliant insights that had gone into creating the character.

I was assured by him that in devising this character I had hit the communications jackpot and had created the perfect symbol, no less great than Mickey Mouse, Donald Duck or even Popeye.

INSIGHTS

Perhaps he was right. After 27 years Louie is as strong as ever in a re-run that is turning a new generation into Louie fans.

I thought that I might share with you the insights into creating a character like Louie so that you might understand the powerful intellectual forces that drive the advertising dollar.

I suppose, in the strictly technical sense, I cannot claim to have invented Louie. What happened was that I was looking through several cans of 16mm film in the film library of McCann Erickson when I came across a can which was marked Louie the Fly.

I ran it through the projector and it was a whole lot of experimental footage of a fly, shot in high contrast black and white film to achieve a sort of animated effect. The experiment was by McCann's senior producer in the early sixties, an irascible old man called Doc Sternberg, who had learned his filming in pre-war Germany and who lorded it over everyone at McCann.

What Doc pronounced on film was law, even if it was filmed out of focus and upside down. The fly experiment was, even for Doc, clearly a disaster. I had only just been made the creative director of McCann and felt that an animated fly of the same name was a nice idea.

I wrote a rough outline and as I remember it, handed it to Brian Henderson (the ad man, not the announcer). Brian, even in those early days, was a brilliant lyricist and not a bad musician and he knocked my idea into musical shape as he had often done before.

Bob Gibson was given the job of putting down the music. A young French animator called Jean Tych conceived Louie as the funny little bloke he became. In those days, animation was strictly Disney rip-off and so Tych's weird looking scribble was seen as very risky and hugely modern, something only a mad French animator would dream up.

I recall selling the initial sketches to Samuel Taylor with great trepidation. Well, the rest is history. Louie de Fly became the Edward G. Robinson of flies and it is from flukes such as these that creative people in advertising earn their reputations.

Therefore perhaps it becomes important to establish who gets the credit. Certainly I have received a fair amount of it over the years, though I have never claimed to be the sole creator.

Without question Brian Henderson in particular has every right to claim Louie as does Norman Godbold the producer, the late Bob Gibson the musician, and of course Jean Tych, the animator.

IMPLICATIONS

Even my son has some small claims as he, now 27, was the baby used in the commercial. What I think we should all remember is that Louie was just another commercial amongst hundreds we have separately and collectively made.

None of us were clever enough at the time to think too deeply about the psychological implications of an animated fly based on the Aussie male ethos. It simply seemed like a good idea at the time and if Louie had died a year later with all the other commercials we made that year, we would not have felt hard done by.

But the client, perhaps the smartest amongst us, kept Louie going and the little fly grew and grew and grew in the hearts of Australians, just as Mr Sheen, another Brian Henderson co-production, this time with Vic Nicholson, has grown to be loved.

When you spend 20 or 30 million dollars on a single commercial over a period of 27 years you increase its chances of becoming a legend in your own lifetime. Nevertheless, it is the genius of Brian Henderson and Jean Tych that made it sustainable for all that time.

Louie has recently been remade by Mojo MDA so that he now appears, not greatly modernised, but in colour. It is a tribute to Brian's talent that the music and lyrics of the new Louie are no better, if as good as the original.

THE AUSTRALIAN MONDAY OCTOBER 24 1988

The answer lies in asking questions

Every day for the past 30 years, I have been making decisions about my fellow Australians.

Decisions is perhaps a rather grand word: what I have been doing is making somewhat arrogant assumptions, or even more bluntly, I have been playing God with my clients' money.

Once in a while, a pang of conscience has caused me to ask that my client undertake a research program. As often as not, my client has looked askance at me and said: "What do you want with my research? We know what the consumer wants."

And in the early years, I think he was probably right. Australians were a fairly homogeneous lot and we had sufficient in common for those of us who wrote the nation's daily sales messages to get it right.

Some years ago, and not too long after I had started my own agency, we scored our first big account. All growing agencies need the one big account to act as a window to the outside world, with budgets big enough to get the agency on to television and into glossy, full-page magazine spreads.

This is the most dangerous time for a small agency which is doing good work. Big clients have a habit of doing things their own way and any impetuous, creative challenge to this conventional wisdom can make a small agency's creatively less-dedicated partners very edgy.

As a so-called creative man or woman, your job is to make sure your client gets the most effective creative work, whereas the job of the account man is, more often, to see that the client is happy. These two job specifications are quite often in opposition to each other.

Anyhow, this big, new, potentially profitable client we'd been fortunate enough to acquire seemed, on the surface anyway, to be making a number of fundamental mistakes.

"May we do some qualitative research?" I asked. "No you may not," came the reply, "we've already spent a fortune on a major piece of research and we didn't like it. It was bloody useless."

Now, if you are silly enough to ask the obvious question, why was it useless, you'd already be ankle deep in very swampy ground.

In an attempt to smother a question so foolishly asked, the accounts service part of your partnership will have kicked you under the table, suggested an adjournment for lunch and changed the subject to the client's children's excellent exam results.

The politics of the situation are that the client has obviously requested a major research project in the recent past and the results have not been to his liking so he has decided, in the wisdom of the board, to ignore the findings.

So you get smart and don't ask the question. Anyway, it is not all that difficult to get the name of the scurrilous research outfit that conducted the hopeless research.

The next day you phone them and casually ask them to send over a copy of the offending research which, as the client's new agency, you're perfectly entitled to ask for. This is what I did.

FEMINIST

The research proved to be excellent and the work we did for this client during the next five years was based on it. The client prospered and the budget burgeoned so that the next time it was necessary to ask questions, we paid for the research ourselves.

Any advertising agency or client who believes they can make the right decisions without asking frequent questions in the marketplace is courting disaster today.

Australians are not the same as they have always been, nor do we have large masses of similar thinking, similar acting people, allowing advertisers to take approximate aim at a target audience and still get an acceptable result.

Too many new influences are affecting our society to talk of a single-minded nation.

The feminist movement alone has made changes not even the most aggressive of its members could have thought possible.

Multiculturism has had the effect of creating all sorts of small, though effective cultural pockets.

Even the older generation has changed. Early retirement and the first effective lump-sum superannuation have helped to give many of yesterday's dependent-on-the-system pensioners a freedom of movement and expression.

Not so long ago, a small agency grew into a giant one selling the ocker image in a gravel-voiced endless repetition of the meaning of Australian life through the medium of beer and ball games.

I'm not at all sure the ocker approach to advertising has much validity in today's marketplace.

If, as an advertising creative person, you are still prepared to go ahead and write copy without asking questions, then you are not working in your client's best interests and, sooner or later, your client is going to find you out.

THE AUSTRALIAN FRIDAY AUGUST 25 1989

With advertising, you'll never be alone

My life is a fairly busy process affording me very little privacy other than that of facing a blank computer screen with a blank mind, which is happening at the moment.

In the fleeting minutes I have to dream, I dream of achieving a little privacy in my life. Real downtime I can spend exactly the way I want to spend it; it's time I can squander any way I like without feeling the least bit guilty.

When you think about it, personal privacy is a commodity in short supply in the marital years with a household full of kids and both parents working.

There is this large section of your life, from marriage to the time you show the last of your brats the front door, shake them by the hand and wish them well out there in real life, when privacy disappears completely as a disposable commodity.

You could say, for most of us anyway, that the only time we get to have a bit of privacy is when we are kids, adolescents and pre-marrieds. And that's exactly the time we don't want it! In a child, privacy equates with loneliness, in an adolescent, boredom, loneliness or both, in a pre-marital situation, desperation.

So when we've got it we don't want it, when we need privacy it isn't there any more.

Yet, more and more, we hear about the invasion of our privacy by advertising. Some days ago I went to my private box at the local post office (yet another attempt, of course, at privacy). Inside were two proper letters, a handful of bills and seven direct-mail letters.

Okay, I make my living as an advertising man so I should welcome this intrusion by my industry into the sanctity of my very own private post office box. But I didn't.

I should have taken it on the chin smiling. Instead, I stuck my chin out and confronted the man behind the counter. He gave me one of those aggrieved expressions much loved by public servants which means "don't give me a hard time, it wasn't my idea". He told me the post office had a lucrative contract with the direct-

ADVERTISING AND RELATED SUBJECTS

mail association that allowed it to pollute my mail box.

I was halfway through throwing one of my better conniptions when I realised I had become the full Judas. I mumbled some sort of half-baked threat and retreated, then went back and retrieved all the direct-mail letters I'd slung on to the counter.

I mean, you never know, do you? There could be something I needed, like a genuine Franklin Mint 1934 De Soto scaled down to one-25th size with white-walled tyres and wheel spokes coated in genuine nine-carat gold.

"A treasure you will have for the rest of your life and one to cherish as it gains in value! Yours for $350 in four easy monthly instalments." Something essential like that.

Having rescued myself just moments before the cock crowed thrice, I gave some serious thinking attention to the intrusion of advertising into our everyday lives. Was it the invasion of privacy the wowsers were making it out to be?

Was it kicking down the doors to our private lives without showing a search warrant? Or was it in fact welcome and not intrusive in the least? I was forced after about 10 seconds' thinking to award a not guilty verdict to my profession.

The evidence, while not complete, is compelling. Every home in Australia has at least one radio and it runs just about all the time anyone is at home. It contains commercial and non-commercial stations and the ones playing commercials are the ones most used. The same is true of television.

Throughout the world, magazines and newspapers which show no advertising remain unsold on the newsstands. A call to the direct-mail association returned the answer that eight out of ten people researched said they would prefer to receive junk mail.

ANYWAY, WHO NEEDS PRIVACY?

This worried me somewhat. If privacy, that thing I crave so much, was such an important commodity, why would people volunteer to have a loud-mouthed radio salesman bawling at them first thing every morning?

Why would they allow the mostly banal crap that pours out of the television set into their nice, clean and tidy, private homes?

Why would they bring the paper home, subscribe to the magazine or open the direct-response letter when clearly they are supposed to despise advertising and know it to be an invasion of their privacy?

So I formed one of my usual dumb, half-cocked theories which goes like this. Most people are lonely, scared and feel themselves to be unimportant.

They live behind locked doors and barred windows and public servants are constantly rude to them.

They spend their lives filling out forms where their names are reduced to numbers.

They try to get a few bucks out of the bank knowing they are a tiny bit overdrawn and their whole life flashes on to a computer screen and the 16-year-old girl behind the counter sends them packing.

The Treasurer tells them daily that things are going to get tougher and he doesn't even have the good grace to apologise. They feel it must be their fault. The tin of tuna from Taiwan bought from the Lebanese on the corner finally broke Australia's mercantile spirit.

Lonely, sad, dispirited and guilty—that's how most people are made to feel in the collective huddle we call the city.

So along comes advertising. It's cheery, cheeky, friendly, making outrageous promises, shouts a lot, laughs a lot, is sometimes funny and most of all it wants to be your friend.

Sure, it has a motive, it wants to remove your hard-earned dollars from you in exchange for something you never knew you needed until it was pointed out that without it, you'd be a socially deprived person.

Who wants to be more socially deprived than they already are? Who wants to take the chance of becoming more lonely, more isolated and more dispirited? Anyway, someone has to take your dollars.

Mr Keating just takes them without asking and then proceeds to slap you down in the process. Advertising is willing to be your friend all the time.

It sings for you. It pays for your entertainment. It fights for your attention. Nobody else does that. Only advertising falls over itself in an effort to be a part of your day, life and lifestyle. Who else does these things for you in exchange for a few lousy bucks? Nobody, that's who.

I know that we are all supposed to turn out strong and resourceful with a set of values that makes us independent of mind and spirit. Our education system, ha ha, is designed to give us the power to think for ourselves.

We are supposed to spend our money on piano lessons for the kids, refrain from strong drink and tobacco, see our lives as an embodiment of nobility, the one animal to rise from the slime and become greater than the subtotal of what had existed. And a few members of the human species have climbed the heights and made it into the school textbooks.

The remainder of us wake up in the morning, scratch our bums, fart, burp, ablute, search for the aspirin and the eye drops, turn on the electric kettle, spill the milk over our toes, warm the baby's bottle, run out of tea bags, break a good cup and grope blindly for the radio switch.

"Good morning, beautiful! You're probably the nicest person I'm going to meet all day. So just for that, just for being your delicious self, I've got this t'riffic deal for you! Siddown, have a cuppa coffee and listen to this! But first a little music to bring the day in. Ready, steady, go man go!"

The advertising day has begun, the invasion is under way. Who needs privacy anyway? It only leads to loneliness.

Why VIPS are very important parts of the advertising system

Several weeks ago, one of the larger multinational clients to whom I grovel gratefully for my livelihood asked me to take one of his young marketing product managers into the creative department for a month.

The idea was for the young bloke to tackle the same problem given to the copywriters and be a pretend copywriter himself.

Because this client spends mega bucks, I didn't tell him I thought it one of the dumbest corporate ideas ever.

Instead, I agreed that it was a worthwhile experiment being a typical sycophantic ad-man, once I had thought about it a bit. I managed to convince myself that it wasn't such a bad idea after all.

I have observed in life that we all have a tendency to think of our own job as being difficult and the next person's is a snack.

That is until we actually find ourselves in a role-reversal situation when we usually discover almost all tasks require peculiar skills, special knowledge and are a great deal more complex than we imagined, looking at them from the sidelines.

In the advertising business young product managers or marketing trainees for large marketing companies are usually trained on the job.

They are given products to look after in the market place and become involved with every aspect of the product's life cycle, which includes advertising.

It is not uncommon for a highly skilled advertising-creative person, earning about 10 times the trainees' salary, to find himself, initially anyway, subject to the trainee's exalted opinions on the work he has produced.

While the final responsibility usually doesn't rest on the youngster's opinion, it is surprising how much damage can be done to a concept before it gets to a level where it can be judged with a modicum of responsibility.

To competent creative people, this can be a very vexing experience.

It is only natural for inexperienced young executives, given the responsibility for making decisions on a brand's advertising, to panic and ask themselves: "What is wrong with this stuff I'm looking at?"

And it is here where the rot sets in. The moment you look at anything in life with a negative bias it becomes almost impossible to isolate its positive aspects.

The good things about the proposition or idea seemed to mysteriously disappear and the bad to expand the moment you start to seek its faults, without first understanding its virtues.

If, on the other hand, you look at anything and simply ask yourself: "Now let me see what's right. What's good about this thing?"

When you take the positive point of view it is seldom difficult to see where the errors lie and usually they can be corrected and the proposition enhanced.

However, being positive is not the opposite to being negative. Being negative requires very few brains and hardly any skill.

Alternatively, being positive requires a fairly high degree of experience, the ability to think and make judgments.

Most young executives have usually not yet achieved these skills and should not be let loose on sophisticated work without having a corporate nanny to hold their hands.

Therefore, the idea of having a young executive trying to solve problems and come up with relevant ideas seemed in the end not such a bad experiment.

At least he would return to his company with some respect for the creative product and a knowledge of how difficult it is to come up with a selling idea in the first place.

In the course of his month with us, I watched a young bloke who wasn't really creative work very hard to try to crack problems. He was eager to learn and anxious to gain as much information as he could in the process.

Fairly early into his time he asked me a very simple sounding question. "How does advertising work?" The answer was also fairly simple. I told him I didn't know.

Which is the truth. I don't think anyone knows what the psychological processes are which make people purchase products. Why one idea works wonderfully well, while another seemingly equally good one fails.

Why research can't consistently isolate ideas that are going to work very well, from others that will work modestly well. The very best it may be able to do is to tell you whether an idea won't work at all and then even research can be wrong!

So I set about trying to teach him the things an advertisement should have in it to give it a chance of working. The best way to remember these components is to use the acronym VIPS. VIPS stands for Visibility, Identity, Promise, Simplicity.

Beginning with visibility, nothing happens unless it is seen, but it isn't the kind of visibility which may be likened to dropping your pants on the Town Hall steps at lunchtime.

You'll be seen alright, but it doesn't lead anywhere useful. Lots of products choose these spectacular environments in which to be seen and usually everything else is seen but the product.

The visibility of your product must be relevant to its most likely end-user. In other words, it must operate effectively in a process of selective perception.

It's a little like never seeing a certain model car until you buy one or are shopping around for one and suddenly you see it everywhere. An advertisement may be invisible to someone who isn't interested in a product and highly visible to someone who uses it regularly.

So, visibility in a product is always devised with the end-user in mind. Advertising for the product should contain those visual elements which catch the attention of its most likely customer.

In fact, for optimum visibility it is important to filter out the people you do not want because, in doing so you increase the likelihood of appealing to the people you do. Allow your regular customers to express their individuality.

In choosing your product they are not responding to your hectoring demands, they are in fact expressing something of themselves. Visibility is the business of allowing people to see themselves expressed in your product.

Identity is simple. You don't have to have your logo a mile high for it to be noticed and it doesn't have to disappear entirely to suggest to your customer that you are a nice product.

Neither brag nor be ashamed of your name. Simply state it so that people will remember it in context and with respect.

If you can work it into the headline that's very good, providing it's a good headline with a real customer benefit and the addition of your name doesn't spoil the proposition, or make it clumsy and self-conscious.

Always make sure people know who you are, but don't stand two inches from their eardrums and shout your name repeatedly. Introduce your product in the same way as you would introduce yourself, with a smile, making sure the person to whom you are talking hears you clearly and enjoys meeting you.

An advertisement without a promise is a very sick corporate child. If advertising is the business of motivating people towards a purchase and in particular towards the purchase of your brand over that of the competition, then you had better make a promise.

A promise you can keep and one which will satisfy your end-user. Otherwise, just like a person, if you keep breaking your promises you lose your credibility.

Remember, the advertisement is making the promise on your behalf, it is you who lets the customer down if he finds your product doesn't deliver.

Remember, a promise is not a list of product virtues or special ingredients. A promise is the meaningful reward your customer gets for choosing to use your product rather than that of the competition.

You make a drill bit. One of its features is that it is made of the finest tungsten-tipped tempered steel, but your customer isn't buying a bit, he's buying a hole.

The promise is a painlessly drilled hole into a concrete wall, which when plugged and screwed will hang a beautiful picture. There is a big difference between these two perceptions.

Finally there is simplicity. Simplicity is difficult because it means leaving things out and clients hate to pay for space and then not use all of it to say everything.

Trouble is that by trying to say too much you can end up saying nothing. Most of the trouble starts when the people the advertisement is trying to please are not the customers, but members of your own organisation.

You try to please too many people inside the organisation and you end up pleasing nobody out there on the street.

Ideally, an advertisement should have no more than four elements: headline, picture, copy and your name.

It should make one strong promise which is visible and relevant to your best customers and they should understand from whom this visually attractive and relevant promise is coming.

That's VIPS. Maybe it still doesn't tell you how advertising works or help you to make a creatively brilliant advertisement or TV or radio spot, but it sure as hell will stop you from doing many of the stupid things you're doing now and take you a fair way down the track to making good advertising.

THE AUSTRALIAN MONDAY JULY 27 1990

Telling you what's already on your mind

Sometimes very late at night I bang on a headset and search the FM dials for a symphony and in the process am rewarded with some very peculiar information from community radio.

This ranges from late night prayer meetings directed to people in hospices to announcements such as: "Calling all Asian lesbians. If you are an Asian lesbian and wish to get together for social and other reasons there is a meeting of the Asian Lesbian Society in the Mosman Town Hall," etc.

I'm quite sure these community stations do a lot of good for minority groups but they do very little for people seeking the concerto at 2am.

Anyway, one of these stations called me several days ago and asked me if I would debate with a person of their choosing on the subject of manipulative advertising.

DEVELOPING A MINDSET

I groaned inwardly but a refusal to talk on this infinitely dreary subject is tantamount to an admission of guilt.

So I agreed, knowing that whatever I said would be ignored. The Anti-Advertising Lobby, generally speaking, has a very confirmed mindset and is not willing to hear a different viewpoint to their own.

Mindsets are interesting, because we all have them. In fact, it would be impossible to operate without them—they tell us who we are and largely what we are.

Humans are, in the main, creatures of their own early experience. The old Jesuit adage that a child's training before the age of seven will largely dictate what sort of attitudes they will hold as adults may not be entirely valid.

But it seems fair to say that we appear to develop mindsets at a fairly early age and these seem to grow static, or put differently, often fail to develop further or modify from that early age.

I'm sure there exists some sort of mean average age when generally our ideas become fixed about things, but for the sake of argument, let's say we change less and less from our late 20s.

In other words, our mindsets are intact and operate largely unchanged from this time for the remainder of our lives.

Now the trouble with this is that things do change around us and often require new learning, new behaviour and therefore new mindsets.

Using the old mindsets, we fail to see the change and we base decisions on redundant information. We see what we want to see rather than what truly exists.

Hence yesterday's red hot manager becomes today's has-been and talks about how things have changed for the worse and how much better they were in his day.

Instead of changing our mindsets, adjusting them for the new information, we use them to make our present value judgments.

In other words, we use the wrong information on which to make the decisions for ourselves and our companies.

Decisions made using the wrong information tend most often to be wrong. So we get fired and a younger man or woman, patently underqualified and totally inexperienced, is given the job and ends up doing it rather well.

But what has this got to do with the business of manipulative advertising?

If behaviour modification is the business of constantly adjusting your mindset to take into account the changes which are occurring around you, then that isn't what advertising does.

Advertising is largely the business of confirming existing mindsets. It tells you constantly and repeatedly that you are right if you act in a certain manner and most products are predicted to appeal to known and established attitudes.

Now there is nothing wrong with this. Products and services in a mass production market exist because of this economy of intellectual scale.

It's just that the usual advertising process of influencing people is to confirm their belief rather than to attempt to change them.

The reason most truly new products fail on the market is because advertising, while brilliant at exploiting an existing mindset, mostly lacks the creativity to modify the way we think.

And this isn't the main argument against those people who talk of the ability of advertising to manipulate minds.

Confirmation of what is already known is not a behaviour modification process. Rather it is a repetitive one.

So, at best, being manipulative means finding new ways of

repeating ourselves, new ways of saying the same old thing and confirming existing mindsets. This can be very clever, but it isn't mind shattering and it isn't even being very creative.

Creativity is, among other things, the ability to modify views, to change mindsets.

CERTAIN MANNER

It is for this reason we think of Picasso and Braque and Cassals and Einstein and the legions of outstanding writers and musicians and artists and mathematicians and scientists and philosophers as creative.

They become so because they change our mindsets and by doing so affect the very substance of our lives.

We don't say "I'm too old to change". Instead, we willingly embrace the change and adjust our attitude.

The moment we embrace and adjust, advertising hastens to confirm. It does so by repeating and repeating and repeating the truth, the new gospel and the new mindset.

Or as Ross Quinlivan, the late creative director of George Patterson, once said to me: "Good advertising is undetected plagiarism."

At the time I thought this was a brilliant and original summation of the advertising business.

Years later he confessed to me that he'd pinched this definition from somewhere else. Oh, well, that's advertising.

ADVERTISING AGENCY–CLIENT RELATIONS

THE AUSTRALIAN MONDAY MARCH 24 1986

Even God and Aunt Dolly couldn't save Gossamer

Do products have a life cycle? A few do, but most products don't.

Many that don't are killed off, if not in their prime, then in their temporary decline. New marketing directors are the principal killers.

There is nothing they like better than to find one or two products looking a little wobbly in the company line-up.

Reputations can be built almost overnight with a couple of ailing products successfully milked before delivering the corporate coup de grace.

Follow this with a modestly successful new product launch and the black, Italian leather swivel chair in the chief executive's office is practically yours.

In my experience, very few fledgling marketing directors know the difference between a product that can be nursed back to health and one that is terminally ill. But the difference is significant.

The new product launch that invariably follows the demise of the old product is very expensive. Statistically, it is more likely to fail than to succeed.

On the other hand, products nursed back to health keep their old friends and are in an ideal position to make new ones.

The difference between a product which may have temporarily lost its vigour and one which has become geriatric is, obviously, dictated by the end-user.

While there is nothing mysterious abut this process, I have seen competent marketing minds turned to mashed potato trying to figure out what may have gone wrong with a once popular product.

You simply ask yourself whether sufficient people still need your product type. If they do, then it becomes a question of meeting their expectations, whatever they may be.

In the process of meeting this expectation, you re-launch your old product, suitably dusted off and presented to coincide with the self-interest of your most likely user.

Rinso has re-launched perhaps fifty times, perhaps even more, so why wouldn't your own ailing product respond to a little high-tech and tenderness?

Of course, re-launches are not very glamourous. The credit for a successful re-launch is minor compared to the accolades that come with a successful new product launch.

A string of successful re-launches is a much harder way to get your bum in the boss's chair. But, in the long run, it is more certain. And when you get there, you may just know a thing or two about keeping your company healthy.

Directly opposite to the new marketing director in a product killing frenzy is the nostalgic chief executive.

He is determined to hold on to a once useful product even when it has reached an advanced stage of senile dementia. This kind of product myopia can occur even in brilliant marketing men.

There was a time, in the late sixties, when women wore their hair in what was commonly known as a beehive. This was a towering nest of hair that defied gravity only because it was held together by hairspray so powerful that one squirt could stop a goods train in its tracks.

AGGRESSIVE

There are women in their early 50s still walking around with these beehive hairdos, not from any desire to recapture their youth, but simply because they've been unable to comb them out.

The market leader in gravity defying hairspray at the time was a product called Gossamer Super Soft, which, in every possible way, belied its name.

Gossamer, part of a product line-up including Mortein, Trix washing-up detergent and Mr Sheen, was one of the major performers under the aggressive and often brilliant marketing baton of Bill Graham, the much feared chief executive and principal shareholder of the Samuel Taylor company.

Graham, a deeply religious man, took no marketing counsel from anyone except God, a liaison which, judged by the enormous success of his company, worked exceedingly well.

A market research program was conducted through the agency in a desperate effort to alert Bill Graham to the fact that Gossamer was in trouble.

But when God has personally had a hand in the formulation of a product, the slender findings of market research do not carry too much weight.

Graham, whether in consultation with God or not I can't say, evidently decided that the research was spurious and promptly refused to pay for it. He called Sim Rubensohn.

Sim Rubensohn was the short and apoplectic chairman of Hansen Rubensohn-McCann Erickson. He had built his agency and part of his considerable fortune by backing Graham, who was backed by God. God, Graham and Sim made a marketing trinity that had kept the hated Proctor and Gamble out of the Australian market for two generations.

To them it was unseemly that the mere fashion whims of the Australian female be allowed to hasten the demise of a market leader as significant as Gossamer Super Soft.

Besides, Sim, who was nothing if not a pragmatist, saw a big spend coming up. Graham always backed his convictions with considerable cash.

Rubensohn was not about to argue with God, or as he may have put it privately, a God-sent opportunity.

Instead he picked up the phone and demanded that I be standing to attention in front of his desk in roughly 10 seconds.

"You've got three days," he said. "Ok, now bugger off and get started."

Sim needed an idea so big that it would blow Graham right out of his seat. I also knew that absolutely nothing I could say about the gravity defier would change the fact it was a hairspray no longer meant for this world.

Two days went by and I arrived home about midnight on the second day still sans idea, with the prospect of a tomorrow sans career.

My wife said the usual loving things about how it didn't matter that we'd lose the deposit on the cottage in Jesmond Ave or whether the boys went to Cranbrook.

In truth she was probably wondering how the hell she came to find herself stuck with an advertising man whose think tank showed empty just when a little extra juice was urgently required.

Too tired to care, I went to bed. At 4 am I awoke. I had the big one. The lollipop. The all day sucker of an idea.

I grabbed our dressing gown, which was one of those red satin garments emblazoned on the back with a dragon entwined with roses and chrysanthemums. Everyone's Aunty Dolly brought them home as gifts from Hong Kong.

If you've ever been the recipient of one of these garments, you'll know that the belt disappears forever after you've worn it but once.

The gown, although it fell open at the front, sort of covered my naked body. Anyway, I was too excited to care and pulling on a pair of gum boots I set off for the beach 500m away.

The idea was simple enough. All great ideas are simple, I told myself.

I made for a stand of dandelions on a grassy knoll behind the beach. It was here where the kids and I had a lot of fun blowing the fluffy heads off the stamens with one huge huff.

In my mind's eye I could visualise exactly the commercial I would make. It would open on a huge close-up of a single back-lit dandelion, the camera would pull back just enough to show a pair of luscious female lips as they blew on to the dandelion, scattering the tiny seeds into the air, leaving only the naked stamen and stem.

I would then fade to a second dandelion and repeat the pull-back but this time we would see a manicured female hand in frame holding a can of Gossamer poised beside the dandelion. The hand would then gently spray the dandelion and withdraw.

Without a cut the lips would enter right of frame and blow. This time not a single seed would detach itself from the Gossamered dandelion.

The visual analogy was perfect. Gossamer super soft was the spray that would hold gently, but firmly for today's soft, natural look.

All I needed was the shot of the beautiful girl wearing today's soft, natural look in the process of being Gossamered and I was practically holding the Logie for best commercial of the year.

REACTION

There I was, standing knee-deep in wet grass at first light, clad in Aunty Dolly's dressing gown and gum boots, spraying a dandelion with hairspray when I felt a large hand come to rest on my shoulder.

"Just what do you think you're doing?" asked a not very friendly voice. Almost before I had started to explain to the police sergeant, I realised how stupid it was all going to sound.

Come along, sir, he said, propelling me into the back of the paddy wagon. I was still desperately clutching half a dozen unsprayed dandelions.

They took me to the local station and booked me for indecent exposure and locked me up. They'd taken away the can of Gossamer but I insisted on keeping the dandelions. My whole future was locked up in those six frail weeds.

At 8 am they allowed me to make a phone call.

I hope it's to your bloody shrink, the desk sergeant said, handing me a piece of rope to tie Aunty Dolly's gown.

Sim Rubensohn usually got to work around 7.30 am. I called him at the agency. His reaction was typical.

"Have you got the idea?" he roared.

"Well, yes . . . not written down, but sort of," I ventured.

"So you had yourself arrested because you knew the idea was no bloody good and you thought you'd be safe in the Darlinghurst lock-up, well I've got a surprise for you, son," he screamed without once drawing breath.

"No, the idea is pretty good," I stammered. "I just want you to get me out of here so I can go home and shave, shower and get changed for this morning's meeting with Mr Graham."

Sim had me sprung and a car was sent around for me. But I wasn't taken home.

On Sim's instructions, the driver took me directly to the meeting with the trinity.

Bill Graham had an office roughly the size of a football field, covered in white carpet with pile so deep it buried my gum boots to the ankles.

Sim Rubensohn, no taller than the seated Graham, stood beside the desk.

The three of them, Sim, Graham and the divine ray of light waited silently for my presentation.

The trinity liked the idea. In fact Graham even tapped the edge of the table lightly with the flat of his hand when, having sprayed a dandelion, I blew upon it and not a single seed detached itself.

Very good, Bryce . . . very good, said Graham.

These creative types are dressing more strangely every day, Sim said disgustedly to Graham as he dismissed me with an upward flip of his hand.

Gossamer Super Soft was duly re-launched and it died in the marketplace. Only God knows why.

Thinking of a change? Call me first

There is a whole subculture in advertising known as the self-congratulation business.

To the writer, art director, typographer, film producer and production manager of modest talent, there are potentially about 28 awards to be won.

These are acquired to enhance the personal reputation of the recipient, to garnish the paspalum-infested foyer in order to impress incoming traffic and to clutter the boardroom for new business presentations.

When the mind wanders from the presentation, it is rewarded with an affirmation of competence.

I'm not against awards, in fact, I rather like them.

Anything that suggests people ought to try harder and that honours them when they do is a good idea.

Most clients seem to like awards. They are often the only confirmation they have that they have chosen their agency correctly, at least in the eyes of the award judges.

While awards for existing clients can be very important, the real pre-occupation in most agencies is the acquiring of new clients.

The advertising agency appetite for growth at all costs is insatiable.

Like the Mr World contest, size and muscle is everything. An agency may be doing meaningful work for its clients, but if it doesn't grow in leaps it's out of bounds.

Before acquisition and size take an agency into the big league where ego and profit fuel the juggernaut, the need for growth comes from a feeling of insecurity.

Agencies can be fired at the client's whim and for reasons that seldom have much to do with the quality of their work.

Typically, agencies are axed for reasons such as: politics (internal, State or federal); the appointment of a new marketing manager who comes equipped with a favourite old agency; as a scapegoat to cover up a poor internal performance; production costs that are thought to be too high; it's just time for a change; we need a more fashionable agency (hot shop); we want a multi-national agency;

we want an all-Australian agency; we want a bigger agency; we want a smaller agency; my wife does not like your last commercial; I don't feel important enough when my friends ask me the name of my agency.

SURVEY

It is even possible to be fired for poor creative work, though this is seldom given as a reason.

All these subjective reasons are lumped under the single heading referred to in the trade as "lack of service".

While there is generally a strong sense of loyalty by agencies to their clients, clients seldom reciprocate this feeling.

They believe themselves quite at liberty to terminate a long-established relationship, often on the whim of a new, untried and unproven marketing man anxious to be seen by his management to be doing something positive.

While there are no new statistics available, a survey done in the mid-70s showed that the average tenure of a client by an agency was 9.6 years.

Hardly a reason for paranoia among agency chiefs. That is, if the statistics still hold good in the mid-80s.

Nevertheless, the fear of account flight persists and the need to grow or perish is deeply ingrained in most advertising executives.

From the agency point of view, new account acquisition has become a catch-as-catch-can business.

If the client is capable of firing you, despite a strong and progressive advertising director (Lotto and OTC are recent examples), then you must find other ways to hold the account.

These other ways are legion and they become the stuff on which cheap novels and cocktail-circuit gossip is based.

Conversely, gaining new business is based on using any advantages, contacts, tactics and form that will give you an advantage over the other agencies in the pitch.

It's no different in any other competitive form of business.

If Phillip Adams, John Singleton, Geoff Wild or Joe Blow has a contact that will reduce the odds, they naturally play it for all it is worth.

That's some of the enterprise that the words "free enterprise" stand for.

The reasons for choosing a new agency are just as haphazard as the reasons for firing the old one.

You can be quite sure they are very seldom based on correct

assessment techniques or hard-nosed business analysis.

The agency guys who win your business will congratulate themselves for the probity of their creative and media recommendations, while knowing that the likelihood of these ever going to air or appearing in print is very remote.

They know that in reality the penny spun and came down heads. It was their day to win.

They got the mix (or the fix) right on the day. The agencies who came second, the euphemism used in advertising for losing, will heap scorn on the winner.

They will point out to anyone prepared to listen that the contest was rigged. The decision was largely made before the starter's gun went off and the whole thing was an expensive exercise in futility.

This is particularly true of accounts appointed from Canberra. Because there is some small truth in this, it too often becomes the whole truth.

To accept anything else is to suggest incompetence, which is seldom true either. The real truth is much more simple.

The client wasn't competent to make a perfectly judged decision. During the course of the five or six presentations, he or she or the evaluating committee saw the truth, the whole truth and the exclusive truth presented so many times that they were finally obliged to make a subjective decision based on anything other than naked advertising competence.

If a prospective client could honestly judge a submission based on proposed media plans and creative implementation for his product, then the best ideas combined with the best media planning would win. But it seldom happens that way.

The client sets out in search of the Holy Grail without even a rudimentary map. Agencies often attract new business because they are generally thought to be hot.

If you don't know the questions to ask, then hearsay is easier than preparing a brief.

There are agencies that have grown from scratch to skyscrapers never having done a speculative campaign. There are others, equally competent, that have had to mortgage the cement mixer because of the cost of unsuccessful new business pitches.

If the agencies that win business simply by showing their house reel and tap-dancing promises of things to come were demonstrably better than agencies that do expensive and detailed speculative work, then the former's clients would all be market leaders, blitzing the latter's whenever they competed in a market.

Which demonstrably isn't the case.

In an age of over-government, where the laws and regulations controlling a dog actually outweigh a cocker spaniel, there are no rules for a company to follow when it decides to change agencies.

In the meantime, if you're thinking of changing your agency, make sure you call me first.

Spend your way out of the recession

Having been through three or four recessions during the past 26 years, it isn't too hard to tell when things begin to tighten up.

Half-a-million dollars cut from a client's advertising budget means it's gone to pad the shortfall in last year's profit forecast.

When these cuts happen, as they are with advertising agencies throughout the land, ad men shake their heads woefully. They tell each other and any of their clients who are willing to listen, that when things are crook they should be maintaining, even increasing, their advertising expenditure.

Money spent when your competitors are not adding to the general cacophony is money doubled in value. But few clients heed this sound, though not entirely disinterested, advice.

When your neck is on the bottom line, the finer points of marketing theory are apt to go unpractised. The next general indicator of hard times ahead lies in the demise of seat-of-the-jeans creative solutions.

Impromptu creative solutions are viewed with a deepening suspicion. The pure creative essence of the heart is diluted with more matter from the head. Creative genius, yesterday urged to walk the wildest unknown way, is today told to stick to the painted line down the centre of the road.

Clients, who in good times were willing to take a punt on an idea way out in left field, now want every inch of the ground rationalised before they commit a cent. And of course, this demand for extreme justification is as dangerous as the previous creative indulgence.

A good creative idea is simply one which presents a familiar product or service to the customer in a fresh and desirable way.

Arthur Koestler called it the defeat of habit by originality. A good idea isn't taking a familiar product or service and making it metaphorically stand on its head, do prat falls and wear a painted ping-pong ball on its nose. Nor is it an idea which has been so thoroughly masticated by research that the meat and the juice is gone and only the gristle remains. There is simply no substitute for a good idea.

The truly good agencies are learning that good ideas are most often the result of good planners and good creative people working together. These days, clients need a lot of confidence to buy unexpurgated creativity. They have been sold too much that hasn't worked. Too much money has been spent on flashy execution of irrelevant ideas.

The downturn in the economy may just be the excuse they will use to put more accountability into creative solutions. Accountability is a funny word. It can mean anything you want it to mean.

In advertising it almost always seems to mean researching the pants off everything that moves. The client looking for a maximum effort from his agency should try to see it as the growing of a sound idea by using all the thinking available to him. Research used without creative co-operation seldom unearths a valuable idea.

The age-old conflict between the planners and the creative people needs to be faced squarely by a lot of Australian agencies. Too many agencies adopt one or the other stance, whereas the answer lies in using the unique talents of both.

While many agencies may give lip service to giving the client a blend of research-inspired creativity, too few actually practise the disciplines involved.

Many high profile agencies are filled with expensive and hard to keep creative talent who tend to be defensive and arrogant and, more often than not, outrank the people in the planning department.

The result is a nodding acquaintance with research where research is only allowed to confirm elements of the creative mix rather than seek to improve the fundamental idea.

In other words, the idea itself is never put to the test, it is simply tested for colour and tone. You can ask a respondent if he prefers the green or the red apple without having to ask him if he likes apples. Our television screens are filled with these passively researched, elaborately dressed up and hugely expensive non-ideas which are all thunder and no enlightening.

A good idea stands naked as a tree on a hill, it welcomes you to its shade after a long climb and succours you with its fruit.

The marketing storms that blow around it leave the idea unaffected, for its roots are deep and its branches strong. You can dress it with lights and bunting, prune it and shape it any way you wish but, underneath everything it still has its feet planted firmly in the ground.

Good planners are those people who test the soil, the climate, the direction of the wind, the degree of frost, the extremes of temperature, the immediate market for the fruit the tree brings forth and the nature of the pestilence which can affect it. If an idea tree doesn't match the prevailing conditions, ignoring the planners' advice is inviting disaster.

Yet this happens too often when arrogant or precocious creative people clutch a half-dead sapling to their bosom, demanding that it be accepted as the tree of life.

There are also those agencies that believe research is all-important, whereas in truth research cannot say that something is wrong—the creative ones and planners have to form a view based on research.

Research is simply market espionage.

Trials of training clients

Brendan picked up his beer and quaffed deeply before replacing it on the bar.

Wiping his foam-flecked mouth with the back of his hand, he said: "Has it ever occurred to you that our job isn't really making ads?

"Our real job is training know-from-nothing brand managers how to do their jobs so that they can succeed in order to be promoted.

"Whereupon they turn around and make our lives miserable while at the same time hiring new wimps as brand managers whom we are required to train and thus the whole catastrophe begins again."

"You're right," I said. "But has it occurred to you that our job allows you to dress like a garbo collector, grow your hair down to your shoulders, shave every third day and belch in meetings while at the same time it pays you more than most doctors and lawyers earn?

"All this munificence in return for being able to rearrange the 26 letters in the alphabet in a persuasive manner or pose a model or a watermelon in front of a camera.

"To do this we require no formal education or even a good telephone manner."

Brendan took another large gulp of the foaming amber.

"You don't appear to hold the advertising business in very high esteem, old mate," he said.

"On the contrary, I love it. Every night, last thing, I'm careful to close my eyes and say thank you for not having been born in Russia, where they have no advertising."

Brendan grew suddenly indignant. "The world needs advertising, it's what the free-enterprise system is all about, you're always going on about that."

"Brendan, be honest now, if you hadn't somehow stumbled on a job in advertising what else could you have done with your life? I mean, what other job needs some bloke who can scribble a bit or who can look through the lens of a camera and say to the photographer, 'Okay, shoot that'."

"Well, I could have been an artist and you could have been a writer."

I looked at him for a moment. "How many writers or artists do you know earn anything approaching a regular six-figure salary? When you're alone with yourself, do you honestly believe that you were potentially as good as Brett Whiteley and could have made it just as big with pictures hanging on people's walls instead of the ones on the packages in their freezer?"

"Well I will, one day I will," he replied emphatically.

"Brendan, you've been in this business for nearly 20 years.

"How many one-man shows have you put together just to keep your hand in? How many books have I written just to show that I have the skills it takes to be any sort of writer I want to be?

"With us it's always 'one day'. In the meantime, we're paying off a big house with a pool and we've got our eyes on a nice little weekender where one day we'll retire and write or paint and show the world who we really are."

NURSEMAID
"Well, what's wrong with that? One day we will."

I laughed. "I hope you're right."

"Peter Carey did and so did Ken Done, so why not you and I? That is if, deep down, that's what we really want."

I handed him another beer. He carefully wiped part of the carelessly poured head off with his forefinger.

"Well, mate," he said, "the prospect of playing nursemaid to the next generation of brand managers isn't all that enchanting.

"For the past 20 years I seem to be making and taking the same layout to the same client to watch him make the same ill-conceived dumb objections to well-wrought work.

"I must have trained a hundred top executives in my day but never once has one of them returned and said: 'Thanks, Brendan, old mate, thanks for making me look good at a time when you could have wrung my ears out like a sponge'."

He took a draught from the new glass.

"I might as well get it all off my chest.

"What about the weekends? The endless cloudless weekends where I've been in the agency putting together a campaign because some stupid client has procrastinated for weeks and has then demanded imperiously that the agency get him out of a jam by using yours and my weekends to make up for his inability to organise his corporate life?

"I reckon I lost a hundred weekends before my kids had reached the age of 10. How about you?"

"Same here," I said. "That's the service industry for you. But I reckon my local doctor has lost more calming hysterical housewives or panic-stricken husbands with indigestion they took to be angina at 2am.

"But I agree with you. I hate the times when you haven't got the facts and an unreasonable client is crucifying you and enjoying every moment. When the agency has goofed and you know you're skating on thin ice and any moment you're going to be up to your ears in ice blocks.

"I hate the client who demands crass and stupid solutions when you've evolved careful and effective ones, or slashes good copy and replaces it with gibberish. I hate the politics and the fear and the toadyism, the pretended friendships, lack of candour and the long, boring lunches.

"But for every managing director you train who doesn't say 'thank you', there is one who does. For every bully there are four kind and considerate people. For every cretin who regards the public as moronic there are three bright clients who treat them with respect. For every mutilator of words there are those clients who appreciate your ability to present or write meaningfully to their customers in a persuasive and polite way.

"You don't have to toady or play politics or to fear the consequences of being forthright and you can decline the lunches.

"Finally, every once in a while, it's probably good to find yourself up to your neck in freezing water because you dropped the ball.

"Brendan, old mate, I would have made a rotten doctor, I'm not sure I have the character or ability to write literature. I hate physical labour. I'm trained for nothing. I can't build a wall or hammer a nail in straight or sew or knit or fix a drain. All I can do reasonably is scribble and for this they pay me a lot more than William Shakespeare ever received."

I lifted my glass. "I think we ought to raise our glasses and wish our clients a Happy Christmas."

Brendan picked up his beer. "I think I'll drink on my own," he said in disgust.

Lovely little earners for the papers

The newspaper supplement is much loved by editors. It fills the paper with ads and makes nothing but money in return for printing a dozen re-hashed press releases and a couple of phoney in-depth articles about an industry or an earth-shaking event such as a new shopping centre opening.

For weeks newspaper reps are out in the concrete jungle flushing out clients who are urged to grab this once-in-a-lifetime chance to be seen and read by everyone who is in the least bit interested in their industry.

Most supplements are filled with small ads from advertisers who never normally advertise. You can almost hear the newspaper rep as he points out that chances like this come but once in a lifetime and to be left out in the cold when all your competitors will be in it with a grin is plain insanity.

However, I have long suspected that the only people who read trade supplements in the newspaper are the people who advertise in them. Apparently research backs this up. Trade supplements seldom enjoy even the readership of the normal day-to-day paper.

I called seven media directors of agencies large enough to have a spread of clients who might be attracted to the special reading opportunity a supplement is supposed to provide.

I asked them, "Do trade supplements work as a special opportunity medium?" and to answer with one of three words, yes, no and sometimes. I got six nos and one reluctant "very occasionally".

It would be interesting to know just how much extra revenue newspapers gain each year by conjuring up trade supplements that must be regarded as doubtful value to their advertising clients.

Another lovely little money spinner for the papers is the opening of a new shopping centre complex or the completion of a very large building.

This is where the developer or big retailer is approached and told that his building is a media opportunity not to be missed, worthy of a big spread or even a couple of pages, or, if he can get enough advertisers, all the pages he wants.

The technique here is not dissimilar to the trade supplement, though it cuts a little nearer to the bone. The newspaper reps scurry around gathering up anyone who had anything to do with the development or the building. Do they not feel that it may be appropriate to congratulate the developer on a successful completion?

Of course they do. They're not bloody idiots. They want the next contract to supply talking toilet seats or venetian blinds that either won't come down or fall on your head when you're not looking. So they all cough up in a flurry of congratulations.

No doubt it gives the developer a nice warm feeling with all those little ads saying thank you. I didn't have to call anyone to find out how well this sort of supplement goes down with the general public.

My advice is stay out of supplements of any sort unless your agency has very compelling reasons and an iron-clad readership guarantee to back the buy. If you haven't got an agency and you're looking down the barrel of a gun, act tough.

Nobody ever lost a contract because he didn't put an ad in a supplement. Send the contractor's secretary a bunch of roses and write on the note, "Enjoy the building I helped to build," signed, Mike's Pipefitters and Drainers.

It will cost you a fraction of the cost of a piece of abject sycophancy you were being blackmailed into putting in the paper and at least you stand a chance of being remembered.

Talking about flowers, on my first trip to America some 20 years ago I wanted to meet the head of Sears Roebuck. I wrote to him and received a polite letter back saying he'd love to see me but unfortunately his appointment book was full for the entire month and was (ha ha) particularly full on the days I happened to be in town.

So when I arrived in Chicago I bought a very large bunch of flowers and told the doorman of the Sears building that I had to deliver them to the lady who had signed the letter.

I was zooped up to heaven, where the king of American retailing lived. At the end of a marble runway, at a desk the size of a billiard table on which stood a vase of flowers in which Ali Baba could have set up home, sat a lady in her mid-fifties.

"Ma'm," I said. "I'm Bryce Courtenay from Australia. You wrote me a very nice letter saying I couldn't see your boss, so I brought you some flowers."

She removed her rimless glasses, looked at me for a few moments, gave a sigh and said: "That's so corny that if it had come from an American I'd be insulted."

She opened up her appointment book and wrote me in for four

o'clock that afternoon. We remained friends for the next 20 years.

Sometimes doing the obvious works best. Remember the advice we all got from teachers, parents, in fact everyone: if you don't know, ask someone. It's such an obvious piece of advice, yet we seldom take it.

Emotion: bottle it up, add fizz, then sell it

This week I found myself driving into the country to a posh resort to speak at a seminar conducted for the middle executives of a large, multinational company who had gathered from around the Pacific basin.

My subject, chosen for me by the course director, was called Emotion in Advertising.

This worried me somewhat, because it seemed to suggest that the kind you find in advertising wasn't the same as you found elsewhere, that advertising emotion was something you could learn and then pass on to young executives who would decide how much of it was required in the products for which they were responsible.

I started to think about emotion in advertising and multinational brands and to my alarm I discovered that in order for a multinational brand of anything to succeed in a market, it is, in a sense, required to export a common emotional response as well as a common ingredient and a common package.

I started with an obvious illustration of this which is, of course, Coca-Cola.

The same package, product and emotional appeal came out of New York and, with minor modifications which local agencies make much of, are dished up to the teenagers of just about every culture.

Coca-Cola is not a product you buy for its taste. Blindfold tests can't separate it from its main competitor or, for that matter, from a dozen different colas.

The thing that makes it unique is its emotional appeal.

However, Coca-Cola's emotional appeal is essentially teenage United States.

So, in effect, in order to succeed, Coca-Cola has to export a US teenager's emotional perspective to the rest of the world. Or so you would think.

But it doesn't work that way. What really happens is that Coca-Cola actually creates a Coca-Cola emotion.

That is, an emotion which is designed essentially for the consumption of soft drink and Coca-Cola in particular.

The Coca-Cola company then merchandises this emotion to the US teenager who, in effect, buys the packaged emotion and not the drink.

When you look at a Coca-Cola commercial there is lots of action and fun things happening to pretty people, but if you take it apart, it has almost nothing to do with how a teenager really feels or lives his or her life.

Or so it seems to me.

The teenagers I know have a reasonably full range of emotions. They agonise over their looks. They are often bored. They take their lives seriously and cry rather a lot and shout at their parents about three times a day.

They lock themselves in their room for hours on end, a few read books and most listen to a great deal of loud music. They have to work pretty hard and most, admittedly with great reluctance, do their share of chores around the house.

Sometimes they get to dance a bit, but mostly life is pretty complicated and Saturday night becomes a bit of a hassle to fill with really worthwhile fun.

In the real world, teenage girls prefer the company of girls and boys of boys and the coming together of the sexes is a sort of biological necessity which requires some part of the week to take place in the company of the opposite sex.

But Coca-Cola, aware of how unpredictable the teenage emotional climate can be, jumps over all this reality and invents a sort of ideal Saturday night and Sunday morning that goes on forever.

This Coca-Cola experience is not remotely like real life or even an approximate expression of teenage emotion.

It is an entirely manufactured commodity which works because it isn't reality. It isn't emotion at all.

It's not at all about emotionally charged teenage problems such as having pimples, or parents who are too strict, or places on their bodies that bulge out where they should go in, or suffering from painful shyness or boredom or sadness or big sisters or brothers who bully them, inferiority complexes, hair that won't stay in place or a boyfriend who gets drunk on a Saturday night and leaves them stranded or vomits in the back of dad's car.

These are the real teenage emotions. The Coca-Cola version is simply simulated lifestyle which looks good on the box for 60 seconds of cutting to the beat.

Now, providing the props are corrected in the commercial to suit the culture to which it is aimed, this ersatz emotion can be readily taken to the four corners of the globe. Teenagers from China to Peru can be reasonably expected to respond to Coca-Cola advertising.

Poor old Coca-Cola takes a terrible hiding from social critics. But really there's nothing else they can do.

They manufacture a simulated emotion and that's the business they're in. If they had to rely on the taste of the beverage they sell, it probably wouldn't rate in the Coca-Cola factory canteen in Atlanta, Georgia.

And so it occurred to me that this manufactured emotion was probably a good part of most successful multinational products.

While the products may be excellent and priced right, the really successful ones seem to have managed to manufacture a corporate emotional stance which is exportable.

A dreamtime emotion which has very little to do with real life.

And perhaps this is why we see so much idealised nonsense on the box.

Parents who are kind, considerate and loving, teenagers who smile and co-operate, children who are always clean and, if they're dirty, they're art-directed dirty and cute. We see young people who eat and drink stuff in large amounts, which any teenager with anything like the body of the model doing the consuming in the commercial knows would blow her to pieces in a couple of weeks.

All these images and the simulated emotions they express have been manufactured to suit the product. In essence, they are the product.

So it may just be possible that real emotion and real advertising have very little in common and that emotion in advertising could well be a manufactured commodity.

Something you could teach to middle-level executives, who could then order up the correct amounts of it to be included in their product.

I must say this depressed me somewhat.

Could it be that the business I had been in for 30-odd years could be reduced to a format as simple as this?

So I started to take the subject they'd given me for the seminar seriously and this is what I discovered.

I discovered that there are two ways to sell a product effectively.

The first is the Coca-Cola way, the way of most multinationals and all it takes is money.

If you have enough money, you can manufacture your own brand of emotional sell by doctoring all the conventional symbols which trigger emotions in human beings and presenting them in a bland, sterilised, homogenised version of their original human selves.

Mums who never lose their temper. Dads who spend all their spare time building kites for the kids. Teenagers who look beautiful and smile their way through life.

But then there is the other kind of advertising, the kind which understands real emotion.

The commercial which reaches out and touches the parts of you with which you can completely identify.

The lonely parts, sad parts, the quirky parts, the often funny parts, and the always imperfect human parts, advertising which understands what it feels like to be a teenager or a working mother trying to pay off the mortgage.

This isn't emotion in advertising at all, it is simple emotion. The real thing, not the Coca-Cola real thing. Now the nice thing about real emotion used in advertising is that it doesn't cost a lot of money.

Real emotion used in advertising doesn't smash through with the sheer weight of the payload.

It walks into your heart unannounced and it's always welcome.

Small can truly be beautiful in advertising

When times are tough companies turn to their advertising budget and pinch as much from it as they can to bolster profits so that head office doesn't give them a hard time.

To point out that this is a bit dumb doesn't help, so I won't.

But here's an idea for anyone who has slashed their budget by 50 per cent or more. Go small.

A good small ad can often work just as well as a dull big one and so I thought we might talk about how to make a small advertisement stand out in a newspaper or magazine.

Small space advertising works best when it makes only one strong point which is of importance to the reader. Clients tend to feel they haven't really had their money's worth until they've bored the socks off their potential customers with loads of corporate codswallop of no interest to the customers whatsoever.

Take, for instance, those pompous corporate ads that go on forever with hundreds of words of self-congratulations. Finance companies are good at these.

They spend a fortune on vainglorious nonsense which no customer in his or her right mind would pause for one moment to read.

But if, as some sort of special penance, you went through the copy carefully you might discover that buried in this double-page broad-sheet advertisement is a statement that the net return on investment for Boredom Inc, was 25 per cent after tax.

What if you took an advertisement in the next day's paper of, say, two columns and 16cm, and placed a polite little headline into its centre which said: "Last year, if you'd put your money with Boredom Inc, you would have earned 25 per cent"?

This tiny little ad with your name and phone number added will work a great deal harder than the previous day's double-page corporate wank.

So what I am trying to illustrate is that simplification, together with copy written in terms of customers' needs, will often be surprisingly well read even though your message appears in a comparatively tiny space.

So, if you want the same sort of advertising reach and frequency as you enjoyed before the recession, why not go half-size or even quarter-size?

The trick is to design your ads to accommodate the smaller format so that you won't lose impact.

The important thing to remember is that small ads need just as much skill in their design as large ones. However, very few small-space advertisements get the loving care they need to make them work.

This is probably because companies which most often use small ads are the ones which can't afford agencies or, if they have an agency, a misbegotten art director thinks it isn't worthwhile to put the work into a little advertisement.

So here are a few tips on how to design a small space to work gangbusters for you.

For a start, small ads can't take clutter. A small ad isn't everything you'd say in a big one, only reduced.

A small-space advertisement is the single big promise you want to make to your customer. Think hard about the one thing you want to say which is likely to influence your potential customers to buy your product.

Your one single big promise should be said in a sentence—even better if it can all be put in a headline without any body copy. Don't simply print your company or product slogan; say something meaningful, promise something.

Then add your logo, phone number or location. This gives you three elements. Your irresistible promise or proposition, your name and your location.

If you are obliged to show a picture of your product or service this becomes the fourth.

A good small ad should not have more than four elements.

Unless your advertisement is going into a glossy magazine and your product photographs well and reduces clearly, don't use a photograph: use an illustration.

To test whether it's going to work, reduce your illustration down to the size it will be in the ad and run it through the photostat machine six times, using the photostat from the machine each time as the one from which you copy.

The final copy you make will tell you, more or less, how your illustration will look in the newspaper.

If you simply must have a photograph in your advertisement, do the same thing with the photograph.

The next thing to remember is to allow your advertisement to breathe. Don't fill every centimetre of space you've bought with words: it may look like value to you, but it won't work.

Leave plenty of white space. Words work best when they are allowed to breathe a little.

The newspaper page you appear on will be filled with cluttered messy advertisements and by leaving lots of "air" around your copy, the reader's eye will go directly to it, even though it may be the smallest ad on the page.

Don't make up for the small size of your ad with a large logo type. Keep your logo to around half the size of the average postage stamp. Don't worry, it will be seen.

If you're smart and you insist your agency takes your small-space ad as seriously as they did your big ones and you do as I suggest, you may just find that you've halved your advertising budget but sacrificed nothing in terms of reach and frequency.

Finally, your advertising message may be more effective in a small space than it's ever been. Small, kept simple, can be beautiful.

CORPORATE COMMUNICATIONS

THE AUSTRALIAN MONDAY JUNE 2 1986

Good manners are money in the bank

How often do you hear the lament that today's kids have no manners?

The phone rings. "Hello?" you say pleasantly.

"Susie there?" rasps a pubescent voice.

"I beg your pardon," you say indignantly.

"Susie . . . can I speak to her?"

You summon your best now-look-here-young-man voice: "To whom do I have the pleasure of talking?"

"Ben," is the droll reply.

You are halfway through a lecture on good telephone manners when you hear the unmistakable click of the receiver being put down at the other end.

Just then your daughter Susan arrives breathless. "Is that Ben?" she asks excitedly.

"It was," you reply.

"Daddy, I hate you," she says, bursting into tears.

She is then forced to listen to your standard lecture on how today's youth are completely without couth.

A look in her eyes tells you that in any choice between the beligerent Ben and her father, the family umbilical cord would be stretched beyond the breaking point.

Switching telephones from domestic to business, I called a business associate recently.

His switchboard operator left me on the telephone for two minutes and then cut me off. When I phoned back she said, "He wasn't in. There was no point in you hanging on."

The comparison between telephone calls at home and telephone calls at work is valid.

Bad manners on the corporate phone, or even an overcasual attitude, may lead to perceptions of your business that can affect its progress.

If you call two suppliers, both of whom are capable of supplying the service you require, and the reception from the switchboard of one is casual and uncaring and from the other concerned and helpful, the result is a foregone conclusion.

It takes a lot of extra expertise to cancel the effects of a recalcitrant switchboard operator.

We all know that good switchboard operators are as rare as chooks' molars.

Do not blame this on today's youth; we ourselves are to blame. We pay a telephonist less than a junior secretary.

Stop thinking of the receptionist as the girl on the switch. Think of her as a member of your sales force, in some cases the only member.

Good corporate manners are money in the bank. Yet today's companies, like today's children, have largely forgotten their manners. The result is affecting not only their turnover but, I believe, the nation.

Sydney-based sales and marketing man Owen Denmeade, one of the few practical people motivators, gives a talk which he calls Catch Someone Doing Something Right Today.

His point is that most management people are unskilled in co-operation and spend most working hours catching people doing something wrong.

This negative environment tends, quite obviously, to foster the traditional alienation between workers and the boss.

Denmeade tells of a company where middle management attended his in-house course, which include his Catch Someone talk.

About 9.30am the next day he was passing through the production department just as the production manager was about to rip the arms off a late staff arrival. Catching sight of Denmeade and remembering the previous day's talk, the production manager swallowed hard and said: "Thommo, I want to thank you for not being as late today as you were yesterday."

Corporate manners are more important today than ever before. One human often has to interface (talk) with five computers, where a few years ago she or he would have been part of a 10-person department. She or he feels lonely, isolated and desperate for the social intercourse humans naturally crave.

Sending endless company memoranda around increases the sense of being in a corporate limbo. Good office manners means calling your people together once a week or more and talking with them about your plans. If they feel a part of a team they'll respond.

Good corporate manners always pay off. They mean remembering a birthday or a birth, a marriage or any other seemingly unimportant trivia which is the very fabric of most people's lives.

It's not public relations and it should not be left to the public relations department. It is the boss's job.

The legendary Bernard Jones, past chairman of Reckitt and Colman, came into J. Walter Thompson twice a year for a drink with the directors.

He would walk into my office and say: "Bryce, I want you to take me around the creative department and introduce me to everyone who works on my account. If I've met them before give me a brief on anything of importance that has happened to them since last I visited."

He would walk around using Christian names he had memorised only minutes previously. With consummate skill he would introduce a personal note of importance to the recipient as he thanked them for their contribution to his account.

The results were, of course, magic and so was the work done for Reckitt and Colman.

A country and a company runs well or runs down depending on whether the people in it care or are indifferent to its future.

Mass caring or mass indifference happens one person at a time. If more of these single units are negative than are positive then, obviously, the results will be more negative than positive. Optimistic people get things done, negative people sit on their hands.

I for one will try to do better. If Ben calls Susie tonight I promise I won't return his rudeness.

Words are all we've got to communicate

I have written about the business of writing in business before. It is an area of communication in which we need to improve vastly if we are to get Australia back on the rails.

Even more fundamental are the skills of communicating orally with each other and, in a business sense, with the world. There seems to be something in the Australian character which makes us deeply suspicious of anyone who can express himself well on paper or his feet. It is as though some sort of race memory persists, a genetic pattern we pass on in the womb which reminds us that we were once convicts and anyone who can express himself beyond a grunt must be viewed with suspicion.

Recently, a client asked me if I would sit in with him to interview the candidates for a senior job within his organisation. The position called for a young executive in his or her late 20s who could eventually assume the top spot in the company. The organisation is a service business with a large staff and one which deals extensively with the public.

The applicants were a varied lot, some excellent, others appalling. It astonishes me that when a job is advertised with a very specific outline of the credentials required it should attract applicants who don't have any of them.

Australians still believe that if the interviewer likes the cut of your jib, you're in. In fact, there may be some truth in this.

In the end, the choice came down to three possibles: an American, an Englishman and an Australian (which sounds like the beginning of a bad joke). Each had sound backgrounds and the tertiary qualifications required.

The American was, as you might suspect, articulate, personable, well groomed and organised. The English applicant, while a little plummy in the mouth and somewhat untidy, in the manner much loved by those who went to Oxbridge, was obviously intelligent and possessed a nice sense of humour. The Australian made it through to the finals by being quiet. He wasn't on my final list, but my client rated him very highly and so he'd made it to the finals.

I was curious. While he seemed a nice enough chap and had a good degree, his answers had been mostly monosyllabic and there had been frequent and awkward silences when he took longer than I believed he should have to respond to a question.

"That's just it," my client replied. "He's obviously a thinker!"

"Hey, wait on! What makes you think that? He said nothing which I recall for its perspicacity."

"Well, no . . . but nor did the others, but you'd ask him a question and he'd really think about it before he answered it. If he didn't know the answer, he said so. I like that in a man."

"Yes, but we asked them all the same questions, the Yank and the Pom answered them well, though sometimes differently. Both were impressive. Conversely, the Aussie was far from articulate, couldn't answer some of the questions and you could practically hear the cogs grinding as he tried to come to a decision to open his mouth."

"Ah, Bryce, you haven't done as many interviews as I have. Take it from me, the quiet bloke has got what this job takes."

Well, I recommended the American girl, the Pom second and mumble-face last. Mumbles got the job.

Is it possible that we Australians try to perpetuate our image of ourselves? That we take seriously the myth of a laconic, sun-bronzed, button-lipped, flinty-eyed, dead-honest, stereotype whom we describe as "the salt of the earth".

The clear implication being that we, too, are built in this mystical image. Do we really believe that the bloke who stands in the corner of the pub and says nothing all night but never misses his shout is a smart guy you can trust? That the university of hard knocks is the only way to judge a man's qualifications? Why are we suspicious of those people who are articulate and express themselves clearly?

Why do we look askance at anyone who has an opinion and knows how to put it across? Why is it that the average Australian business executive can't write a two-page letter that makes sense or a single paragraph that isn't awkward or over-complicated?

Is it that we've always been a nation of farmers and miners and you don't have to do much articulating in a paddock or down a hole?

PEASANTS IN BUSINESS SUITS

Above all, why do we actually admire our inability to communicate? From the Prime Minister down, we mumble and grunt and aahhh ourselves into punctuation. Our teenagers, particularly our young women, speak with a rising inflection at the end of every sentence, thereby turning it into a querulous statement, as though they totally under-value their opinions.

Is it that we really do believe we're second class? Peasants in business suits?

Words, in the final analysis, are all we've got. Everything begins with words. If we are to square up to a hostile world and take it on as a small, but dynamic, antipodean trading nation then we will need to begin with words.

When you learn to communicate something extraordinary begins to happen: you discover that the only way to communicate effectively is to know something about the person or country you hope to influence.

Before you know it, your mind starts to broaden, you begin to think of ways to reach them, serve them, influence them. Not in your terms, but in theirs.

Put into a nutshell, you begin to sell to them, you sell products, services and ideas. Next thing, you're competing effectively and, what's more, enjoying the process.

The sign of a first-rate nation is its ability with the written and spoken word, its pride in language.

The surest sign of a second rate one is its inability to articulate and its disregard for the written and spoken word. At the risk of being smart with words: It's never clever to be dumb.

The writers who really earn their money

I receive a dozen or more calls every week from people who want to be writers.

Some even get it right and say they want to be copywriters. Others, proud of their research, point out to me that, while they want to write copy, they perceive that people such as me, with a weekly column, a reputation as a copywriter and now a successful book, are essentially writers.

They cite Phillip Adams, Peter Carey, Leo Schofield, Paul Wilson, Geoff Pike, Bani McSpeddan and, in fact, any of the dozens of advertising men and women who have written beyond advertising.

They believe this training as a copywriter will essentially train them for (implied, never stated) the real business of writing, and that advertising will prove to be a highly paid, not to be taken too seriously, apprenticeship for the real thing. And, of course, they're quite wrong.

After 32 years in advertising I'm still unable to pick a potential copywriter from scratch. One thing I do know: very few of them actually start out by writing beautifully.

I used to think that, with someone who could write, it was only a matter of training. All they had to do was learn the advertising side and they would take the words they already had and cunningly fashion them into persuasive and effective advertising.

For a while I hired young poets and uni graduates who had done well in English. I even hired Bob Ellis, who at 20 already wrote beautifully. But I don't think I ever managed to turn any of these talented young writers into copywriters.

Then I tried hiring journalists, those who were writing interesting stuff in the papers. They arrived in advertising with a healthy disdain for the business.

It was the money that brought them in, along with the idea that it was going to be an easy way to make a quid, a one-hand-tied-behind-your-back sort of vocation which would allow them to get on with important things such as writing their book.

The only journalist I ever heard of who made the transition was the late Alex Dumas. The ones I tried, anyway, stayed good writers but made hopeless copywriters.

The funny thing is that just about every great copywriter I know is a good writer. But, with very few exceptions, they didn't start out that way. John Singleton started conventionally enough as a dispatch boy at J. Walter Thompson, Leo Schofield as a junior in the advertising department of Anthony Hordern's and Wayne Garland at Grace Bros.

However, Lionel Hunt, perhaps the greatest of them all, is said to have started as a labourer, and Ted Horton as a waiter. Mo started in his dad's ad agency and Joe started life as a jackeroo, while Derek Hansen worked in a bakery.

I'm not sure Phillip Adams counts because he started as everything all at once and has stayed that way.

While I'm told Peter Carey from his earlier days wanted to be a proper writer, he certainly started from scratch in the mail room of an advertising agency and ended up being one of the truly great advertising copywriters.

What's interesting about all of these people and a dozen more like them is that almost none had a tertiary education and some of them left school at the youngest permissible age.

Most of them probably didn't know a great deal about the rules of grammar and syntax, yet all of them write well and some of them brilliantly.

Now I know there are a great many critics of advertising who will agree that the rules of correct grammar are seldom, if ever, present in contemporary advertising and that the lack of formal, university-trained thinking is all too apparent.

THE MOST SERIOUS CRIME IN ADVERTISING IS TO HAVE A CUSTOMER KEEP HIS CASH IN HIS POCKET

But if you think about it, the advertising copywriter has perhaps intellectually the most difficult writing job of them all.

He or she must persuade people to read their copy and, having done so, to part with money for something they hadn't seriously contemplated buying in the first place.

They have to write words which change people's minds for long enough to make them take an action which is both time-consuming and expensive.

The journalist or the magazine writer simply has to keep the reader occupied for as long as the reader is willing to be informed or entertained.

The job is essentially passive. Simply by buying the paper or the magazine, this kind of writer's reader has agreed to co-operate. The advertising copywriter has to place his or her writing in an environment where it almost always plays second fiddle to the magazine or newspaper writer.

From this distinctly disadvantaged position the customer has to be flagged down and physically moved from a passive to an active state of mind.

Now the ability to do this with words and pictures on a page is not a talent to be sneered at. It takes a very special type of persuasive power and you don't get it by simply being good with words.

The truly great copywriters seem to have an ability to make people feel good about themselves.

Contrary to what the intellectuals tell you, people seldom buy things because they are depressed. They may follow peer group pressure, but that's more likely to be an upper than a downer, and they like to feel part of something and not left out.

The kind of advertising to which they respond is the kind that makes them feel they're part of something worthwhile.

Sure, there are a lot of symbols in there working their little socio-economic heads off, people aspiring to be what they ain't, keeping up with the neighbours, the aspirers and the achievers.

Advertising thrives on this sort of stuff and clients pay good money to market researchers to divide and categorise, refine and define. And some of it even works.

But the talent the great copywriters have is to simply have the ability to know what will touch people enough to have them dig into their pockets.

They don't need the purchase-factor analysis; they don't need the lifestyle and aspirational charts.

They simply think of why their mum behaves in a certain manner, why their dad stays at the pub longer than he should and why their little sister locks herself up in her room for hours with a friend and seems to do nothing but giggle.

They know how ordinary people feel and behave. They are in touch with the ordinary level.

Keeping the common touch may seem simple. But most of us spend most of our lives getting away from it. People who have the task or aspiration to write are often the worst offenders.

Proper writers strive to write literature—words and meanings that are seen to be beyond the comprehension of ordinary people. Books are often rated literature in direct ratio to the number of copies they didn't sell.

Despite the fact that just about every masterpiece in literature was a bestseller in its day, today we rate the seriousness of a writer by his inability to touch the common man.

Serious journalists talk and dream of serious analysis, beautifully researched and in-depth journalism that will win them the acclaim of their peers.

No magazines are rated backwards. The ones that sell only a few copies are good and the mass sellers are obviously trash. We talk about serious journalism, serious literature, serious broadcasting.

Now I think the thing that makes great copywriters is that you simply can't talk about serious advertising in the same idiom.

Serious advertising is judged by the common factor of sales and those who write well for it understand this. They understand that the most serious crime you can commit in advertising is to have your customer keep his or her money in their pocket.

So if you want to be a great copywriter, it's not the same thing as being a great writer or a great journalist.

The great copywriter always puts the reader (the customer) first. "How can I make the reader devour the words I write?" That's the question they ask.

Now if you're going to be a serious writer that's not the place to start. Start with that sort of assumption and you may end up writing a bestseller. Then where will you be?

How to make audiences sit up and listen

I thought I'd talk a little this week about talking. That is, the business of making a presentation.

Every year a great deal of valuable information is lost because people who have an expertise don't know how to put it across.

Seminars are filled with speakers who have worked very hard on their presentations but bore the pants off the audience when it comes to delivering it.

So let's start with a few don'ts.

Don't use an overhead projector unless you are going to draw on it. Sheets of typed paper placed endlessly on to one of these projectors are the best way I know to kill a talk stone dead.

In fact, as a general rule, don't put words up on a screen at all unless they are key words and absolutely essential to your talk.

USE SIMPLE LANGUAGE

If you must, put words up on a screen, make sure you never put more than a single short sentence up and try to put a picture up with them at the same time, a picture which illustrates the point you are making. Words are always better spoken than written anyway.

When you prepare your talk, do it like this: Take a sheet of A4 paper and cut it in half. On this half sheet type, in capital letters, double space only, as much information as your eye can take in two glances. Which is about 20 words.

Position these in the centre of the page. Place the next 20 words on a new page and so on.

Now, with a little practice, when you stand at a podium or rostrum you can appear to be delivering your talk with only a few notes, as though you know your subject intimately and are talking off the cuff.

When you've written a talk, shorten or alter any sentence which doesn't come naturally or sounds too convoluted.

When you've completed writing your talk, leave it overnight or a couple of days before coming back to it. Then come to it with a questioning pen.

Ask yourself: "How can I make this talk sharper? Can I make the sentences shorter? Am I repeating myself? What information in this talk do I think the audience may already know and what can I eliminate?"

Make the changes and read it aloud again, but this time slowly. Most talks are delivered too rapidly. Slowing down a little gives your voice more resonance and gives you more presence.

In any talk you're giving never try to impress the audience with how much you know. Instead, ask yourself who they are and what they need to know.

And tell them in simple language. Do not use jargon or technical language unless every member of the audience knows and uses the same jargon in their everyday life and there simply isn't a plain English equivalent of the word.

Never go over time. In fact, always write your talk five or 10 minutes short. The reason for this is simple—most seminars start late and there's always some boring idiot who hasn't timed his talk, which goes 20 minutes over time, and by the time it's your turn the audience is bored and restless.

If you tell them you're going to cut your talk by 10 minutes they'll sit up and listen to you.

Try to vary your inflections when you talk. A monotone sends people to sleep, so write the inflections on to the page.

Where you feel you need emphasis, underline the sentence, so when you get to it you raise your voice. When you feel you should go softer strike the sentence with a magic marker as a reminder to lower your voice. When you need to pause, write "pause" on to the page.

When you've written all these instructions down, then read your speech aloud to yourself and see how well they work.

Don't feel you have to know the talk backwards. Nor should you read it dozens of times. Read it aloud as you're working on it.

When you've written a paragraph, read it back aloud to yourself immediately and test it for tempo and ease of expression. Then read it again a few times, always aloud, and put it to rest.

When you get to the rostrum, remove the bulldog clip holding your talk and lay the pages out so they can be read, lifted and put to one side almost without looking at them. Never staple your talk at the corner—always keep the pages loose. If you're nervous, then just turning over the pages will calm you.

Again, if you're nervous, take a small sip of water before you start to speak. Do this in front of the audience; they will decide you're pretty cool and this will help you.

If you lose your place, take your time finding it again. What seems like light years to you won't even be noticed by your audience.

NUMBER EACH SLIDE

If you show slides then make sure they illustrate the precise point you're making, and if you're activating the slides yourself mark the position they come into your talk clearly on the page and colour the spot with a bright magic marker colour so you can see a slide is coming.

Don't keep slides up after you've made the point to which they relate. Use a blank between it and the next slide if the slide points you're making are spaced far apart in your talk.

When you've got all your slides in the right order and the right way up in the slide cassette, put the lid on and seal the slides with a small piece of scotch tape on either side so that, if the cassette drops, your slides don't fall out and scatter everywhere two minutes before you go on.

Number each slide with the number on the top right-hand corner facing you so if they do scatter they can quickly be replaced the correct way up.

Always arrive one speaker before you or more so you can get the feel of the room. Brief the operator yourself on the slides or video tape and give him or her a copy of your talk with all the slides and tape clearly marked.

If you can get to the microphone, test it and make sure it is the right height. If you're the first speaker on in the morning or afternoon test everything!

Now, when you've done all of this, take three deep breaths and walk up to the rostrum, smile and begin slowly, speaking clearly. The rest will take care of itself.

Oh, one final thing. If you're not a good joke teller don't try to tell a joke. The best talks follow the KISS method. Keep it simple, Simon.

Beware vulgar language of the quick buck

I think I'd like to talk this week about being polite.

Writing words that knock respectfully on the customer's door or wait quietly to make a point.

If you likened the average advertisement to a person, you'd most likely conclude that a great deal of advertising today was a bit of a yobbo—empty headed, loud, conceited and, above all, exceedingly ill-mannered.

The sort of person who jumps queues, pushes past old ladies to get on to the bus, talks and throws popcorn in the cinema and forces his way through crowded traffic by pressing the horn and a digit finger hoisted above the roof of the car pointing to God.

Too many clients believe that it's good to be intrusive, to shout and carry on and generally misbehave; that by paying for a page in a newspaper or time on the air they are entitled to come into our homes with a high-decibel verbal assault.

In this last decade of the 20th century the world is manufacturing more emptyheaded noise in one year than a person living in its first decade would have encountered in an entire lifetime.

The cacophony of commerce is resounding and becoming increasingly ineffective.

In my business anyway, I think a lot of the reason for this loud and empty banging of propositions and proposals has come about because we've forgotten how to write; how to say things in such a way that they go straight to the heart.

Good copywriting is about making people see old familiar things in a new and desirable way. And for the most part, the best way to do this is with words.

The Australian language was evolved in a tough environment blessed with few of the niceties.

Our first settlers, unlike their American counterparts who left England to the promise of a richer and freer existence, were dragged kicking and screaming from the dungeons of Newgate and the rotting hulks of Bristol to the living death of an isolated and barren land.

They had no time to pack a copy of whatever the equivalent

of Fowler's Correct Modern Usage was at the time.

Our language bore the marks of shackles and carried the inflictions of the shanty Irish.

From this unpromising beginning grew a language which was laconic and often recalcitrant, but which, used properly, had a blunt vigour and an ability to enchant.

Lawson and Paterson used it well. Malouf, Keneally, Carey and a dozen others writing in the Australian idiom still do.

But mostly, this rough, blunt, but meaningful and often exhilarating language has died out.

The traditions of saying something cleanly and well have lost out to words that fall joylessly on to the page like cold spaghetti.

Our propositions are filled with frantic declamatory words that soil white space—Now! Only once! Last chance! Bargain! Huge discounts! Three months to pay! Buy one, get one free! Hurry! Super sale!—and all the other vulgarisms of the quick buck.

Then there are the sycophantic, self-indulgent, matey words much loved by banks and governments and large insurance corporations that plop into headlines like fat grey grubs.

Corporate, concerned, integrity, endeavour, meaningful dialogue, share with consumer, rollover, annuity, superannuated, budget, mortgage and a host of other depersonalised sluggish, slow-moving words.

We use words in business and in everyday communication with one another as though they are unimportant people, which they are not.

They are very important people indeed; if you can get them on your side they will lift you on their wings and fly you to the moon.

Because television has become so big a part of our lives the advertising business will only tolerate words if we set them to music.

And sadly, mostly it doesn't matter anyway—the lyrics are silly moths flying into the light, attractive for their metre and not their meaning. The pander of bleat.

Print advertising, once the pride and joy of copywriters, the chance to flex a literary muscle or two and turn a dull product into a bright shining prospect for the buyer, now uses a bunch of stock words that have been so thoroughly sedated by corporate lawyers and which are so starved of nourishment that they have to lean drunkenly against one another for support and need lots of exclamation marks to prop them up.

Print is the playground of our language. It is where you go to run and kick and shove and sweat and shout and laugh and generally have a lot of fun.

To take the blood, sweat and tears of laughter out of the playground with a bunch of sterilised, homogenised and pandering words is to render them useless.

If you love words, try to use them well and treat them right, respect their functions, see their colour, feel their texture, understand their constraints, know their weakness and how to use their strengths, then it is difficult to write a bad advertisement.

If you insist on great writing for your ads, using words that move people to action—vital, alive words—you'll no longer need to shout and wave your arms and drop your corporate pants in public.

Your advertising will reach out and touch people politely and they will be happy to respond to you.

THE AUSTRALIAN FRIDAY NOVEMBER 2 1990

Stimulation always beats information

It's rather nice when you write a column and the information within it appears to be useful to readers.

Some weeks ago I wrote about making a presentation; some of the dos, and perhaps more importantly, some of the don'ts.

I've received quite a lot of mail and calls from people anxious to know more. So let's talk about making a talk that works. Here are a few small things which may prove to be helpful.

The most important thing to remember when you're making a speech or giving a talk is to understand the difference between information and stimulation.

We've all been brought up to believe that it's pointless getting up and saying nothing. Which is true, of course.

But most of us make the mistake of believing that a talk should be filled with information, whereas it is probably far more important that it be filled with inspiration.

Our society may be said to suffer from information overload.

I recently needed to know something about potatoes. This ought not to be too difficult, I thought; the potato is a pretty basic commodity. After all, how much is there to know?

The answer is a library full. The common potato, I want to inform you, is blighted with information overload.

Now, suppose I wanted to make a talk about the potato I would have two choices: information or stimulation.

MONOTONOUS VERBAL CHAIN

If I belonged to the school of information through oral communication I could put together a hundred carefully researched facts about the potato and confound the audience with my knowledge and bore the pants off them in the process.

In effect, I would show my audience that I knew more about potatoes than they wanted to know.

And this is what most people do when making a talk. In effect, they make lists and string each item on the list together into a monotonous verbal chain.

Now that's really not the idea. The idea is to make your audience want to know more about the potato.

Your job is to stimulate them to see the potato as an infinitely fascinating plant or vegetable with an entire social history that became one of the main reasons why Australia is the kind of place it is today.

In effect you should tell a story. And the story, as we well know, generally makes one of two points very well and leaves us stimulated.

So, here's how to begin. When you're talking on a topic, list all the things you know about that subject.

Next eliminate all the items on the list which you think the audience might also know about it.

If you're an expert you may find you're still left with a sizeable list.

So now eliminate any information which isn't important for your audience to know and which may be thought of as dull, plodding, pedantic material.

Keep on doing this until you are left with one or, at the most, two positively dynamic points.

These should meet the following three criteria: the information should not be known to your audience, it should be interesting and useful to them and it must stimulate them to respond, to take some sort of future action.

Put into simple terms, it should be excitingly new to the audience, and stimulate them to want to know more or to simply respond by passing your stimulation on to someone else.

But be careful about exciting information; one man's excitement is another man's head cold.

The dynamic point you decide to make should be exciting to your intended audience, not simply to you.

It is critical therefore to know and understand your audience.

The first question you ask when you're asked to give a talk is: who am I talking to?

The next question: what am I trying to say to them?

And the third is: how do I say this one thing in the most stimulating manner possible to get the most response?

By now you're over halfway to making an excellent talk.

The fact that you're a chronic stutterer, have a habit of snorting loudly between each sentence and have a bad facial tic is suddenly unimportant.

You have material which is dynamic, material designed to stimulate.

Information can be obtained from almost anywhere; anyone wanting to know about anything can, in a matter of days, sometimes hours, gather an enormous amount of hard data.

But stimulation is always in very short supply.

And when you talk you are more often in the stimulation than the critical information business.

An ounce of stimulation is often worth a ton of information, because it leaves your audience ready to think, to dig later for themselves, to find out and to experiment with their own minds.

We learn best when we willingly gather information by ourselves.

If the audience leaves your talk wanting to know more, in other words, they are stimulated to take action, then you have been successful.

If they leave with a pad full of hastily scribbled notes, which they will never again refer to or simply regurgitate for an examination, then you have failed.

Which brings me to one more aspect of making a talk, or more correctly, telling a story, a fascinating story which will inspire your listeners, and this is controlling the audience.

This can be difficult and often takes courage when the speakers before you have been dull and have allowed the audience to get out of hand, but here are a few pointers.

Your hands and your eyes are very important, so don't stand and clutch the podium, or what is known in the parlance of speech-making as giving a "white knuckle talk".

Stand back a little, if you wear glasses put them on and then stand back and take them off and appear to be looking at your audience, taking in the entire room, your eyes sweeping right to left. Eye command is critical.

Then step forward again and make your opening remarks verbatim.

Do not look at the piece of paper in front of you. You have about 30 seconds to get their attention, and you won't get it mumbling into your notes.

Pause long enough for the audience to become interested in the pause, maybe 10 seconds, which will feel like an eternity to you.

Then move your hands slightly forward over the podium and above your shoulders or head and make one fascinating opening point.

"Did you know that if it wasn't for the common potato, *Solanum tuberosum*, Australians would today average a height of four feet two inches, and be a race of dark-skinned, Spanish-speaking dwarfs?"

"Oh? How come?" is the mental response from the audience . . . you're on your way.

Then make it seem casual.

With this promise of things to come (don't over-promise—you must be able to deliver) you have captured the audience unto yourself; now it's up to you to stimulate them so that they may truly respond in a manner befitting all your many hours of preparation.

For the final rule is: work on your talk until it is perfect.

THE AUSTRALIAN BUSINESS ENVIRONMENT

THE AUSTRALIAN MONDAY DECEMBER 1 1986

FBT just a symptom of the disease

Flicking through this paper a week or so ago, I was assaulted by a full-page, government-sponsored advertisement which attempted to justify the fringe benefits tax.

I have always maintained that advertising anything, providing it is legal, is what a free society is all about. It is this fundamental right that frequently leads to the accusation that advertising is a whore.

You pay your money and, providing it isn't illegal, you get your sales story. And of course, in the process, advertising is one-eyed and has a tendency to be simplistic.

None of these things is necessarily bad. The free enterprise system (when it is allowed to work) allows us all to compete equally. The democratic system allows us to say what we believe in the hope that we can persuade others to see our point of view.

Political advertising, even if it is disguised as being in the public interest, is almost always scurrilous and usually does all the things consumer protection legislation specifically forbids anyone else to do.

What appalled me about the advertisement—which showed 53 people standing on top of each other with the top 11 people standing happily on the shoulders of the remainder—was that it singled out businessmen and women as the villains.

The headline next to the 11 people (all but two in business suits), who were standing triumphantly on top, read: "Of course, some people were perfectly happy with the old tax system".

The same tired and over-used implication was back again. The implication that business has been ripping off the rest of us, living off the fat of the land while the workers endured with blood, sweat and tears.

The workers were cunningly shown mostly as young people, with the obvious inference that business is to be blamed for their dilemma.

Well, nobody can say that isn't one-eyed, divisive, class-war rhetoric at its very best.

The only real tax redistribution which has taken place is not from the top 11 in the advertisement to the bottom forty-two on the pile, but from all of us to the Government. Government at all levels now absorbs 43 per cent of our gross domestic product.

May I remind you that in the life of this Government we have had five new taxes imposed on us. The onus for collecting the major portion of the monies from these taxes has fallen on business.

I am constantly appalled at the lack of understanding bureaucrats and politicians have of how business works. Common sense dictates that when a business is squeezed for profits, it is forced to do three basic things.

It has to increase its prices, cut its costs and reduce its investment. Put into everyday language this usually means the business charges its customers more, fires some of its employees and doesn't hire or train any youngsters or replace old equipment.

This leads to higher prices, more unemployment and inferior goods. The latest tax reforms promise the average pay packet will increase by $14.20 per week. What does the Government think the effect fringe benefit and other taxes imposed on business will have on that $14.20 a week?

As a small but practical example of how that $14.20 will be eroded, most small businesses will be forced to discontinue the 17.5 per cent holiday loading.

Put into weekly terms that is already $4.36 per week slashed from the $14.20. A nation can only spend what it makes. When it spends more than it makes it goes broke.

The Government has an income from taxes of $78 billion dollars. Last year it spent $91 billion. That's $13 billion, or 15 per cent, more than it makes. So it borrows money from other nations to make up the shortfall. By now the interest rate on the money we owe other nations is $10 billion.

That means every family in Australia owes Japan or France or Germany, etc, $15,000.

The problem isn't tax redistribution. The problem is mismanagement by government on a monumental scale.

In Japan, 7 per cent of the workforce is employed by the Government, while in Australia it is 26 per cent. Doesn't that suggest that your taxes and mine are not being redistributed, but are simply propping up a hugely inefficient, government infrastructure?

Taxing a dwindling resource in order to prop up a non-productive one is ultimately terminal. Now, Australian business is, by classic definition, a dwindling resource. It is costing more and more to produce less and less.

Labour costs have increased, productivity has decreased. Taxes have increased, plant and machinery investment has decreased. Competition has increased, research and training has decreased. The demand for quality has increased, quality control has decreased. The more successful you allow industry to become the more successful the workers become.

Redistribution of wealth is a direct result of wealth creation. You cannot hope to make a poor man rich by making a rich man poor. History has proved that people only work for personal incentives. A nation only has one task: that of wealth creation.

With enough money it can achieve all the social and spiritual niceties.

If you agree you'd prefer to be rich, then the government you appoint must be dedicated to the creation of more wealth, not the redistribution of existing resources. In effect, it must go into business against the rest of the world and make a profit.

To do this successfully it will need to reward its high achievers and its wealth creators disproportionately to the rest of us, who stand to benefit from their entrepreneurial skill. In taxing fringe benefits they withdraw this reward.

Why are we paying top price for a banana?

One lunch hour last week I stopped to purchase a banana from the fruit and vegie shop in the building where I work. Not wishing to look like a guts I selected a medium-sized banana from a pile and handed it to the dark-eyed lady behind the counter.

To my astonishment she put it on the scale, squinted and announced, "44". "I don't need to know how much it weighs, just how much it costs," I said a little testily. Her coal black eyes stared dispassionately into mine. "Forty-four cents," she repeated. I pocketed the warm 20¢ piece I was clutching and gave her a dollar. There goes another political milestone.

I have not quite adjusted to being part of a banana republic and now I discover that we're already past that point and can't afford bananas any more. I received a call from a business associate in London around seven that evening.

"What's the price of a single banana over there?" I asked him. There was a pause on the other end. "Well, I haven't bought any futures in bananas lately, to tell you the truth I haven't a clue. Wait on, my secretary is on a health kick, I'll ask her."

His answer came back, around 15p. which, translated into Australian banana republic money, is about 35¢. Now it seems to be that Jamaica is a lot further away from London than Sydney is from Coffs Harbour.

My final call in the great banana-republic banana price scandal was to Flemington markets in Sydney to check that we were in the banana season and that there haven't been any cyclones or tropical storms in the north which may have devastated the banana crop. They assured me that bananas were plentiful at this time of the year.

I'm prepared to bet, in London, New York, Amsterdam, Frankfurt, Paris, Rio, Moscow and any of the Peter Stuyvesant capitals around the world, that 44¢ in Sydney is the top price for a medium-sized banana this week.

Last week Keating fiscally beat up the States with the excuse that the world had let us down, giving him the right to let the States down. Take this argument to its logical conclusion and it leads to the price of bananas.

Because this Government, and to be fair the one before it and the one before it, spent more than the country earned and because a lot of other countries produced more than they could sell, we find that the things we traditionally sell to the world are being undercut in price by these other countries selling their surplus.

This means the money we make from selling our stuff, such as wheat and meat, isn't coming in which, in turn, means we can't pay those nations to whom we owe money.

So Mr Hawke and Mr Keating create bigger taxes for business and manufacturing so that they can get their money this way.

Everyone then adds to the cost of the goods they make or grow so that they can pay the bigger taxes. Before you can say scumbag, Keating's favourite word, a medium-sized banana costs 44¢ and the rapidly rising cost of all the little, ordinary things people need to live on, none of which appear to depend on the outside world, are what is driving the average family bananas.

I get quite a lot of comment on the hoof about my column being, well, not really about marketing. People say, "Liked this week's but what's it got to do with marketing?"

What they're really saying is that marketing should be all about facts and statistics, trends and prices, demographics, research and advertising, the whole dreary litany of business complication.

In fact, marketing products, locally or for export, is about quite ordinary things like bananas, about the cost of growing bananas, making people want to eat more bananas, the cost of earning a reputation for the quality of your brand of bananas and the skill in growing bananas efficiently so that you can price your bananas competitively against the other bloke's bananas. And then people will buy yours, not simply because they are competitively priced, but because they're bigger, firmer, more yellow with no little, brown spots on them.

Marketing, when it's all boiled down, is about going shopping and coming home with a whole heap of things you need to keep body and soul together for the same quality and price as you generally expect to pay.

When a government takes more and more of the banana manufacturers' money in taxes and passes more and more legislation, making it harder and harder to turn out your basic banana, then inevitably the price of one medium-sized banana gets to be 44¢.

So there it is again, the price of bananas and everything else is as a direct result of a government which is in the process of taking as much as it can from the people who make things in order to use the money for a whole heap of social reforms and minority programs we didn't vote for.

If this government were a good marketer it would be forced to make one very large decision—to pay our overseas debt. To do this it needs to make our goods more competitive. That is, cheaper and better than the countries with which we compete.

Instead, by taxing business and manufacturing at the highest level in history they have raised our costs, compromised our quality, increased our overseas debts and inflated our cost of living.

In marketing terms, they've plainly gone bananas.

It's scrape, bump and thump from here, son

Last week, my 19-year-old son began his own business. He had thought about it quite a bit and decided he wasn't the type to work for someone else.

What can you say? You go through all the arguments about gaining experience and all the usual wet-behind-the-ears stuff. But secretly you know that scrape, bump and thump is really the best way to learn how to make a quid.

I waited until I was 40 before breaking away from the security of a guaranteed pay packet. The only real regret I have is not to have begun 20 years earlier.

Anyway, the youngest of three was polite enough to ask me if I had one or two hints which might be useful to him. This is the same bloke who, when he was seven, would ask me a question and, while I was in the process of answering it, his hand would go up. What? I'd ask. That's already more than I want to know, he'd say.

He's gone into desk-top publishing and the first thing he published was a car window sticker that contained his corporate slogan: Hire a teenager today, while they still know everything. This was followed by his name, what he does and his 'phone number.

So we sat down and I cleared my throat. He interjected and said he'd already been to see Gareth Powell, Australia's desktop publishing guru. Mr Powell told him all he needed to know about DTP, so would I confine my remarks to money as he had an urgent need to acquire a Ferrari before he was 25 and was too old to enjoy it.

I had to confess to him that I hadn't been remarkably successful in this area but that I could tell him a few things I'd learned in 15 years of business. His eyes glazed over but his expensive education saw him through and he remained seated.

The first lesson is very simple. The bank will only give you money when you don't need it. Without a good credit rating or a house to mortgage, money from a bank for starting a business is generally not forthcoming. Banks take very few risks and even fewer on 19 year olds.

"How do I establish a good credit rating at my age?" he asked. Not easy, but you can take the advice Victor Kiam, the multi-squillionaire who owns the Remington shaver company, gave to a young bloke who asked him the same question. The quicker you get a friendly bank on side the better, so here's what you do.

Go into the bank and ask for a personal loan, I'll act as your guarantor, say $2000. But only borrow it for six months. Then take the money and go down to a building society and open an account with the best rate of interest you can get over three months. The shortfall, or the money you lose between what the bank interest is and the building society pays, won't be very much.

Then after three months take it out and pay it back to the bank. Making sure you see the manager and tell him, while it was a personal loan, it was for your business which is doing well and so you can pay the loan back early.

Wait another three months, borrow an amount again, do the same thing. Wait four months, ask to see the bank manager, show him how your business is expanding and why you need a loan for new equipment etc. The bank manager will think he's discovered the next Alan Bond and it's all over bar crossing the cheques.

SERVICE

Lesson two is never to anticipate business. Forward projections are what you give bank managers, but don't make the mistake of believing them yourself. It takes between three and six years for a business, any business, to create a customer rhythm independent of force feeding.

Lesson three is: a client on the books is worth a multiple of five. That is, five new clients. Service is everything. People hate changing arrangements and once a satisfactory one is established, provided it delivers, they will continue to give you work. Smother your clients with love. Call every client every Monday and ask them how you can help. You'll be amazed at the amount of business this once-a-week 'phone call generates.

Lesson four is about paying your accounts. If you are starting a new business with very little capital you're going to need credit. There are going to be times when you're caught short. Always negotiate the terms of credit before you begin, then stick to your side of the bargain. Go to your supplier, explain to them that you need 60 days, then pay on the 59th day.

In my experience very few suppliers will knock you back after you've kept your word. But do not think this means you have a permanent 60-day facility. If you're only half smart you'll see that this particular supplier is paid on his own terms the next time. That way you can go back when you need to and ask for an extension of credit without having to mumble.

Remember, always, to stay loyal to the supplier who helped when you needed it.

Lesson five is obvious, though one which is most often neglected. Understand quite clearly that the world doesn't owe you a living. Work harder than your competitors with the bit from the neck up.

It's your head that makes money, not your hands. Hands can be hired cheaply, hired heads are expensive, so before you hire one use the one you've been given free to its maximum potential— you'll be surprised how good it is.

Lesson six is perhaps the hardest of all. Maintain your enthusiasm to your staff and your clients. Everyone likes to share in a dream and people will work their butts off if you give them personal goals and inspiration.

Lesson seven comes out of lesson six and is the first rule of management whether yours is a two- or 2000-person company: before you make a decision, consult with the people who will be affected by that decision and take their point of view into account as part of the process. Good luck, son.

THE AUSTRALIAN MONDAY OCTOBER 17 1988

Our cult of failure is the biggest obstacle to success

How often do you see a product that seems so simple and useful you can't understand why it wasn't invented before?

Like those little pieces of yellow paper you can stick to your notes with additional comments.

Or the bloke who thought of tying a piece of string to the ear pieces of glasses so you can carry them around your neck.

There are marketing opportunities everywhere for those who are prepared to think a little harder.

Within hours of the Soviet Cosmos satellite coming apart in space with bits from it supposedly heading for the United States, a small insurance company in California was selling a policy for $10 covering the recipient for a million dollars should a piece of satellite harm them on re-entry.

It's all a matter of initiative and imagination.

A friend of mine, now retired from the British Department of Customs and Excise, tells this story of how he had his eye on two dockside workers who, he was sure, were smuggling stolen goods from the dockyards.

They had the job of cleaning out ship's hulls and they would take their barrowloads of muck out of the gates all day long which, of course, provided them with the ideal opportunity to get things out.

My mate, the Customs officer, would diligently examine every wheelbarrow load of dirt as it passed through the gates but found nothing.

At the end of the week when the job was done, he was forced to conclude that the two dockside workers were innocent.

They had made at least 100 trips through the gates and he had not discovered a thing.

Some weeks later, he met one of the dockers in a pub and the man immediately offered to buy him a drink.

After they had relaxed over a pint or two, my friend admitted that he had been wrong about them and started to apologise for having given them a hard time. The dockside worker stopped him.

"You was right, mate," he said.

"Impossible," replied my friend. "I went through the contents of every wheelbarrow with a fine tooth comb."

"We was, you know," the docker insisted.

The Customs officer was consumed by curiosity.

"If you tell me what it was you were smuggling out of the dockyard, I promise not to report you. I just have to know," he pleaded.

"Wheelbarrows," the docker replied. "We was nicking wheelbarrows."

I guess it's all a matter of taking the initiative.

I have the theory that winning and losing are habits, that we don't win because we are lucky or lose because we are not.

We win or lose because we program ourselves to win or lose.

CHANCE

People who show great initiative seem to gather a sort of winning momentum around them.

One action sparks off another until opportunities to make a buck appear everywhere.

They simply get good at seeing opportunities around them.

Action seems to beget further action and they can't help succeeding. Life is one big, golden opportunity.

It's not that they work a lot harder than you or me but that they have a trained eye for the big chance.

Here are the characteristics I have found most lucky people possess.

The first is energy.

They have lots of momentum. They make the calls, do their homework, follow up leads, make contacts, write letters, keep promises, give service and, above all, show initiative.

I have never seen a winner yet who was not constantly on the lookout for opportunities to improve in performance or exploit a situation.

I have never seen a winner who whinges about his working conditions, boss, systems, or the product he makes or sells.

Winners are, by nature, enthusiastic about life, ready to find a way around obstacles.

One of the biggest obstacles we have as a people is that we are deeply suspicious of personal initiative. If a mate breaks away from the pack and succeeds, we call him a tall poppy and we try very hard to bring him or her undone.

We make a cult of failure, out of being ordinary. Even our schools teach that the competitive instinct is not wholesome and that the whole is more important than the sum of its parts.

Collectives, on the surface capable of so much, have been proved not to work. The whole is seldom more important than the individual parts. We have to start breeding winners for the future.

We have to start rewarding initiatives rather than taxing them. We cannot hope to succeed as a nation if we do not create incentives to win, if we do not make it worthwhile for the individual to dream dreams and set goals.

The most important product a country has is not the crops it grows, the minerals it mines, or the things it makes in its factories; it is the people it breeds.

Most humans have roughly the same equipment when they're born.

How you train this raw humanity will largely determine what sort of a nation you become.

If we are losing our initiative as a nation, we have only ourselves to blame because, of all the countries in the world, our kids, in the material sense, get about the best start there is.

Why is it that with such splendid clay, we fashion a country that is finding it increasingly difficult to compete with other nations?

Surely it must have something to do with discouraging personal initiatives and therefore nipping our fair share of winners in the bud?

THE AUSTRALIAN FRIDAY SEPTEMBER 27 1991

Entrepreneurs prove power corrupts

I have always been fascinated by the effect of power on people.

I don't mean leadership, which is an entirely different thing, though good leaders earn power and also exercise it.

What I am referring to is that mixture of autocratic action and special circumstance which bestows someone with the right to do things and behave in a way which would simply not be tolerated in anyone else.

It's a new kind of power and hopefully it's almost had its day, for it differs entirely from the institutional types of power we've all grown up with and basically understand.

The most typical example of institutional power, for instance, is someone like the Governor-General or Prince Charles.

He may in fact be a born leader or a rotten one, but we are never going to be allowed to find out.

The power which has been vested in him is institutionalised and is going to ensure that people do as he bids without his having to think too much about how to seek their co-operation.

Power lies in the position he holds rather than in the man himself.

It used to work in business much the same way.

The chairman or managing director was respected and obeyed for his position and not because he was particularly good at his job.

He had a title and he was referred to as Sir or Mr, and people were actually a little scared of him, not because he threatened them or was in a position to fire them, but simply for what he was: the big boss.

The big boss was from a different class, the royalty of the factory or business.

Thank God, very little of this sort of mindless touching the forelock exists these days on the job; business, for the most part, is about hard work which leads to profits, and management is expected to perform at every level.

But until recently there was still one section of the business community which continued to be treated with all the trappings of power.

We coined the word entrepreneurs to describe them.

They were not managing directors who came to work in a Merc and stayed all day and sometimes worked until late at night.

These new men of power number hundreds, big and small.

People at every level in society seemed happy to give them unquestioning power, even though, in some cases, by every definition, they were the most unlikely people to be trusted with it.

Many had never demonstrated a personal history of integrity and intellect, or any real ability or training; many of them couldn't even read a set of books properly.

What's more in the main, they showed no, or very few, natural leadership skills. Some instead used other people's money and treated their donors' money as though it was their own, spending it unabashedly to enhance their personal reputations and to lead a lifestyle of extraordinary extravagance and vulgarity.

Nevertheless, they were able to exercise real power with prime ministers, premiers, politicians, churchmen, judges, policemen, small investors and, of course, bankers. Especially bankers.

The more they raped business and stripped assets and borrowed against assets they didn't have, except on paper, the more they were admired and allowed to run riot.

Nobody questioned their power, though many of us admired it and responded mindlessly to it with our cash offerings.

Part of the answer must lie in the fact that people trusted their savings with them and, for a while, anyway, this turned out to be very profitable.

But it doesn't explain the millions of people who weren't motivated by pure greed and who didn't invest a cent in any of their enterprises and yet seemed prepared to allow these men to behave in a bizarre and unseemly manner.

LARRIKIN IN US SECRETLY ADMIRED THEIR ABILITY TO GET AWAY WITH IT

Collectively, we seemed rather proud of them. It was as though we suspected that many of them were pirates, robbing the poor to pay the rich, but the larrikin in us secretly admired them for their ability to get away with it.

After all, Alan Bond was one of them and wasn't he the guy who gave us one of our proudest moments when we watched the last race in the America's Cup and we knew that after a hundred years or so we'd made those bastards in New York unscrew it and hand it over to a kangaroo who wore red boxing gloves?

We never asked him where he got the money to build the boat. It never occurred to us that we were watching a race designed for the gratification of the world's richest and most self-indulgent men, who were prepared to spend as much as it took to win a race, which was the almost perfect parody of a sporting event.

The America's Cup was no contest of muscle and brains and sinew, of beautifully trained athletes, but simply one of money.

Our rich men against their rich men, our expensive sails and winches against theirs.

We loved our rich men and we willingly allowed them to purloin our money to show us how much they loved Australia.

And when Bondy won the Cup for Australia our Prime Minister put on a funny jacket and allowed people to squirt cheap champagne all over him and to take a sickie from work to celebrate.

I hasten to add that I was no wiser at the time than you were; like you, I didn't see how ridiculous this all was.

Instead, I joined in with everyone to applaud the self-indulgence of the very rich; just like everyone I gave them their power by approbation.

But the power these men had they hadn't earned. Nor did they have permanent institutions such as royalty or government to cover for them or to back them when they finally failed.

In the long run they needed real ability to match the power and now it seems this is what so many of them so utterly lacked.

The banks which scooped up millions of dollars and threw it willy-nilly in armloads at these entrepreneurs begging them to help themselves withdrew the hand of friendship.

Rugby success shows worth of team spirit

Do you recall the Cameroons in the Soccer World Cup? The never-before-heard-ofs who shook the soccer world and scared the pants off the world's most powerful soccer nations?

Now again, in the Rugby World Cup, tiny Western Samoa has taken on Wales, Australia and Argentina and demolished two of these big-reputation sides and, while narrowly losing to Australia, managed to scare the living whatsits out of us in the process.

When you look at the components required to excel in anything, you come up with a list that goes something like this.

You must have a good product priced right, sound knowledge, high skills, the ability to work hard, some imagination and even originality in promotion, the ability to adapt to changing conditions and lots of determination. In business these are the determinants of success in the marketplace.

But if you are a small nation, these essentials are not enough; they're fine for Germany, the United States, Japan, France and other big nations where enormous money, capacity and power push their enterprise, but they are almost worthless in a small nation trying to compete.

The point is that they are all self-cancelling; the big, powerful nations also do all of these things, or enough of them to make it very difficult for us to compete with them.

It is not so different from a rugby or a soccer team; nobody goes to the World Cup if they are not thoroughly prepared.

The extra ingredient needed by a small nation or a small business which faces powerful competition, while being ephemeral and very old-fashioned, is nevertheless the only element apart from total originality that will take the bigger nations on at their own game. It is, of course, spirit.

Now spirit is an interesting thing. It isn't something you learn at a business school and it isn't something you can buy; it is something you have to give yourself.

It is the collective giving of an enterprise or a country that creates spirit. That means it must be made up of individuals, it must come from each one of us as a part of our personal belief system.

There was a series run on SBS which told the story of post-war Japan. How a country completely destroyed came back to win the world.

The thing that struck me most about this particular and often-told miracle was how it went right down to the grass roots. Factory workers spoke of working, eating and sleeping on the premises and of being allowed one day off a month—most chose to work on their day off.

The point is that everyone was involved, everyone was prepared to give of their individual spirit and, of course, the sum total of this spirit became unbeatable.

Now it's easy to say that they had nowhere to go but up, that they were forced to work as they did.

BACKS TO THE WALL

It wasn't only the work, it was the spirit they took to their work which made the essential difference. It was the same spirit the tiny Cameroons and the practically insignificant Western Samoans have contained in their soccer and rugby teams.

It is time we looked upon ourselves as being under siege and with our backs to the wall. More than one economist has said that Australia has nowhere to go but down. Now I don't accept that.

You can show me all the forecasts and all the charts in the world, but if we have the spirit to win then we are going to give the rest of the world a severe nudge. We're going to be contenders. What chance do you think the world gave Japan after Hiroshima?

This all sounds pretty gung-ho; all we have to do is rally the boys and girls and off we go. We all know it isn't as simple as that.

But as the Chinese proverb says, every journey of a thousand miles begins with one step. The first step for all of us is to start respecting each other again.

We seem to have divided ourselves into factions and every faction believes the fault lies with the other. We have to start being a national team, to believe that each of us must and can contribute to getting Australia back on its feet.

Let's begin with government. We have a two-party system based on what we fondly call the Westminster System. What the Westminster System calls for is lively and honest debate on the affairs of the State.

The resultant decision should lead to the best possible outcome for the country. But, of course, no such thing happens.

We vote a party into power and they in turn select a handful of ministers who sit in the party room and decide what to do. Often our entire future is decided by two or three by no means highly qualified politicians.

The issue is then debated in Parliament along party lines and accepted. Woe betide any member of the party if he or she happens to disagree. In fact, crossing the floor, as it's called, is practically unheard of and is regarded as the worst possible crime a politician can commit.

What this means is that the politicians must put the party before his or her country or conscience and so the man or woman you selected has little or no say in what happens.

Parliamentary debate becomes a complete sham and leaves the nation, in effect, with a one-party system led by a virtual dictator and a few close aides. The hundreds of people we elected, on either side, to run things, to fight for our views, are completely impotent and spend their parliamentary days sitting on their hands.

Can you imagine what this does to the spirit of our Parliament? Can you guess what it does to the very soul of the backbencher? Most importantly, can you imagine how it affects the spirit of the nation?

If we are going to win out in the big, wide world we must do so with a spirited Parliament that's open to the kind of debate that contains things.

We must believe we can win at the things we believe in. We must believe that each politician, each Australian, can make some sort of valuable contribution to the Australian team.

In all endeavours, it's nice to have leadership what works to bring us together collectively, but it may just be that we have to lead ourselves, that each one of us has to be the minder of our own spirit and select ourselves as members of a national team that cares.

We must become fanatics about being the best; the best trained, the best at all of the things it takes just to get to the starting line. But when we've done this, we have to be possessed by our own spirit.

We have to start believing in ourselves, believing that we can make a difference, that each one of us can add to the spirit of Australian enterprise in the competitive world.

What is defeating us is our own profound sense of defeat, our own distrust of each other, the fact that we believe it is someone else's responsibility to take charge and to run our lives.

SENSE OF DEFEAT

In fact, each of us is responsible for himself and also for his brother and sister Australian. We are a team, the Australian team. That's a fact. The task is to become a great team, capable of beating the biggest and the best. We can't do that without spirit, enormous individual and collective spirit.

Our task is to go into the world with the sort of skills and spirit the Cameroons and Western Samoa, two tiny island nation Jacks, who were and are determined to be giant killers, brought with them to the World Cup.

Now some smart arse is bound to say: "But the Cameroons didn't win the World Cup!" Well, I personally think they won a great deal more than a single trophy.

As for the Western Samoans? It's not over yet.

Being taken seriously is not a bad place to start in the competitive world of trading nations.

But if you won't take yourself seriously, if you won't take personal responsibility for yourself as well as the other team members, how then will we begin to build Australia into a small-nation team with great ability and spirit of the kind it takes to be a giant killer?

THE AUSTRALIAN FRIDAY NOVEMBER 1 1991

A dumb way to become a clever country

I guess what I'm going to talk about this week has been heard often enough before.

The small company or inventor who comes up with a breakthrough in science or engineering or whatever.

The attempt to keep it in Australia for Australians, hoping that it will eventually earn export dollars for a small country with brains.

From time to time, the papers pick up such a story and we all tut-tut and talk about how the government should step in and help, then the story disappears into the bottomless black hole where tired old media stories go.

Several years later we buy the product and see that it is made in another country, our original idea having come back to us at great profit to someone else.

It's a tedious story and you must forgive me for repeating it, but each time we let an opportunity to be clever and unique slip out of our hands and go to some other nation to be developed and marketed, we get just a little more dumb.

Instead of the clever country, we increasingly become the incredibly stupid country.

Now, it is easy to blame government but really they are not to blame, they don't know how to make money, only how to use it.

They don't know how to create anything new, but simply how to recycle moribund and reactionary ideas.

One of the reasons governments loved the now disgraced entrepreneurs, was that they didn't make anything.

They simply bought and sold and miraculously the money seemed to roll in.

Nobody appeared to be taking any risks and certainly nobody was producing any original ideas to spoil things. It was political heaven.

The point is, that risk capital is the very essence of doing business.

The dinner doesn't grow on the plate ready cooked; considerable time and management and risk goes into creating the steak and beans, potatoes and broccoli, together with the power to transport and cook them.

Unless we take risk we can't grow. We can't grow as a nation and we'll never become a rich and competitive people.

When Alan Bond bought Mr Packer's television station for about five times more than it was worth and then Mr Packer bought it back from Bond for about half what it was worth, in fact nothing happened to help anyone but Mr Packer.

NOBODY APPEARED TO BE TAKING ANY RISKS AND NOBODY WAS PRODUCING ANY ORIGINAL IDEAS

This kind of business requires a large money resource and absolutely no imagination or real risk-taking.

The one man made a stupid decision and the other a smart one, but nothing worthwhile was made in the process and none of it made Australia more valuable, stronger or more competitive against the outside world.

Australian business is constantly doing this; we live off the misfortunes or stupidity of each other.

We do not make things, we simply recycle old ideas and call it business momentum.

No country ever survived in the end by trading with itself.

If we hope to succeed as anything but a grower of commodities or digger-up of minerals, then we must start thinking of useful things that do not already exist and risk developing them for export to other nations.

If we win, we make a huge contribution to our own and our nation's welfare; if we lose, well, actually, we are not a lot worse off and in the process we will have learned something useful as we venture out into the world market.

This week, the phone rang and a voice introduced himself as coming from one of the more prominent national research organisations in this country.

He stated that he and his colleagues had been working on evolutionary biology and he thought that I might be able to help.

I gulped. "What is evolutionary biology?" I asked.

"Well, putting it in the most simplistic terms, we have cause to believe that the theory of evolution as it is taught is somewhat off the mark.

"We have, in a sense, been working on a new one or perhaps more precisely, a greatly modified one and we think we've made several important breakthroughs with significant commercial potential."

"Oh, yeah." I didn't recognise the voice, but several of my friends are pretty good mimics and not above this sort of highbrow prank.

"No please, Mr Courtenay, give me a moment to explain."

"Who the hell is this?" I asked. I was busy and wanted neither a friendly prankster nor a nut in my life for the moment. I do get some pretty weird phone calls during the course of the week.

"Mr Courtenay," the voice said, sounding a little anxious and not at all like a shyster.

"Look, I am very busy. I don't even understand the old Darwinian theory of evolution properly, you have quite obviously got the wrong person."

"May I send you a letter and a paper?" the voice inquired politely.

"By all means," I replied with relief, "thank you for calling." I put down the phone quickly just short of being rude.

The following day a letter arrived with several attachments.

The writer obviously thought me rather more intelligent than I am, because, for me anyway, it was fairly difficult reading.

But what it semed to be saying is that using new evolutionary theory on how living organisms are biologically composed, we can start making significant corrections.

An example used was that we can breed race horses to run faster and perform better under racing conditions, another being that people or animals who carry genetic problems may well be prevented from passing these on to future generations.

I won't go on, as I run the risk of misquoting him badly and besides I haven't asked permission to quote from his paper or letter.

GRAB WITH BOTH HANDS

However, the gist of what he said was that the technology involved was largely Australian with great commercial applications in many easily demonstrated ways and yes, you guessed it, if Australian business is unwilling to embrace the technology with risk capital and imagination, other nations will grab it with both hands.

What the writer wanted to know was whether I might in some way advise how they might go about the business of helping to find Australian organisations prepared to listen to some pretty radical commercial science ideas which could fairly easily be shown to

ADVERTISING AND RELATED SUBJECTS

be viable in manufacturing and breeding technology.

But as I read on I became very excited—here was something unique and wonderful and all our own work as a nation.

That is, if we had the faith, the guts and the imagination to embrace it.

As an idea it was bigger than Christmas, New Year and Easter thrown in together.

Wow! Up good ol' Oz!

Then my heart sank.

Would we again walk away from a great and original idea?

Would our big manufacturing companies and investment organisations dismiss the concept because it required a bit of thinking and risk-taking and wasn't in the familiar field of buying and selling each other's internal assets?

We are so used to using our money to buy and sell, without adding anything or making anything useful or contributing anything worthwhile, that we probably were incapable of thinking out of the square.

I got a nasty sinking feeling in my stomach just thinking about the difficulties that lay ahead of this seemingly brilliant bunch of innovative scientists.

I don't know if I am the person to advise the writer and his organisation.

But I sincerely hope I can make some sort of contribution or know someone who can.

Just once, let's get a really good idea, originated here, to stay with us.

Give jobs to the young—our future depends on it

I was out for my usual run with a group of friends one day last week and, as is usually the case, someone started talking about business.

This is a fairly high-powered group of marketing, advertising, insurance, media and public sector thinkers, and running with them is probably as good a briefing on the economic situation as is available.

Always on the lookout for a column, I asked what they thought needed to be done long term to give Australia the competitive business environment it needs.

Pretty soon I'd gathered most of the conventional answers—a national plan to get out of the recession, wage restraint, union modification, finance restructuring, privatisation, reform of government, venture capital on a national scale, reassessment of our global opportunities, and the like.

We reached a rather formidable hill and the talk stopped as the effort required to climb it increased.

Finally, only Alex Hamill, the chief executive of George Patterson, Australia's largest advertising agency, was strong enough to talk while he was climbing. As usual, he was short on theory and came directly to the point.

I shall try to interpret what he said: "My agency has always maintained a policy of promotion from within. We believe it was smarter for our business to take kids out of school at 18 and have them learn the wisdom of the street rather than the campus.

"Advertising is about people and their needs and aspirations and these are skills best learned at ground level.

"We figured that a bright young guy or lady with five years' of practical experience behind them could cope with our business a lot better than one whose head and expectations were filled with the expectations of a university training which entitled them to a soft ride to the top.

"We started all our kids in the dispatch department, where they ran the messages, delivered the mail and papers and got kicked around a bit.

"From here, they progressed through every agency department until they were eventually given a junior account or media job and became entitled to wear a three-piece suit or its opposite gender equivalent.

"It didn't always work, but it was one of the better guarantees of a practical and well-trained executive continuity we'd found in the 57 years of our company's existence.

"In a recent review of the agency, I realised with some dismay that we'd changed this fundamental part of our corporate culture.

"Last month, we had 83 applicants for a start-up job and they all had one thing in common—sheer desperation.

"Most were aged around 18 or 20, most had been out of work for a year—in other words since writing their final school examinations—and all said the same thing: That they were getting no nearer to being employed.

". . . I interviewed several of these applicants myself. I soon discovered that a great many had simply lost their way and their courage.

"How would you feel if you had sent out 40 letters and got two replies—both negative? Or made a hundred phone calls to have them mostly cut off at the switchboard?

"How many times can you pick up the morning paper and hope something might turn up? How many friends can your father or mother ring to see if they can use an old favour or some influence to get you an interview? How long do you believe your courage would last?

"The answer, in my case anyway, is not too bloody long.

"At this moment, I am told, 37 per cent of kids aged between 18 and 20 are out of work and most of them have been so for at least a year.

"My own kids fall fair-and-square into this statistic. Fortunately, I can afford for them to continue their education, which is not the case with a lot of other parents.

"Besides, even education is getting more difficult. The marks required for business courses have increased dramatically and it is becoming harder and harder to aspire to a tertiary education.

"The irony is that to be unemployed is no longer a stigma. Like divorce, it's become accepted as a part of our lifestyle. But getting rid of a wife or husband is not the same thing as getting rid of the next generation of Australians.

"How do you think these kids will feel about life in five years' time? What do you think we, the business leaders, plan to do about it?"

We had reached the top of the hill and I stood with my hands on my knees gasping. "Frankly, I'm sick and bloody tired of hearing about this recession we had to have.

"I don't give a damn that the consumer price index is only 3 per cent. The solution, like most of the world's 'too complicated' problems, is dead simple!

"Let's begin with advertising, my business, which is said to have been hit harder than most. There are 172 advertising agencies in Sydney and Melbourne and half a hundred in other capital cities.

"If every single one of us decided to employ a young person tomorrow and pay them the minimum salary of $16,000, there's 172 kids gainfully employed.

"Maybe that won't make a big dent in the 37 per cent, but it's the beginning, if every company with more than 10 people in its employ was prepared to hire one person . . . we would be on our way.

"Let's negotiate with the unions to freeze wages for the first four years of employment.

"I assure you, there isn't an unemployed kid out there who would knock this opportunity back.

"Our future isn't in the hands of Hawke and Kerin, it's in our own and those of the young kids who are increasingly sitting on their hands, wondering what the hell life is all about.

"If we don't want the fear and urban violence we read about in cities like New York and Chicago, which is caused by the militant anger of deprived minority groups, we've got to do something fast.

"If our young lose their faith and turn inwards, it's a long, long way back. Please, hire at least one kid tomorrow. Please."

SALES AND MARKETING

THE AUSTRALIAN MONDAY MAY 26 1986

In the service of tomorrow's sales

The worst thing you learn about the advertising and marketing world is that yesterday is dead and tomorrow is too distant for concern—today's sales are all that matter.

The preoccupation with the immediate is manic.

If sales are down: pump in the cash, pile on the incentives and undercut the opposition.

The skirmish is more important than the war and it soon becomes apparent that long-term planning is what you talk about at sales conferences but never get around to implementing in the field.

If you live to tell the story, the past can always be packaged with examples of cunningly contrived tactics, nerve, skill, patience and predatory know-how in the asphalt jungle.

In marketing parlance this is known as a case history.

In most free-enterprise marketing, five-year plans are no more successful than those that Stalin and Mao continuously and unsuccessfully implemented.

In marketing, survival is the only fixed rule, all others are expendable.

Multinational organisations view the Australian market as an opportunity to make profits as quickly as possible.

The chief executive sitting in a mega-storey, glass high-rise in New York, Osaka, London, Dusseldorf or Hong Kong looks only at the bottom line.

Business is not fair, it is simply business.

The small and the big, local and multinational are all in the same ball game.

Winning in industry happens not because you play a great game of corporate chess, but because you are prepared to get out on the street and slug it out in the daily brawl.

The average Master of Business Administration graduate is still picking the fluff out of his navel when the skirmish is over and the day is won or lost.

If my observations are accurate and if this scenario is close to the reality of business in Australia, then one begins to speculate as to how a company might find a long-term marketing edge in this environment of sudden death.

It is reasonable to assume that most goods perform more or less equally at a given price level.

While new product development is a part of marketing, most of the goods for sale have been around for a while.

The difference between this year's model and the one before is likely to be more trim than all new within.

Five-year plans are not much good for the stoves, refrigerators, dishwashers, driers, microwave ovens, toasters, mixers, television sets and hi-fidelity players that clutter our cottages.

It seems as though suburban man is programmed to have at least one piece of electronic "indispensibilia" break down on him weekly.

Just about every manufacturer has mastered the technique of making appliances that are guaranteed to turn mild-mannered brides into screaming harridans.

This particular neurosis is brought about from dealing with any after-sales service department.

After-sales service is the traditional marketing Achilles heel.

I have yet to meet a chief executive who made it to the top from the after-sales service department.

Yet, when you think about it, after-sales service is a potential long-term marketing strategy that cannot fail.

Provided, of course, your goods are built roughly to the same standard as those of your competition.

The purchaser of your goods views your paid propaganda on the television, compares your price in the newspaper and discusses your brochure with her husband at the kitchen table.

She never gets the chance to actually talk to you before she makes the decision.

Hers is an act of pure faith, even good faith for which you are about to kick her in the teeth when you meet her for the first time.

She meets you at her kitchen door. You are usually a couple of days late for the appointment.

You walk into her kitchen with muddy boots and after a cursory examination of her lifeless appliance you tell her that the part she needs is out of stock and will not be available for two weeks.

You then charge her $25 for the privilege of cleaning up after you.

You call it a service charge and you charge it for not servicing her appliance.

After two weeks of eating out of tins she calls you to be told the part is still not available—it will be at least another two weeks.

When she yells at you, you say: "Don't blame me, madam. It's not my fault."

If it is not your fault, then who is to blame? You will probably blame it on the wharfies' strike, the union or the government. Anyone but yourself.

You are too busy trying to beat up the competition for today's piece of the sales pie to concern yourself about sales past.

What you are doing, in fact, is missing the greatest long-term marketing advantage any company could have.

You are missing the only safe investment there is in the future.

If survival is the daily creed of the marketing department, then the only long-term marketing rule is to create customer loyalty.

Every refrigerator or whatever you sell to my wife has the potential for at least two more sales if you treat her the right way.

Why is it that when she meets you for the first time or the 10th time, her impression is of a man in a slightly dirty dust-coat with mud on his boots? A recalcitrant, if not belligerent, person with a lack of concern for her predicament that borders on sadism?

Apart from ensuring you have a warehouse full of spare parts and a reasonably efficient way of getting them to your service vans, the rest is easy if you think about it.

A person with an appliance breakdown is in urgent need of two things.

A gentle manner on the telephone and a serviceman in a clean jacket who dispenses hope.

Oh yes, and if you do not have the part to fix her appliance, do not charge her for the privilege of receiving the bad news.

If I ran a large concern where servicing the goods I sold was a part of my corporate responsibility, I would have a psychiatrist choose my service personnel.

She, because a female would have a better understanding of the customer, would choose only extroverts who enjoy their jobs and are proud of the name embroidered on the pocket of their spotlessly clean dust-jackets.

I would pay them well above award rates and devise a form of incentives based on customer satisfaction.

How long is it since you took a hundred servicemen and their wives to Hawaii because they went daily into the suburbs to battle for you, winning the hearts and minds of your existing customers and by so doing swinging the market your way for years to come?

Maybe, just maybe, there is an idea buried in there somewhere.

Greener pastures across the Tasman

February rain has kept the grass from burning the usual mid-summer umber and Sydney is greener than I can remember it.

Flying home from New Zealand a fortnight ago, an American passenger sitting at the window seat next to me remarked with disappointment that Sydney looked more like New England than the outback shed he had hoped for.

It's coloured Bicentenary green. It's only like this every 200 years. Well, how about that she exclaimed, apparently taking me seriously.

I had spent four days in New Zealand hopping from Auckland to Wellington and on to Christchurch, doing a three-hour lecture at each of those places. Standing up and talking to half a hundred hairdressers at each venue for three hours was more than a daunting task.

New Zealanders are made of sterner stuff than most of us: hardly anyone seemed to fall asleep.

It was kiwifruit time in New Zealand and a bowl of the furry green eggs greeted me in my hotel room. I ordered an omelette from room service and four slices of kiwifruit decked the plate where the ubiquitous tomato ought to have been.

At breakfast, bowls of sliced kiwifruit sat next to the All-Bran and yoghurt. At lunch the fruit garnished a plate of blue-lipped mussels and appeared again as the predominant ingredient in the fruit salad.

At dinner, kiwifruit appeared sliced like a cross-section of a giant's brilliant green eye on my fish where I would have expected to find a sprig of parsley.

Despite hailing originally from China as a chinese gooseberry, the kiwifruit is very New Zealand: a country where green is the dominant colour.

If you close your eyes and think New Zealand, you instantly think green. And kiwifruit is just the right colour of green to be the fruit to represent New Zealand as the grape does France, the cherry Japan, the apple England, the mango the tropics, the banana the Caribbean, the orange California, the melon Spain, and the pineapple Queensland.

REMARKABLE

I can remember about 15 years ago asking Tony, our local fruitologist, about the funny-looking hairy eggs neatly set out in the green plastic tray.

"They call him kiwifruit . . . you wanna try?" He sliced through the kiwifruit with his cabbage knife, and deftly removed the skin, offering me a slice of bright green eye on the point of the well-honed knife.

I recall tasing it and puckering my lips. "Not a hope, won't sell, tastes like wet socks dipped in sugar."

I was witnessing the beginning of one of the most remarkable agricultural marketing exercises the world has ever seen. Only the jaffa orange from Israel can compare with it and it took nearly three times as long to establish itself as a household name.

Today, New Zealand boasts several hundred kiwifruit millionaires as the fruit finds itself on tables throughout the world and always at a premium price.

I recall seeing half a dozen kiwifruit in the fruit section of Harrods with a £2 price tag on each.

In fact, my impression of New Zealand last week was of kiwifruit and Japanese tourists. They came together as I left the Hyatt in Auckland: a hundred or so Japanese tourists climbing aboard a luxury bus and, as they approached the door, a pretty girl with a tray of kiwifruit handed each of them a big, plump, furry specimen, whereupon the recipient would give a small bow, smile and say "ah so . . . kiwiflute".

It seems to me the New Zealanders may have worked their marketing priorities correctly selling the fruit of their land to the world while selling its beauty to the Japanese.

At the three hotels I stayed in over four days, every time I climbed into a lift I seemed to be the sole Anglo-Saxon surrounded by young Japanese honeymooners, in between holidaymakers and retired folk.

The menus were in Japanese, at least one Japanese clerk could be found at the reception desk, and a great many tourist notices of the kind that are common at tourist resorts were also printed in Japanese.

Even the instructions on how to regulate my shower were printed in Japanese. All the large shops had half a dozen Japanese shop assistants and prices were often shown in yen as well.

One reads about Japanese tourists returning from Australia with money in their pockets.

WAIT

I cannot say whether this is true of New Zealand, but at Christchurch Airport every Japanese tourist seemed to be laden with sheepskin rugs, jackets, hats, boots, as well as containers of frozen lamb, rounds of cheese and, yes, cases of kiwifruit.

No doubt their suitcases were filled with other local treasures.

One gets the feeling that New Zealand is taking the Japanese tourist very seriously and, for the first time in the 30 years I've been crossing the Tasman, I received less New Zealand money for the Australian money I exchanged. The dollar now buys NZ98¢.

At Christchurch our Air New Zealand 746 got halfway down the runway before jolting to a stop and turning back with engine trouble. Three hours later a jumbo had been diverted from Auckland to pick us up.

In the superior way airline people have of apologising, the Air New Zealand representative told us that the almost-full jumbo from Auckland could not accommodate all the business-class travellers and, using a random selection method, 12 of us would have to be downgraded to tourist – whereupon 12 Australian names were read out, followed by those selected for business-class, all of whom had names such as Nakamura and Takasami.

In tourist terms, once again, the New Zealanders had got it right. We arrived in Australia with a jumbo-load of Japanese with a yen to spend, only to be told that the baggage handlers had gone on strike.

We stood in the baggage area of Sydney's international airport for the next six hours waiting for our bags to be unloaded. There were no refreshments offered and Customs would not allow anyone out.

During this entire period no tourist official attempted to either explain or to apologise to the several thousand thoroughly disgruntled tourists, most of them Japanese.

I cannot help feeling that the wide brown land is still very green while the green one across the Tasman isn't green at all.

Instinct beats expertise on success scale

Marketing is just a tiny word for all the things we do to make a sale.

I have worked with men who hold brilliant marketing degrees and who know nothing about marketing. I once hired a kid who helped his dad sell chicken manure off the back of a truck and I could teach him nothing he did not instinctively know.

We research and measure, evaluate and pontificate, and still the new product fails. Eight out of 10 new products on the market are destined for the scrapheap. We refer to marketing as a science— if it is, it's a very primitive one; a 20 per cent success rate in any other science would not be tolerated.

Most new products are researched for longer than they actually remain on the market, which forces one to ask the logical question: "If, instead of spending squillions on research and development, we simply guessed, could we do any worse?

Some years ago I was invited to Indonesia to act as a consultant for the Bentoel Tobacco Company. You have probably never heard of them, but in Indonesia they are bigger than Rothmans and produce more than 100 million cigarettes a day.

By any standards, Bentoel is big business. The company is owned by a Chinese family which has been in Indonesia for more than 300 years. The Bentoel factories are largely computerised, so much so that they are compelled to create new jobs for the quota the Government insists they employ.

From the stripping of the leaf to the rolled cigarette, the printing of the pack and the stamping of the foil, the machines do it all themselves. A couple of dozen white coats seem to keep several acres of sophisticated machinery humming away for 24 hours a day.

The Bentoel Tobacco Company doesn't seem to make too many mistakes, with 14 leading brands and the countless lesser ones they put on the market. Every year they launch a new brand to replace the least profitable of the leading brands, allowing the old brands to join the successful also-runs. Somehow, they've worked out that

14 brands is right for their structure—and certainly it seems to work.

Then someone must have told them that they should do with their marketing what they've done with their manufacturing—they ought to employ a marketing and advertising consultant to prepare the new brand for the coming year.

I'm not sure how I was selected, but I found myself on a plane to Indonesia. I was being paid by the day and naturally my hosts were not too anxious for me to hang around for too long. The factory tours could only have been faster if we'd been wearing rollerskates.

I discovered to my dismay that they almost never have a new product failure: that I wasn't there to nurse them into a potentially profitable new brand but to give them a new, super-profitable one. The idea of failing had never entered their heads—or if it had, they kept it concealed from me.

I thought about this for a while. If they were as successful as they seemed to be, how the hell did they do it?

The following day I asked to meet the bloke who did the research and development. He turned out to be a German who ran a spotless lab and who talked a whole heap of jargon and wasn't any help at all.

REPLENISH

So at the afternoon conference, where the whole family met to drink green tea and discuss the day's business, I asked who decided what the new brand would be? Mr Lee, the head of the family, pointed to an elderly lady seated in the corner and introduced her as Miss Lu. To my surprise, Miss Lu spoke tolerably good English and by spending the next couple of days with her I managed to work out how she made the selection.

Miss Lu was to tobacco what fine winemakers are to wine and coffee blenders are to coffee. She instinctively knew how to blend tobacco. The day after Chinese New Year she would start and during the next month would blend half a dozen flavour styles of cigarette. These would then be made up into batches and left conveniently near the women tobacco sorters.

Indonesian women do not generally smoke but almost all the men do. The women would pinch the cigarettes and take them home to their men. Miss Lu would replenish the cigarettes and, during a period of six months, carefully note which batches were stolen most often. At the end of six months, with about 2000 tobacco sorters as her test market, she had a very good idea which blend worked best. This became her choice of brand for the coming year.

"Why not simply allow them to help themselves and then let them tell you which blend their husbands like the best?" I suggested.

Miss Lu seemed shocked at the idea. "If the cigarettes are not stolen, then the husbands' tastes will not be so keen," she said. "They will lose their concentration."

She gave me a deprecating smile and then added: "But I am too old now, these are old ways and Mr Lee says the German must make the brand for you because we are going to spend a lot of money and you are an expert."

I went out and bought the old lady an expensive gold locket and chain and persuaded her to give me the blend she had selected for that particular year.

This I took to the German, who analysed it. Then I fixed up some of the more fundamental advertising mistakes they had been making and put together a fairly decent sort of advertising campaign.

Bentoel launched the new brand with a fanfare of marketing trumpets and I'm happy to say they had an even better than usual success.

Home repairs—
plumbing the depths

I have given up urban living and the scream of police and ambulance sirens and have left my jumped-up workers' cottage for an apartment in a leafier, quieter suburb which, though much less yuppie, has a view of the Harbour.

It has a proper suburban quietness where fat labradors lie on the pavement in the sun and give you a cursory wag of the tail as you pass.

The flat I moved into was announced in the sales leaflet as brand new with nothing to do.

It turned out to be just over 90 years old, but the nothing to do bit seemed true. It positively glowed with renovation.

Now I wasn't entirely taken in by all this.

You see, the place I had just sold said the same thing in its ad and, while it was in pretty good repair, "nothing to do" was stretching things a bit. So it didn't come as a big surprise that the dishwasher hose needed replacing and the oven switch on the stove, once switched on, refused to switch off.

Replacing the hose on the dishwasher didn't seem like a job for a plumber, despite my wife's earnest plea that I should immediately employ one from the yellow pages.

I trotted down to the hardware shop and purchased a new hose and tap connection. Roughly four hours later, with both my hands in bandages, I announced that the dishwasher was ready for action.

My wife turned it on and away it went, chuffa-chuf-chuffing as the water swirled around its stainless steel belly. But very soon a second stream of water appeared to issue from the bottom of the sink cabinet.

I inspected it to find the tap connection was leaking. When this sort of thing happens I am apt to believe the fault is mine. My incompetence in the area of household repair is profound and my inferiority complex is well developed.

Another hour later, with my bandages practically dripping blood, the beggar still leaked, so I took it back to the hardware shop.

"Don't worry, a lot of men do that. Give it back to me and I'll give you another one," the bloke at the hardware shop said calmly.

"You mean it really wasn't me?" I asked, amazed.

"No mate, we have two or three of these returned a day," he replied.

Now it seems to me that ever since mankind can no longer afford plumbers, the price of do-it-yourself plumbing gear has rocketed and the standard of the merchandise has gone down.

Things that used to be made of brass and which lasted a lifetime are now made of plastic, don't last a year and leak anyway.

And since when is plastic twice as expensive as brass? Since slobs like me went into do-it-yourself plumbing—that's when!

And while I'm on the plastics plethora, why do I have to pay $2.50 for four two-inch plastic pipes with which to connect two hoses when I want one small piece of copper piping that used to cost 10¢?

Surely the principles of marketing are that the more of something you make, the less they ought to cost. Isn't economy of scale what manufacturing is all about?

Well, it doesn't work that way in the home handyman business.

The second tap fixture worked and, counting the fact that my hands were out of commission for two days, so that I couldn't earn a living as a writer, I reckon I got out of this particular repair for roughly $506.50.

Being a reasonably fast learner, I decided not to tackle the oven switch.

I promptly called the manufacturer, who immediately checked my stove on his inventory to discover it was three days off its warranty period.

How do they do that? How do they manage to make things break down within nano-seconds of the expiration of the warranty?

"It will be $40 for the house call and $15 for every half hour period or part thereof thereafter," the girl at the other end rattled off, in a voice which sounded as though she was talking with her mouth full of dry Saos.

"Can't fit you in until next Thursday some time."

"Some time? What's with the some time? Can't you be a little more precise?"

I could hear her sigh of exasperation.

"We cannot anticipate the whereabouts of our vans or their ETA (estimated time of arrival) at any given time," she said.

I was forced to give her nine out of ten for pedantic grammar and nil for co-operation.

"Just a moment, miss, I'd like you to know that I'm a brain surgeon who has to operate next Thursday on the Prime Minister, who is in urgent need of cranial adjustment so we can get the bloody pilots flying again. Some time Thursday isn't the kind of answer I expect."

"Well, let me see," she said in a crisp voice. "If you don't take next Thursday we can possibly do you the Tuesday after that. Are you operating on that day, doctor?"

Anyway, around two o'clock Thursday the company serviceman arrived.

"Switch, is it? Yeah, they all go. Just out of warranty, is it? Thought so."

What I don't need on a Thursday at home, when I should be at work, is a cheerful Pommie repairman who works for a white goods company that has got built-in obsolescence down to a matter of seconds.

"Can you hurry it along please, I'd like to get to work."

Nearly an hour later, at $15 a half hour or part thereof, he had the switch in his hand.

"Broken," he announced triumphantly.

I restrained myself from hitting him.

"Needs a new one," he said, sounding genuinely sympathetic.

"Fine, put a new one in, what's a new one cost?"

"$4.50, but it's not just that."

"I can afford $4.50 but can you hurry, please," I said.

"Yes, sorry guv, 'aven't got any. We'll have some in about a fortnight's time."

He wrote me a bill for $70 and left.

Okay, so what does all that add up to in marketing terms? Well, it all makes some kind of sense.

Instead of making products that will work, you make products that don't work. These you sell for a lot of money with a little sticker on them which says they are made in Australia so you've got to buy them or else.

Then you make your service department a big profit centre and you collect a second tidy little profit.

A tap fitting that is punched out in an injection mould at 2000 units an hour, and costs 5¢ to make, retails for $4.50, so it doesn't much matter if a few faulty ones are returned and a switch that cost 10¢ to make retails via your service department for $70.

And another $70 no doubt when they return with a new one in a fortnight.

Now that's a pretty smart marketing ploy.

The tariffs on an imported stove, or washing machine or whatever, are so high that people can't afford them any more.

What a neat trick. Shoddy workmanship, built-in obsolescence, profitable service departments, little local competition and government-aided tariffs to keep well-made imports off the market.

Adding to this are the national man hours wasted as tens of thousands of people on any given day are forced to stay at home waiting for the serviceman to arrive.

Now I ask you? Is this not a serious attempt by at least one local white goods manufacturer to bring Australia to its industrial knees?

If not, then the white goods manufacturers and the plumbing and home handyman industry have invented a whole new area of marketing which, for want of a better name, shall be known as The Shoddy Goods Principle of Marketing.

Now I know what the Prime Minister means when he claims that we Australians are a clever and innovative people.

THE AUSTRALIAN FRIDAY FEBRUARY 8 1991

Here's how we become leading manufacturers

I have just come up with a way of making the world beat a manufacturing path to Australia.

All we have to do is pass a law making all service calls for the repair of appliances free for the first eight years of the life of the appliance and all parts replaced at the original cost, the price published in the handbook when you buy the appliance.

Just think about it for a moment. If your fridge breaks down it costs you $50 just to get someone to the door. If he works for an hour that's another $35 and if he puts in a part it costs roughly four times what the original part cost to put into the refrigerator.

If you make a call the chances are that it will take three or four days for the bloke from the service division to come and if you belong to 70 per cent of Australian households you have to stay home from work for half or even the whole day waiting. Let's put that cost at around $100.

So the simplest thing that can happen to your appliance can end up costing you a couple of hundred dollars.

Last week my fridge went berserk and froze everything. Perhaps $40 or $50 worth of fruit and vegies and a few other bits and pieces.

I called the manufacturer, my wife stayed in all day, he came late, looked at the thermostat switch which was located in the freezer, said it was wrong, leaned over, clicked it two notches, took my $50 and left.

I went out and bought $40 worth of fruit and vegetables telling myself that idiots such as I deserved to be penalised, but puzzled as to why the setting was wrong when it hadn't been touched for the year or so we'd owned the fridge.

The next morning I chopped everything out of the fridge again. Another $40 worth of vegies had used up our precious oxygen resources for nothing.

I called the service department, waited two days and a different guy switched the thermostat back to where it was originally set.

"You've got the thermostat set wrong, mate. Just leave it where we put it and she'll be right."

I explained that I hadn't moved anything, that the two clicks he'd just cancelled had already cost me $50.

Covering for the Richard-cranium who'd preceded him, he said: "Yeah, well, thermostats can be tricky, no two are the same, they have minds of their own. That will be $50."

When I objected he politely asked permission to phone his service department and after what appeared to be a fairly complex conversation, someone on the other side decided magnanimously that I needn't pay.

For reasons I fail to understand, the fridge now seems okay.

SERVICE CALLS FREE

But just imagine if the manufacturer had been forced to make the service call free, he'd soon go broke with thermostats and belts and hinges and nobs that have a habit of falling off or wearing out or going berserk.

He'd have to make appliances that don't need servicing except for spare parts which wear out after eight years or so.

Suddenly he'd be a lot more careful about the materials he puts into his products and the way he designs and tests them.

He'd know that every time he introduced a new model into the market it would have the potential to send him broke if he didn't get it right.

People wouldn't have to put up with shoddy merchandise because the market would soon find the manufacturer out.

However, the manufacturer who met the new specifications would become very rich indeed and the world would be delighted to buy his merchandise.

Now I am not silly enough to believe that left to his own devices the manufacturer is going to see the virtue of this little idea.

In fact, in the sector of the appliance industry which concerns fridges and washing machines, one giant manufacturer produces the three best-selling brands of refrigerator and washing machine and owns nearly the total market.

In other words, this one company is competing with itself, which is not a crash hot way to encourage quality control, value for money or consumer goodwill.

This huge company complains that its service department, at $50 a call, runs at a loss. That's just another way of saying the goods they make are so bad that they can't afford to fix them.

Now, if it's okay in a country for one company to buy out all the other companies making fridges and washing machines so that they have no competition, why isn't it also okay for a government to set a quality control standard which they have to meet?

Why isn't it okay to make this standard the highest in the world? After all, we have the raw materials, we have the know-how and presumably we have the intelligence. All we lack is the desire to be the best at everything we do.

Imagine if we measured everything we did as a nation by only one criterion: the best value for a dollar spent in the world.

Two things would immediately become apparent. We'd soon learn where we could intelligently compete and where we couldn't.

So we'd only work in those areas where we were potentially the best for a dollar spent. This way everything we made would be readily exportable because it represents great value.

The government wouldn't have to prop up and subsidise industries which can't compete and manufacturers wouldn't have to run service departments which sent them broke.

I'll bet in no time flat we'd find someone in Australia who knows how to make a thermostat that isn't schizoid and doesn't go berserk and run amok causing grievous bodily harm to tomatoes and suchlike.

By the way, why is it that tomatoes don't taste like tomatoes any more?

THE AUSTRALIAN FRIDAY MAY 3 1991

Cattlemen stake their export claim

City met the country this week when I was asked to talk at the Australian Beef Expo in Rockhampton.

Though I was only in the north for 48 hours it was sufficient to challenge a number of attitudes I'd formed, if unconsciously, about our brothers from the bush.

Like most ad men I have a baked bean and raspberry jam mentality, which means that most of the products I help to sell are not among life's major decisions.

The subject of beef is rather grand and important and one on which politicians are continually being put on the spot, facing prying cameras and demanding questions.

You wouldn't exactly expect the Minister for Primary Industry to answer to the people on national television because IXL or Cottee's had taken the whole strawberries out of the jam.

But beef is one of those important subjects you don't dispose of with glib advertising.

Besides, I knew very little about beef. While I would have agreed it was important, I suppose I regarded beef as one of those rural commodities handled by a bunch of country reactionaries who were reluctant to change their bush-based ways.

Along with beef, I would have lumped wool, wheat and fat lambs, in fact all the present semi- and complete disasters known as the rural plight.

A VALUE-ADDED IMPRIMATUR

Isn't it nice when a pre-conceived opinion is so totally shattered you have to go on to your knees and pick up the pieces and make something entirely new?

What I saw in Rockhampton left me feeling that not all of our rural industry was on the ropes with wobbly legs trying to last out the final round.

It was I who was to learn a lesson in open mindedness and over a period of 48 hours I was to meet a breed of Australian who wasn't taking a lifestyle for granted.

These were men and women who saw beef in consumer terms, not as I did, as lumps of meat sent to Japan or to the great hamburger mincer in the United States but who regarded beef as a product to be as carefully considered as any product on the world's supermarket shelves.

I discovered that beef is rapidly becoming a niche marketing exercise and not simply carcasses with blue ink stamps sold by the ton.

Dr Rhonda Miller, assistant professor at Texas A & M University, told us how beef is being bred for specific consumer needs.

For instance the steak, cut thin, that will deliver tenderness and flavour and can be cooked in five minutes needed to be bred in the beast—in effect, designed into the genetics of the breed.

People dieting will be able to get beef for diets, a fat-free steak with a low-calorie content that nevertheless tastes like one which is rich in delicious flavour-enhancing fat.

Beef exports to the Japanese will need to have at least a 50 per cent fat content and so on.

The beef industry is learning how to breed for peculiar needs in a variety of quite specific ways—they have discovered niche marketing with a value-added product.

I'm no expert on rural matters and so should probably keep my mouth shut, but it seems to me that one of the problems we may have with wool is that we simply grow it, pack it in hessian bales and send it off elsewhere.

Of course there are grades of wool and, I imagine, even types of wool, but it seems to me that we're doing very little to create a value-added wool product.

If I suggested we go into the milling business there would probably be a thousand studies to show why we couldn't compete.

But when you add value to a basic product, what you're doing is giving the raw material a characteristic for which you can command a premium price.

Perhaps if wool producers took the same outlook as beef producers are doing and started to work on niche marketing opportunities we might not be held to ransom by the rest of the world quite so often.

Another aspect brought up at the conference was the idea of a national label for produce from Australia.

Douglas Shears, the mercurial executive chairman of ICM Australia, proposed a logo which simply stated the words, "Australia Fresh".

It would be something we, as a nation, could own for our agricultural product and which other nations would grow to envy, a sort of national added-value imprimatur.

This idea was supported by the hugely clever Dr John Stocker, the chief executive of the CSIRO, who pointed out that Australia was an almost unpolluted country compared with the other big agricultural exporters.

We could be seen to be a place where freshness originates.

Freshness is an idea which is both believable and supportable and one which could become part of our agricultural product ethos.

A country known for the freshness of its agricultural product would give us a huge emotional advantage in a world becoming increasingly health and environment conscious.

It could be regarded as a national treasure, as indeed the environment is.

And so I came away without the usual feeling of despair that, once again, the word-seeds of the speakers had fallen on barren, untilled soil and that the delegates would go home, unchanged and unrepentant.

Instead, the tiny lamp of hope still flickered within me. Here were a bunch of pretty hard-nosed rural people looking at their future and ours through a set of clear eyes.

It was a very nice feeling and I thank all at the Australian Beef Expo for their hospitality and their hope.

Pride in products and services comes before a rise in business

The success of Germany was based initially on the Volkswagen, the unprepossessing hunchback little motor car.

The US, Britain, France and Italy all made cars in the immediate post-war era with Japan following not too long afterwards, so you could say the choice of cars was fairly wide and ranged from the boxy British makes to the extravagant Yank tanks with an ostentation of chrome, wings and width which brashly pronounced the American way.

But only the Volkswagen was observing the needs of supply and demand. What was needed was a car only sufficiently large to carry the post-war family of two children with economy and complete reliability.

The VW did this without the benefit of the traditional motoring marques. Its proud owners soon grew to love it for what it was and dubbed it "the Bug" or "Beetle" and proceeded to create a personality for it which has become legendary.

In other words, it filled all of the needs of a product. It was cheap, reliable, did the job required of it and was emotionally satisfying.

Germans were regarded as skilled, conservative engineers who produced products that represented good value for money.

Today people pay a fortune for a Mercedes or a BMW for more or less the same reasons that they bought a VW for a song.

SUPPLY AND DEMAND

They are convinced that they can have ultimate performance and luxury in a car which is superbly made, will give them trouble-free motoring for years, add to their personal prestige and hold its resale value.

The combination of pragmatism and emotion which has become a powerful purchasing force, but which is little different to the reasons which motivated their mums and dads when they bought a post-war Beetle.

The basic customer rules hadn't changed.

So, if as a nation we accept that these rather simple rules apply, how can we use them to our advantage in a highly competitive world market?

Well, we're going to need a single magic ingredient to begin with and once again it is an ingredient which the Germans and the Japanese have demonstrated they have in abundance.

Pride. We have to be proud of ourselves as a nation which supplies things for other people to use or experiences for other people to enjoy.

Now I'm not talking about a jingoistic, chest thumping, football crowd pride, but rather an emotional quality which contains as its essence the two words "quality control".

We have to earn a reputation among our customers for being a caring and careful producer of goods or services, whether these are practical or emotional.

We hear an awful lot about innovation and invention and, of course, both are important to a small nation, but they won't save us.

Being perceived as being the best at filling quite ordinary existing needs is what will make us a competitive force.

For example, much is made of our tourist potential.

Facts and figures abound which prove that Australia as a tourist destination is likely to become hugely attractive to a world looking for a new and different holiday destination.

But if we are going to make tourism work for us we have to start to observe the same rules as Germany used for the Volkswagen and Japan used to create its industrial muscle.

We have to be seen to supply unique value.

But our cultural cringe and lack of self confidence forbids this sort of excellence.

Really, it isn't that hard once you set your mind to it.

We have the same set of hands and our brains are no smaller, all we have to do is adopt the right attitude and use a little basic intelligence.

If we set about finding out what the majority of people from overseas really wanted from a holiday destination, then if we designed our resources to fill these needs so that tourists left us and returned home, having decided that they had received optimum practical and emotional value for their money, then the world would flock to our shores.

I'm willing to bet that what the great bulk of tourists in the 21st century want will be contained within the following criteria:

SPOTLESSLY clean accommodation which is not extravagantly priced.

GOOD cheap food based on freshness and health.

A TRANSPORT system that works, is simple and comfortable to use and isn't over-priced.

SAFETY in personal movement.

ABOVE all, a host nation which appears to welcome tourists and is anxious to see that they enjoy themselves.

If we can work at just this set of "VW" characteristics for tourism, in other words, understand the customer's needs, both practical and emotional, supply value for money, be reliable in performance, and demonstrate pride in our work and unremitting quality control, we will become one of the world's leading tourist destinations.

What we could do for tourism we can do for meat and wheat and wool and fresh grown stuff.

We can do it in education, a highly exportable commodity, and we can do it in light industry and mining.

All it takes is an ability to find out what our potential customers want and then a determination to be the best.

THE AUSTRALIAN FRIDAY AUGUST 30 1991

Why you keep buying that same warm, friendly brand of soap

Any psychologist will tell you that it is very difficult to change an attitude. The same is true of a purchasing habit.

This is because we do not simply buy products for their function but also because they confirm our attitudes and the way we look at life.

Modification of an attitude is what advertising is mostly about.

Because most product purchases are not major decisions the trick is to try to get someone to sample your new product, to buy it once or twice in the hope that something about the product is sufficiently enjoyed to place it in a mental short list.

Once on this list it is possible to start the long-term job of bringing it to the number one position in the individual mind for its product category.

In fact there is evidence that we all carry a sort of product contingency list in our heads which consists usually of three brands.

If we can't buy our usual brand there are up to five alternatives, but usually only three. These are placed on this preference ladder in a pre-determined order.

Firstly, there is the brand you like and always buy, then the one that is allowed to replace it if your usual brand is missing, because it is thought to be almost as good.

Then, if it too is not available, there is the number three choice, which often becomes a fairly reluctant purchase.

This is known in marketing jargon as giving your product top-of-mind awareness.

Top-of-mind awareness is the first stage in the long-term business of becoming a part of a customer's regular buying habit.

If you don't believe you have a potential preference list, testing this for yourself is simple.

Take a piece of paper and write down five brand names of each of the following product categories, taking no more than 30 seconds per category: cigarettes, washing detergent, toothpaste, hair shampoo, hair spray, toothbrushes, toilet soap, toilet paper.

You'll agree all of these are common enough products with multiple brand names.

For instance, there are 116 brands of hair shampoo and at least 50 of these are in your supermarket or pharmacy at any given time; you have to nominate only five.

Not only will you have difficulty completing the exercise but you'll often be stumped after writing down only three brands.

This is because the brain seems to store up only the product information it needs in order to function efficiently in the marketplace and, presumably, if you can't get any one of three brands on your personal hit list then obviously something is very wrong and you are going to have to re-evaluate your purchasing environment.

In advertising terms this very seldom happens; supply almost always meets demand and so marketers see their jobs as reinforcing their product cultures and not upsetting the purchasing environment.

Advertising for old, well-established brands is more often in the business of keeping the peace, of reinforcing existing attitudes rather than trying to make a sale to a new customer. That is, it has the task of convincing you that you've made the right choice.

It is for this reason that new products so often fail. Traditional brand names, provided always that they are seen to be working hard to keep up with the times, are extremely hard to dislodge from their share of the mind.

Nor do product loyalites operate in isolation; they are the result of a number of factors impinging on them.

The product lives your kind of life style. The most obvious example is the product relationship passed on from mother to daughter or father to son.

The brand of soap or washing detergent or the type of motor oil. It is not simply the advertising that's working but a number of covert warm and nostalgic associations.

We call this feeling about the product its "brand loyalty". A smart marketer does all he can to maintain and increase this loyalty and as little as possible to disrupt it.

A brand is a touchstone, a part of the progress of the user through life, and ultimately it can be said to be a "product friend". This friendship between the user and the product is the product's most precious possession.

However, it is in recession times like this that a product friend can be placed in the most danger, and when an old and respected product friend can be dislodged.

There are two reasons for this, the first being that the manufacturer, desperate for sales in hard times, decides to improve his product formulation, change his pack and adopt a new advertising platform.

In other words, he changes the physical makeup, the looks and the personality of your product friend in the mistaken belief that what the market needs is a boost and his product friend needs a stimulus to buy.

This can be a big mistake and it's not smart to play around with your product during a recession.

A product friend which changes too rapidly when times are hard is contrary to what loyal customers want.

In down times and times of economic stress your loyal customers need dependability and continuity in his or her life and product innovation, pack changes and variant advertising messages lead to discomfort and insecurity.

It opens the opportunity for your brand-loyal customer to invite the actively advertised brand that is one down from you on the top-of-mind awareness ladder for a solid and considerable home trial.

The second, and even greater danger is to severely restrict or to stop advertising altogether during a time of recession.

Quite often products which are market leaders and have been in the market a long time, and so have considerable brand loyalty, make the mistake of believing that their long lifestyle associations with their customers are so strong that they can afford to stop or greatly reduce advertising in tough periods and rest on their past performance laurels.

This can be a big mistake. When you stop advertising, your product is, in effect, no longer visiting your brand-loyal customer's home as a good friend.

Your customer feels ignored, even rebuffed, and often responds by inviting someone else home, a potential new product friend.

This is one of the few times when brand attitudes, usually so hard to change, can be modified reasonably quickly.

It is also an opportunity for entirely new products with a good performance story to gain a solid toehold in the market.

There is some real evidence to support the theory that manufacturers who advertise during recessionary periods gain a bigger market share more quickly than when times are buoyant.

More importantly, they gain this new share of mind and of market at a considerably lower cost and keep it when the market returns to normal, providing always, of course, that they maintain their relationship with their new customers.

So, if one of the market leaders in your field has slashed its budget, see this as your greatest opportunity to increase your position by upping your ad budget: there may never be a better time to topple them from the mental priority ladder and to usurp a share of mind which may have taken years and tens of millions of dollars to build.

A little courage on your part and the recession could be the best opportunity your company ever has to increase your market share and to make new, brand-loyal friends in the homes of Australia.

THE INTERNATIONAL SCENE

THE AUSTRALIAN MONDAY MAY 12 1986

Why Japan catches world with industrial pants down

Have you ever noticed that when a speaker attempts to substantiate a fact by prefacing it with its nation of origin, we automatically weigh the statement by whatever our preconception of that country is?

For instance, if I were to claim that United States scientists were training cockroaches to carry tiny electronic bugs into Soviet embassy dining rooms, my audience would accept this statement as being, at least, possible.

Each of you would quickly review the stereotype data you personally hold on US attitudes.

You would then conclude that Americans are positively neurotic about spies and spying and are technically competent enough in neuro-entomology, microsurgery and electronic miniaturisation to pull it off.

If I asked, in percentage terms, how likely they were to be successful most of you would give them a very good chance, say 85 per cent.

Were I to make the same claim about the British, you would probably conclude that it was a delightfully eccentric idea and might just succeed.

The British chance of success would be put at about 60 per cent.

The insect side would be easy, given their love for animals, but the electronics might prove a bit too tricky.

The Germans would have no trouble working out the technology involved, and would produce a highly disciplined spy-roach that would lack the initiative to act on its own.

Let's give the Germans a 50 per cent chance.

The French would quickly produce an inspired prototype but the wiring would be so complicated that they would never get two spy-roaches to behave in the same way.

Besides, they would never really trust the cockroach (a German insect) to stay loyal to France.

The French would have about a 35 per cent chance of success.

The Italians would put all their effort into redesigning the cockroach.

It would look terrific on the outside and go very fast, but would be prone to breakdowns. The Italians would get a 25 per cent rating.

The Soviets, who have always had trouble with electronic miniaturisation, would need to breed a new species of cockroach about the size and shape of a rugby ball.

While this new bug would work very well, it would be impractical for the original task. But what if I told you that after the Americans had successfully produced the spy-roach, the Japanese had entered the electronic bug business?

You would instantly conclude that in a very short while every home would be able to afford its own spy-roach to spy on the neighbours, take telephone calls and generally do the eavesdropping around the house.

GAMES

Before any other nation could snap its industrial fingers, the Japanese would be marketing the next generation of spy-roach, spy-bug 2—an even smaller cockroach with a 50-byte memory that played several sophisticated electronic games and could be used to spy out exam papers.

In the April 26 issue of The Economist magazine there is a brilliant article on how and why the Japanese keep catching the rest of us with our industrial pants down.

A part of this article appeared in *The Australian* last Monday and I quote from other parts of the original article today.

The Japanese, The Economist explains, are less concerned about who had the original idea for a gadget and more concerned with turning it into a mass-produced quality item at an affordable price.

It works like this. The high-tech-obsessed US military want a new piece of equipment.

They then place huge orders in Georgia and the research and development is allocated to the big high-tech US electronic companies.

These companies are so stuffed with defence projects already underwritten by the US Government that they are loathe to risk their own capital to enter potentially risky commercial ventures.

These are left to the little companies, typified by the Silicon Valley enterprises, which show tremendous entrepreneurial flair in commercialising new technology.

It is not simply that the Japanese are clever copiers. The Japanese do not place the same importance on originality that we in the West do.

Their culture is perfection based, while ours is ideas based. The Japanese believe, quite rightly, that our culture is the major breeding ground for original ideas, so why duplicate a process which is already producing more ideas than can be commercially harvested.

A typical Japanese high-tech research project in a large company starts collectively with targets set for the quality of the performances and end price required.

They are not concerned with its origin but only with achieving a superior and marketable level of sophistication at an affordable price.

It all begins with the Japanese education system which, like everything else, is competitive.

Schools are graded and children compete for entry with their brains. We used to do the same thing with our opportunity schools and selective high schools until we decided that the dumb should inherit the earth.

In education, the system of group co-operation works well when groups are equally matched in intelligence.

Group achievement gives a higher degree of satisfaction without necessarily discouraging individuality.

Like-talented children use each other to hone their intelligence. It is only when interaction takes place in an atmosphere lacking peer-group pressure to sparkle intellectually that a group sinks to its lowest common denominator.

The results of this type of competitive education shows that the general level of examinable intelligence is higher in the Japanese 16 year old than in British children and, presumably, also in our own children.

Less intelligent children who may end up in lower standard schools are not destined for the labour junkpile. They too are trained in group co-operation and they too are required to sit for company examinations to gain employment.

Schooling does not end at school for the Japanese. They continue to sit for examinations at their place of work for the first 15 years of employment.

No employee is neglected: everyone is encouraged to reach his or her optimum level in group interaction.

The net result is a happy, highly motivated workforce that co-operates naturally and with maximum effect.

There is no proof that the Japanese are naturally smarter than we are, yet they seem to outsmart us every time.

What if Australia were left behind because we had become clogged with systems that did not ideally suit a small antipodean country placed more or less in Asia?

What if the cherished principle of individualism had deteriorated into a system where the lowest level in the community became the mean average?

Where our educational system produced individual creativity at a very low level rather than collective and competitive excellence at a very high one?

MERIT

Where job remuneration was set by the unions or legislated according to age and not by merit, skill or effort?

It all begins to sound alarmingly like a certain country we all know and love.

Could it be that we need to do a bit of a national business rethink to see if where we are headed is where we want to go?

Does our approach to new technology and the new markets it creates make us confident that we can compete in the future?

It is just possible that the Japanese and others among our Pacific neighbours have one or two ideas about doing business with the world that we can use without losing our unique culture.

The Japanese once eagerly took advice and borrowed know-how from us without losing their culture.

Right now, on a percentage basis, what would our chances be of successfully modifying and training a cockroach that could carry a bugging device into President Suharto's dining room?

THE AUSTRALIAN MONDAY JUNE 23 1986

Home-made excellence could make its mark

A month ago most Australians felt that things were more or less all right here on the biggest island.

We were, after all, supposed to be the fastest growing economy in the West.

While some of us could not quite see how this equated with 9 per cent inflation, we were sufficiently bamboozled by the explanations of the economists to hope they were right and that, unlike the dollar, things would settle down.

Then, while the Prime Minister, Mr Hawke, was away telling the Chinese leader, Mr Deng, how smart we were for a little nation, the long dark shroud (the Treasurer, Mr Keating) made his historic banana republic speech. We all sat up with a jolt.

Mr Hawke rushed back from China to tell us not to listen to Mr Keating, but that it was all true, except the bit about a banana republic. He told us that we are deep in the proverbial; in fact, in debt up to the Snowy Mountains.

He told us we would have to tuck our Pelaco shirts into our moleskins, tighten our hand-plaited, Australian-made belts, pull up our computer socks and buy Australian.

He promised to run a campaign to tell those of us who have not been listening to what Michael Carlton so aptly calls his television mini-series what he wanted us to do.

He wants us to stop buying from our Pacific neighbours—Japan, Taiwan, South Korea, Hong Kong and Singapore—whose goods come to our market with the landed price approximately doubled because of the import tax he levels on them in order to protect local industry.

Not so long ago, Japan was a shambles with two big nuclear holes in it; Korea was divided and smashed; Taiwan was a small island off the coast of China to which a beaten general had fled with a handful of thoroughly depressed people; Hong Kong and Singapore were snoring blissfully as outposts of Her Majesty's curry tiffin and chopstick empire.

In roughly the time that it took Mr Hawke to go from the Guinness

Book of Records entry as the fastest consumer of a yard of ale to becoming our most admired wowser, each of these countries has become a significant economic power.

In a very short time, these neighbouring nations have made something out of nothing, while we have been busy making nothing out of something.

They do not have mountains of raw material like we have, they do not have an educated population like we had, they did not have oceans of fish, miles of wheat, billowing dust clouds of cattle and snowy horizons of merino sheep.

All they had were energy and enterprise. That was enough.

They bought our mountains of minerals, canned our fish, wove our wool and boosted the energy of their increasingly educated populations with our wheat and meat. What they made they sold to us at a handsome profit. We were laughing: all we had to do was dig, grow, muster, dip and clip.

Sure, we made a few traditional things, but every time some young corporate larrikin came up with a new idea we forced him overseas to sell it.

The national priority is to underwrite ailing industries which are making things less efficiently and more expensively than our neighbouring countries. But still many Australian companies have made it.

Despite taxes, discouraging legislation, disincentives, union interference and bureaucratic obstruction, they have made it on to the market with goods that are as good and as competitively priced as any in the world. They are the entrepreneurs who care.

Although I heard one such company chief executive remark recently that he believed his company deserved a better country.

The triers and the people who care are still out there and they are the people from whom we ought to be buying.

The idea that we are expected to buy Australian-made goods without comparing them for value with overseas goods is at best stupid and cynical.

Why should we buy a car which has fewer features, breaks down more often, is more expensive to repair and uses more petrol than one we can buy less expensively from elsewhere?

If that same car were made in Japan, would we import it for the price it is selling on the Australian market? If we did, would we buy it? I am not suggesting the cars we make are all lemons.

I am suggesting that if we protect and subsidise our industry, the least we can expect is superior products. People should be falling over each other to buy a Holden, our quasi-Australian car. Instead, this year General Motors-Holden's Ltd has shown a $100 million loss.

The industries that queue up in Canberra for help or protection are most often the ones that produce a less-than-competitive product. It may be an overworked principle, but when you know the competition is good you do not ask the judges to handicap them, you run harder, smarter, better and cheaper.

If we are going to ask each other to buy Australian goods and services, why not create a national expectation for Australian-made products?

Why not confer a symbol on any product which can demonstrate clearly that it is as good or better than anything that can be imported?

A mark that cannot be bought, only earned by competing and winning against imported competition. A mark you can earn each year or for each new model, not one you can use in perpetuity.

When the buyer sees the mark, he or she knows that the product or service represents the top quality available for the money. What an expectation that would be. We would take pride in buying that product or service. The advertising campaign could be simple.

It would first encourage companies to submit their goods or services for independent evaluation by a body that was not government-controlled. It would then show people what the mark was and what it meant.

Such an advertising campaign could rightly have an emotional component because it would be based on the desire most peole have to do something good for their country. It would exercise the power of one. That is, each of us could make an active contribution, willingly, knowingly and happily.

For once, the people would be in control which, for the free enterprise, democratic nation we claim we are, would make a nice change.

Brain strain a national gain

Ideas, we all agree, are good to have. Most of us readily accept that without ideas, time and circumstance tend to tread water.

Without ideas, it is simply not enough to be in the right place at the right time.

The Americans are said to have and bring the most ideas to fruition, while the Japanese are thought to be fairly short on ideas of their own but very good at developing the ideas of others.

They have developed the knack of taking a raw idea and polishing it to a high mental sheen.

The English, who are also very good at ideas, some say the best, tend not to believe in themselves any more.

This means that the Japanese and the Americans have a fresh harvest of English ideas to add to their own every year.

This gain from brain strain is any country's most important harvest. The Americans are careful never to sell their ideas to the Russians, or anyone else at a discounted price.

However, we in Australia invariably sell our limited harvest of good ideas at a heavily discounted price.

It has almost become a general rule to send our ideas overseas and have them come back to us with a made-in-some-other-country name tag and an expensive price ticket before we accept them.

We are basically labourers. We dig stuff up, run it once through the crusher and send it abroad.

The idea of using this raw material for product ideas of our own seldom occurs to us.

Other nations have learned that raw material plus idea equals profit. It's the simple arithmetic we haven't yet grasped as they pay less and less for the stuff we dig up.

When it runs out of ideas, a country quite obviously becomes mentally barren, although it may be argued that we have never been burdened with a good enough crop of ideas to recognise the drought.

Perhaps for the first time, we find ourselves needing ideas to survive in a world that has a surplus of everything else except ideas.

It's tough starting way behind everyone else while having to build idea factories.

But like the Japanese and the Germans after the war, starting to scratch our heads from scratch may not be such a bad idea.

It means we can build new idea-manufacturing techniques and can take bold initiatives. It means we can afford to have ideas where others fail to think.

The nice thing about the idea business is that anyone can get into it.

Small countries can have big ideas without being bound by treaties or having to knuckle under to unilateral agreements that big countries break at will and small ones at their own risk.

Our culture suggests that we have a very good mental growing climate for ideas.

It is just that we haven't bothered to turn the mental soil over and have come to rely mostly on expensive, imported food for thought. Mental food for thought is a little like real food.

The first escaping convicts starved in the midst of a bountiful Australian bush.

According to an article by Julian Cribb in this paper last Monday, we have ignored a wealth of native grains and seeds, a delicious variety of native plums, raspberries, cranberries, currants, grapes, gooseberries, pomegranates, figs, guavas, apples, peaches and passionfruits.

These are natural crops that are adapted to our soil and climate and are resistant to our insect life. With a little horticultural breeding, this produce could supply a new bounty.

New Zealand managed to doctor the humble Chinese gooseberry from a small, tart fruit, which I recently bought from a roadside stall in China, to its present delicious, rotund state which the world buys at a premium and gobbles up in boatloads.

MEAT

In a world where saturated fat is a major health hazard, kangaroo meat, of which we have an inexhaustible supply, contains 0.6 per cent of saturated fat as opposed to 55 per cent in pork and 46.2 per cent in mutton.

If it is possible to make soya beans taste like steak, it shouldn't be too hard to make kangaroo palatable to a world where lean meat sells at a premium.

All it takes is a few ideas formulated in a quiet corner of one of our brand new national idea factories.

We are a nation of knockers and tall poppy choppers.

We seem always to know why we shouldn't undertake something

and we're experts at digging up reasons why things can't be done.

We have to start looking at an idea and asking ourselves what's good about it.

Confront the idea with a positive attitude and you'll find the negatives can usually be eliminated without damaging its intrinsic value.

Here's an idea. Under the able chairmanship of Phillip Adams, Australia has a Commission for the Future.

Why don't we create a national register of ideas?

It shouldn't be too hard to create a method that makes it simple for an idea to be evaluated.

If your idea makes it into the register, you might be paid a holding fee.

The register would then be printed each year and sold to industry and anyone else for that matter.

If your idea were used, you would be paid a royalty.

Now you can probably think of a dozen reasons why it wouldn't work but try to think of just one reason why it would work.

Send me your suggestions on how, as a people, we can generate idea productivity and I'll publish the best one in this column and perhaps have a chat to Mr Adams.

Remember, we're all in this together and in the idea business there is no pecking order, your idea is just as good as anyone else's.

An idea has four stages. The first is to dig up enough relevant information to think about, the second is to feed it into your head and start to think, the third is to stop thinking when you're exhausted so that your mind can do the work for you, and when your idea comes to fruition, the last stage is to open it up for discussion with positive people.

OK then, take three deep breaths, close your eyes, relax, start up the idea generator and think for Australia . . . Chuga, chuga, chuga, choof, chuga, toot, toot.

THE AUSTRALIAN MONDAY OCTOBER 19 1987

How to sell to those dreadful foreigners

If you work for a multinational advertising agency, sooner or later you have to deal with an overseas client who demands to make his own global advertising decisions.

So you write up all your marketing cunning into an unnecessarily large document, padding it with pictures and graphs and population trends.

You spend lavishly on doing finished creative work with word perfect, highly polished print ads, TV commercials and radio tapes all integrated into a slide presentation in two languages.

Armed with 100 kg of excess baggage, you catch the plane for Mecca. If your client is European you arrive in Zurich or Paris, Dusseldorf or Rotterdam, where your client feigns surprise to see you, or alternatively adopts a pose of professional boredom affected by those who feel they come from a world much older and wiser than yours.

You may be one of a dozen global teams gathered for the annual advertising genuflection. Your trail is scheduled in what turns out to be some sort of sociological order, with your presentation almost always somewhere after America and Britain.

These two nations have special status and often do their thing separately, or at least while the judge and jury are still fresh and interested. You pray that you won't get to tap-dance directly after lunch.

The Europeans, I have observed, are not particularly good after lunch. Too much wine blurs the senses, or, worse yet, stirs them. Judgments about Australia, never good at the best of times, may become quite bizarre.

After the trials are over, when several months of work has been shot down by bombast, you lick your wounds and meet Brazil, Argentina, South Africa, New Zealand and half a dozen Asian countries in the hotel bar and try to pick up the collective pieces.

Europeans seem to regard the bits Magellan, Vasco da Gama, Christopher Columbus and Cook discovered as still faintly distasteful. Although, of the Americas, the northern version merits the respect Europeans have always shown for money.

The southerners, Asians and antipodeans are lumped together for scant consideration. The Japanese, while also placing countries in rigid pecking order, do so according to the order book. Your ranking and importance is directly correlated with your export value.

This is because the Japanese see themselves as the only socially acceptable race anyway. To the pragmatic Japanese, he who buys most comes first in all things. Unlike the Europeans, particularly the Germans, the Japanese are seldom rude.

Japan is a country where consensus rules in all things and the committee is everything. Committees are by nature faceless and a presentation in Japan is never sudden death, as it can be in Europe.

Instead, you are killed off by attrition, one tiny incomprehensible verbal droplet at a time until finally all is awash. A presentation to the Japanese may take a week. It will begin at 8 am and end at some hugely expensive night club and eatery at midnight. This may continue for half a dozen days and in front of twice that many committees, all of whom come to the meeting having read the copious notes made by the committee which preceded it.

Even the slightest deviation from a previously expressed sentiment or idea is picked up and tossed back for an explanation. The Japanese worship consistency and any presentation team going to Japan hoping to tap-dance on the day confident in their ability to improvise is in a lot of trouble.

The Japanese like things to be precisely ordered and totally predictable. In their minds what we regard as mind-numbing consistency means that you have done your homework and reached your conclusions after a great deal of blood, sweat and tears.

This over-rehearsed approach runs contrary to the Australian personality, which likes to play things by ear. We do this, not always from lack of preparation but because we become suspicious for exactly the opposite reasons to the Japanese. If a man's patter is too perfect we suspect his purpose.

Last weekend I attended the Caxton Awards seminar, a get-together of Australia's advertising creative elite. In a presentation by Mr John Newton, the creative director of Leo Burnett, he used a real Encyclopaedia Britannica salesman.

To gain our attention and to make his point, he claimed that this salesman earned over $500,000 last year. His customers, mainly blue collar, are anxious to gain instant wisdom for their kids, perhaps so that they might grow up and learn how, among other things, to resist encyclopaedia salespersons.

This super-salesman demonstrated how he made a typical sale. While his technique was polished, even brilliant, it consisted mainly of appearing to be inadequate to the task of making a sale.

Unfortunately, clumsiness and carelessness is not an export commodity. If you're doing business in Europe you must be in and out of the boardroom within an hour showing a competence and an assurance that takes them by surprise and forces them to give you exceptional status.

If you're presenting to the Japanese you must be word perfect, rehearsed to the point of being able to recite your presentation verbatim 50 times or more. If you're facing the Americans, or New Yorkers anyway, your presentation must be in the local idiom: Americanised, homogenised and sterilised.

The point I'm making is, if we're going to sell the beloved country's bits and pieces overseas, we need to learn to ask ourselves three simple questions: What are we trying to sell? To whom are we trying to sell it? How best do we sell our things to a particular people?

If, when we go overseas to sell, we demonstrate we know these answers, we will become a much richer nation. If we don't ask ourselves the questions, then we are destined to be a poorer one. In the end the customer is always right. Or in the Australian idiom, he who pays, says.

We've got it, and they want it, but . . .

It's easy to whinge. It's also easy to be smart after the event. And it's easiest of all giving advice when you don't have to walk up to the workforce and turn your wisdom into action.

We all agree the beloved country is in terrible debt and we all acknowledge that when you owe someone a lot of money you have to make more and spend less until you've paid it off.

Or, there is another way. You can sell the bloke to whom you owe the money your services or even some of your possessions and ask him to deduct the value of them from the money you owe him.

You sell him the dining room suite because you all eat in front of the television anyway.

Then you cut down the dead tree in the back yard and turn it into firewood and get out the rake in the fowl run and put all the chicken manure into a rubbish bag and give it to him for his azaleas.

But there's a trick to paying back a debt when you can't find the cash. You can't simply give him all the junk you don't need.

You have to find out what the bloke to whom you owe the money needs. So you find out he's just built a house for his old mum and he needs a dining room table and chairs.

You find out azaleas like chook manure and he is an azalea fanatic.

In business terms this is known as market research. Pretty obvious really. You find out what people want and you give it to them.

Now it seems to me a nation like ours, which for the past few years has been importing more than exporting so that it owes, for instance, the Japanese more money than it has got to pay them back, may have to start sending stuff the creditors want in order to pay off the debt in kind.

Stuff we've got which they really need. We've got to find out whether they like open fires, grow azaleas and need a table and six chairs or whether they still sit on tatami grass and play around with teapots.

Not only have we not attempted to find out what they need but, according to an article from Alan Goodall in last Monday's issue of *The Australian*, most major Australian business organisations don't even have an agent in Japan.

In other words, while the Government has made some attempt through Austrade, private enterprise hasn't bothered to find out what the Japanese want. The Japanese, being patient but not stupid, realise that we're a little backward.

'JAPANESE ARE PRETTY ANNOYED'

In fact, if we were any more relaxed we'd be fly-blown. They can clearly see that the prospect of getting the money we owe them is looking pretty bleak so they make up a billion-dollar shopping list of the things they're pretty sure we've got and hand it over to us.

There you go, mate, fill this list and you're a billion dollars better off. That should help you pay us back a little of the money you owe us.

The list is mostly medical and computer equipment and, unlike us, they've done their market research and they know we can make what they want.

So the boys at Austrade in Tokyo think Christmas is early this year. They're sitting around devising ways to get promoted to a European trade consulate when out of what passes in Tokyo for a clear blue sky comes a billion dollar order.

Holy Keating. Wait till the birdman hears about this.

Australian business will be tearing each other apart to get a piece of the Japanese action.

But alas, birdman's Buy Australian advertising campaign has been so successful that Australian business can't be bothered talking to the Japanese as they're too busy true blueing the local market.

According to Goodall's report, only one Australian company has tendered for a slice of the billion-dollar Japanese order.

Half the companies Austrade approached and which, presumably, could make the goods required, didn't bother to reply and a further 20 wanted more information.

The Australian article goes on to say that another 64 Australian companies have brushed aside offers from the Federal Government's Austrade office in Tokyo.

One of the reasons given by manufacturers was that the need to process documentation in Japanese made things too difficult.

There are approximately five million Japanese who speak and write Engish sufficiently well to process papers from English to Japanese.

I feel sure at least 65 of them could be persuaded to come to Australia for a reasonable salary and membership of a golf club.

Now, as you might expect, the Japanese are pretty annoyed. Do you blame them?

They've found out what we've got and then told us how many chairs and tables they want, how much firewood they can use and when they got to telling us about their love of azaleas we turned around and said: "Sorry, mate, we're not interested in chicken shit."

A little serious dreaming may do a world of good

As usual, I'm not quite sure how well what I'm going to say this week is covered by a brief committing me to a column on marketing and advertising.

But I was thinking about the beloved country, which is something I do quite a lot. I was thinking about a country's hidden attitudes, the things that make one country work and another sit on its bum with its hands held out.

Korea has been in the news lately, having recently staged the best high-technology Olympic Games in history. Like all of us, they wanted the Olympic Games for the glory, but they also had another reason. They used it to show the world what they could do. They wanted us all to sit up and take notice.

It's perfectly obvious that they cannot compete with all those muscle-bound countries which export sport for prestige, so they used their brains instead, and with the whole world staring at them through the tiny glass window of satellite television, they had the opportunity to market the pants off us.

The Japanese used the same trick when they held the Olympic Games in 1964. We all came away bowled over by Japanese technology, and before long there were Toyotas and Toshibas, Nissans and Nikons everywhere you looked. Now, it's the turn of Korea—time to say "hi" to Hyundai.

A friend of mine who travels regularly throughout the Pacific Basin told me how he had gone to a barber shop for a haircut in the Ginza shopping district of Tokyo.

The bowing and nodding, hot towelling, brushing, clipping, tidying up and laying down and taking up of scissors in an elaborate and exquisite finger-movement ceremony made a Japanese tea ceremony look like a cup of Bushells taken on the run. It took an hour to receive an excellent haircut that cost him $50.

The next time he needed a haircut was in Korea, several weeks later. He checked into a barber shop where one bloke, who moved so quickly he could have been on roller skates, proceeded in a blur of fingers to scissor, snip, wash, trim, blow dry, brush and comb his way to a perfect haircut in 10 minutes flat at a cost of $30.

It seems the Japanese, now the richest people on earth, are slowing down while the Koreans, hungry for the good things in life, are speeding up.

The source of energy has moved from Japan to what economists call the Little Dragon. Energy is an important idea in a nation. If you've got a lot of energy that is not the sort you make with coal but the sort that makes you sweat, things begin to happen.

When it comes to energy, Korea's is the perfect case history. As a country, it's divided roughly in half. One half hasn't got any energy and is poor, the other has lots of energy and is beginning to be a large industrial power. The same people, but a different inspiration.

About 12 years ago there was hardly a tree in South Korea except for those in parks and a few private gardens. The country's landscape had rice paddies, rocky hills and gullies, soil erosion and no trees. The trees had been used up for fuel generations before.

But the South had energy. So every man, woman and child undertook to plant a given number of trees and to care for them until they were old enough to take care of themselves. South Korea today is blanketed by 12-year-old trees. All it took was the idea to germinate a few seeds and a lot of energy.

When you cross the 49th parallel into North Korea, you are aware straight away that there are no trees. There is also no energy to plant them.

Now, you could say that Korea, South or North, is hardly what you'd call a country at peace with itself. On alternate evenings, when we aren't watching teenagers firing machine-guns at random down brick- and debris-strewn Lebanese alleys, we're watching South Korean students hurling molotov cocktails at "Darth Vader-type" Korean police, who return the compliment by beating up the students with metre-long batons and showering them with tear gas.

I am aware that I am not talking about the ideal society. The energy the Koreans generate as a people has nothing to do with the fact that they may need the odd lesson in peace and quiet, as well as human rights.

Nor does their energy come from being threatened or beaten up. We have seen in the North how this does not work. The people's energy comes from enthusiasm.

Despite everything, the overcrowding, the tough laws, the lack of freedom and true democracy, the South Korean people are enthusiastic about their future. They can see that if they get off their backsides they can create a rich country, one that can more than pay its way in the world and one which will eventually give them all the good things they want.

So, we see how energy comes from enthusiasm and enthusiasm comes from having a dream. Without a dream, where's the point? You have to be able to dream. You have to have a dream for the future.

So, I thought a little more about the beloved country. Where was our dream? What was that thing nations need to give them direction and the enthusiasm to strive for something better? If a country such as South Korea could have a dream, and a tiny cramped and rather dull island such as Singapore could have a dream, when neither of them, like Japan before them, had any resources other than their enthusiasm and their energy, then why can't Australia have a dream, with all the things we've got?

Why, I ask myself, is the beloved country sitting on its backside staring into the distance without a dream?

If we could only find a dream. Something about which we could become really enthusiastic. Something for which we could agree to pull together, sweat over, argue over, then have a go.

I reckon before you could say "wool cheque" we'd be about the best damn nation on earth.

Or am I, as usual, wasting my time dreaming when I should join my mates on the picket-line who are demanding shorter working hours and more pay?

A perfect opportunity to cash in on Japanese buyers

I've always had a bit of admiration for the Japanese.

It seems amazing to me that a country with no resources, not even enough to feed itself, can rule the economic world.

I read somewhere recently—although I forget the actual figures, so please don't quote them—that if all countries were suddenly cut off from each other and all imports stopped, the United States could exist for around two years, England about a year, Canada indefinitely, Australia the same and so it went.

I remember the exact figure for Japan, which was 2.5 weeks.

The Japanese are entirely dependent on the outside to feed the inside—not just food, but raw materials as well.

I've heard it said that if you look at most self-made men, blokes who have a squillion dollars, it is surprising how many of them come from broken homes.

I'm assured by a psychiatrist friend of mine that there is some truth in the hypothesis that unhappiness in childhood is often the spur to success.

Do you imagine this can happen to a country as well?

After a war, defeated countries seem to recover faster than the winners. Germany and Japan are prime examples of this.

Is it that a little poverty and hopelessness can get a nation with the right leadership and work ethic supercharged again?

Take the Japanese. After the war, they borrowed a heap of money from the US to buy steel and stuff from people like us and then got cracking. But think about it: they couldn't just produce things for sale.

I mean, who is going to buy the stuff from the people who tortured our troops and generally behaved in an uncivilised manner?

Not a hope—unless they could produce goods that were cheaper by far and better by a wide margin. When this happens, the greed factor comes into operation.

We forgot about water torture and bamboo up the fingernails and other nasty little warlike habits.

We happily clicked on the Made in Japan watchermacallit and

told each other we'd let bygones be bygones. Greed has an alarming effect on the long-term memory, and it only comes into play when the bargain being offered is irresistible.

Your average Japanese man on the street who worked a 12-hour day, six days a week, with only two public holidays and a week's vacation a year found himself with money in his pocket to burn.

He'd already bought all the Japanese gizmos his own factories turned out and so he looked round to buy other things—things that didn't have Made in Japan stamped on them. For example, he looked at lead crystal.

THEY PRODUCE GOODS THAT ARE BETTER AND CHEAPER

He went to Europe to look at the lead crystal factories in France, Sweden, Belgium and Bulgaria—factories that had been turning out beautiful crystal for 200 years.

To his delight, he discovered it takes seven years to learn to blow a perfect crystal goblet and five years to be able to cut the intricate designs. He knew he'd found something special because every process in the making of crystal is by hand.

You couldn't do a clever Japanese thing to crystal and turn it out better and cheaper. This was tradition, craftmanship, pride and the Japanese love of doing things.

So he decided that crystal was a good way to spend his money. But something very strange had happened to him since the war when he'd picked himself up, dusted himself down and started all over again.

He discovered that having spent all his working life trying to make things better, he had developed a desire for perfection.

So he went to a world-famous crystal factory in Ireland, to people who'd been blowing and cutting and generally earning a reputation for turning out the world's best crystal for 200 years.

He also went to France, which had a similar reputation for smooth crystal and to Sweden and Bulgaria and, in fact, everywhere.

Soon he knew an awful lot about crystal.

Then he went back to Ireland and he said this to the proud and superior craftsmen: "We'll buy boatloads of your crystal, we'll buy $100,000 vases and hand-cut glasses and anything you can make if you'll pull up your socks and do things properly round here."

Now that's not a very nice thing to say to proud and dignified craftsmen who have been patting themselves on the back for several dozen generations.

"Properly? We're the best. That should be clear as crystal!

"Five years just to learn how to blow one of them buggers, a lifetime to get it right, cutting secrets passed on from father to son unto the fifth generation—what do you bloody mean, pull up your socks?"

"It has to be perfect," the Japanese man in the street said. "It has to be the very best."

Well, the happy part of the story is that someone listened. To their enormous surprise, the cloth-capped craftsmen, pride of the old sod, found that they could improve their crystal markedly—no little bubbles where bubbles ought not to be.

In the old days it didn't matter, tradition was everything and a bubble or two added a bit of character and a design not quite perfect was regarded as artistic licence.

But not any more—the Japanese man in the street is watching.

The Irish crystal factory is booming and the traditional craftsmen are proud of their new sense of direction.

Now they positively know they are the best in the world because the Japanese are ordering by the boatload.

Is the notion of getting things right unfair?

All the Japanese man in the street wants is that you produce the things you sell to him as well as he does the things he sells to you. That doesn't seem unreasonable to me.

He doesn't want to lower his standards. He isn't even greedy. Unlike you and me, he isn't asking for our goods and services to be cheaper and better, only better.

I am told that the average Japanese couple who have decided to take their one holiday in a lifetime in Australia arrive here with a barrowload of money, quite prepared to redress our balance of payments.

Right now, every Australian owes a Japanese family $12,000 and they want to give us the chance to get some of it back.

But they end up taking most of it home. It seems they just can't find anything to buy that meets the minimum standards they set.

Pity about that—the money is there for the taking.

THE AUSTRALIAN FRIDAY MAY 11 1990

Let's ditch our desire for failure

This week the Russians told us they were broke and couldn't pay for the wool they bought.

So now Keating can tell us we're having a recession rather than having the recession we were having when we were not having a recession. He can blame the whole thing on the Russians.

Most governments are pretty good at passing the buck or blaming others for their own shortcomings but this one, elected by default, has turned blaming others into an art form.

Which brings me to the subject of blame.

As countries go, I reckon we're near the top when it comes to blaming anyone and anything for our misfortunes. Read the newspaper on any morning and you'll find it's almost entirely composed of articles blaming someone for the failure of something.

Companies who've blatantly behaved in a reprehensible manner blame other factors for their dilemmas. Politicians who neglect their brief blame anyone and anything but themselves; teachers blame the government; businessmen the unions; sports teams the ref; the people the public service, and so it goes on.

IT'S ALL THE POM'S FAULT

If it wasn't for someone or something else we'd be perfect.

The trouble with always having someone to blame is that it gives us an excuse not to do anything. It's not our problem; someone or something beyond our control is to blame. So we all end up sitting on our hands while the beloved country sinks deeper and deeper into apathy.

Blame is the result of an attitude.

An American friend of mine finally left our country because of the frustration of doing business here—"the Australian desire to fail". He claims we actually like the idea of failure. More than like it, we worship and desire it.

Now, before we dismiss him as another know-all Yank, he may well have a point. We have just spent several million dollars sending a bunch of nice old guys back to Turkey to worship at the shrine of our greatest failure. A place where the flower of our marvellous youth, from a country which at that time was claimed to have the highest standard of living in the world, needlessly threw their lives away. The result was that the beloved country, always short of men, was virtually crippled for the next couple of generations, its building blocks destroyed.

Somehow the idea of being incredibly brave and stupid in the face of insurmountable odds captured the imagination of Australians. We've ignored several spectacular wartime wins in both world wars in favour of this one monumental disaster. Nice old blokes with necks like turkey cocks are carted over to a dawn service where the Prime Minister sheds his accustomed and mandatory tears so we might be reminded that our greatness as a nation lies in abject failure.

And, of course, while we have learned to worship this particular failure as an illustration of our greatness, it wasn't our fault. The Poms did it to us! So there's the format. Fail hugely, even brilliantly, but find someone else to blame.

The tall poppy syndrome is yet another expression of the national desire to remain mediocre, to fail.

Success requires long hours, loneliness, determination, some originality and an ability to follow your convictions. All of these characteristics call for individualism and the desire to achieve a result.

Mateship has come to mean being the same as everyone else, not pretending to do anything beyond the common denominator.

Now, if the common denominator is geared to blaming the system or anything else for our lack of success and sitting on our collective hands, then basically failure is perpetuating itself.

It all comes from an attitude: the attitude that something or someone else is to blame for our misfortunes.

In private, politicians from both sides nod wisely. The world economy has gone global, the decisions are made elsewhere. Australia is too small, too unimportant. No matter what we do we can't influence the decisions which affect our wellbeing. Macro-economics is to blame. So there it is again.

But nobody told the Japanese this after World War II.

Nobody said to them: "Hey, Japanese. Look here, chaps, we've bombed you into oblivion. You're history.

"You don't have enough land or equipment, you have too many people, you can't feed them, house them, you don't grow enough food for them, you have no raw materials of your own.

"We're not even going to let you make any decisions. All you've got is your heads and your hands. You might as well sit on your hands because your heads are no good to you. Go ahead, blame the war! You lost! You are entitled to stay losers.

"Here's a good idea! Build a national shrine to your greatest defeat, start worshipping it, send all your old samurai over for photo opportunities. There's a lot of comfort in knowing you were incredibly brave and steadfast in the face of the enemy. It may be all you've got to clutch on to, the metaphorical dead baby you clutch to your national chest, but hold it tight, it's better than nothing and it entitles you to mediocrity!"

The Chinese who were defeated by their communist countrymen and forced to retreat to a small island previously used for growing vegetables didn't celebrate their failure. They built the vegetable garden into Taiwan!

The South Koreans, destroyed by a war between north and south, were quite entitled to mumble that they were blameless and entitled to a better deal. But they didn't. They got off their bums and built a modern miracle with very few resources.

THE JAPANESE SHOW US HOW

Japan, Taiwan, Singapore, Korea, the big and the little dragons on our doorstep, they too failed but they haven't made a glory out of failure, haven't turned it into mateship, poppy-chopping and blaming someone or something else for everything that happens to them.

They may have troubles but they're not of the kind that comes from sitting on your hands.

Can't we all stop, take a deep breath, look around us and accept that we are all equally to blame? Not macro-economics, or unions, or politicians, or teachers, or rapacious business, or J curves, but all of us.

Let's all forget about failures of the past and start working our butts off for success of the future.

Work for the success we could so easily deserve as the small but brilliant young country so beautifully poised on the lip of the Pacific basin. The St George of the Pacific ready to compete with the dragons, big and small, for our share of the good things to which a country with brains and resources and an ability to work is entitled.

Then, perhaps, the stupid, needless but nevertheless wonderfully brave deaths at Gallipoli and elsewhere can be rewarded and turned into something worthwhile.

THE AUSTRALIAN FRIDAY MAY 24 1991

How Japan and Germany beat the rest

In April this year the GATT report showed the latest trade figures for the world's industrialised countries.

GATT stands for General Agreement on Tariffs and Trade and is pretty well the last word on what is happening in world trade.

The report showed that Germany had become the world's biggest trading nation, the world's biggest exporter, passing the United States for the first time and pushing Japan into third place.

Germany, even as a divided nation, was finally on top again a mere 45 years, or one full generation, after the Allied forces had more or less razed her.

It is interesting to speculate that of the world's top three trading nations, two—Germany and Japan—have almost no natural resources of their own.

They are essentially traders. They buy from elsewhere, add value to the raw material they buy and sell it to someone else at a higher price.

So, when you think about it, Germany and Japan are doing something anyone could do.

The only value they add to the raw materials they buy at the same price as everyone else is their brains.

So it may be said that what Germany and Japan essentially do better than anyone else is think. And, of course, having done the thinking required, to work very hard.

In other words, the miracles both these defeated and largely devastated countries have performed in the post-war world are based on something any other nation could just as easily have done.

After all, lots of nations work hard and there is no measurement which suggests that 6½ ounces of brain each of us has been given is better when it performs in German or Japanese.

What then was it which made these two beaten nations crawl out of the rubble and take on the world, and in a little over one generation become two of the three most powerful trading nations on earth?

Well, it's easy to say it was pride or, put differently, the humiliation of defeat and the desire to vindicate themselves, but lots of proud countries took a hiding one way or another and haven't emerged as winners during this period.

Russia and Britain, for example, didn't lose the war but they took a terrible hiding and were forced, more or less, to start from scratch.

Both these countries are known for their pride and character.

Only the United States enjoyed an unfair start as a country whose factories were intact and going flat out with a people who were energised in an industrial landscape that remained unscathed.

So great was her start that it has taken 45 years to haul her in.

So it must be said that national pride and a willingness to work hard are both essential ingredients in the success of a nation and most Australians will reluctantly admit that we are not the world's leading exponents of either of these ethics.

But if we look at Germany and Japan there is something else besides brains and guts.

For want of a better name, let's call it simply a particular expertise.

While Germany and Japan do lots of things well they each do one thing very well indeed. With the Germans it's cars and with the Japanese it's electronics.

They each have this one area which has allowed them to become and remain dominant in world trade and which has given them a sound industrial base on which to expand into other manufacturing areas.

According to a recent article in the Spectator, the Germans originally based their entire success on the Beetle, the tiny hump-backed Volkswagen originally designed by Austrian designer Ferdinand Porsche in 1937, two years before the war began.

Volkswagen, as most people know, simply means "the people's car", named first by Hitler, who aimed to put German families on wheels.

The Volkswagen was pretty well all Germany had to offer as she lined up on the starting line after the war.

Even this was a start from scratch, for while they had what must have seemed like a set of somewhat dated plans for this ugly little car, the VW factory at Wolfsburg was in smouldering ruins.

But the concept of a cheap, reliable car wasn't out of date. The idea was valid and up for grabs and available to any country who wanted it.

The Germans grabbed their chance with both hands. The Volkswagen was to become the car that would put the post-war world on wheels.

This was Germany's singular idea.

The car wasn't pretty, it lacked almost any real features, it didn't hold the road very well. In fact, all it had going for it was that it was cheap, reliable and didn't use a lot of petrol.

PARTICULAR EXPERTISE

Fifty years after the first model was produced in pre-war Germany, 20 million Volkswagens, the last model little changed from the first, have been sold worldwide.

The basis for the German car industry and expertise was built by this simple little machine and the rest simply followed.

What the Germans did with the Volkswagen, the Japanese have done with electronics.

Both found a basis to begin work and took it from there to become hugely diversified industrial nations.

There must be a lesson in all this for a small country like our own.

What Germany and Japan did was create a need or, in smart marketing talk, they discovered a niche, albeit a very, very large one.

The Americans were making big gas-guzzling cars and the British were making small, unreliable ones. The Germans filled a niche for a small car that never broke down and ran forever on a gallon of gas.

The Japanese saw the need for reliable and portable entertainment and they took the pompous, round-shouldered radiogram out of the lounge room and put it into the pocket of every teenager at an affordable price.

Provided always that as a nation we use our brains and work hard, what we then need to do is find out what we can do potentially better than anyone else and then seek out who most logically will want to buy what we make.

What are the ideas which we as a nation might explore and which could give us a basis and a niche in the markets of the world?